Organizing Chaos

A Comprehensive Guide to Emergency Management

Dr. Mark Chadwick, CEM, TEM

This page is intentionally left blank.

Dr. Mark Chadwick, CEM, TEM
6018 Bear Canyon
San Antonio, TX 78252
texasemergencymanager@gmail.com

Printed in the U.S.A.

First Edition 2021

Library of Congress Control Number: 2021918733

ISBN: 978-0-578-25532-3

Cover photo from Pixabay.com

Dedication

This book is dedicated to my loving wife Rebecca "Becky" Leigh (Bass) Chadwick. Becky has been my inspiration for every accomplishment in my life. She has been there beside me through all my years in the military, while working catastrophic disasters across several States, and during the countless hours of activations for localized disasters. I also dedicate this book to my adult children Mark Chadwick II, Ariel Kellogg, and Bronwyn Payne. I have given the vast majority of my life in service to try to make the world a little bit safer for my wife, family and friends. Now I have grandchildren who also provide me with encouragement to face the dangers of disasters to attempt in some small way to protect them. In the dark hours when my physical strength has wavered, I remind myself that I do not do the things I do for myself, but for them. I pray that I may continue to be granted the strength to stand in the face of disaster and endure the hardships of separation for my family and my loved ones.

Mark

Contents

Preface

Writing *"Organizing Chaos"* has been both a labor of love for the profession of Emergency Management and a personal journey. I began an Emergency Management Internship program nearly ten years ago to do my part in training up and preparing the next generation of Emergency Managers and this book is a continuation of those efforts. Early on, as I set out to write this book, I was determined to not rush and to thoughtfully record factual evidence along with personal experiences. To promote integrity, I purposefully selected two of the highest caliber professionals to review my book and to provide their honest comments. Their comments are provided in the Foreword and I have included their biographies to allow the readers to comprehend the value of their testimonials. While their biographies will provide an in-depth glimpse into their qualifications, I wanted to extract and highlight a few of their achievements which make them more than qualified to evaluate this book. To use a poker analogy, having these two as reviewers is like holding two aces in your hand.

Paul Hannemann is one of the founders of the All-Hazards Incident Management Team (AHIMT) concept which is implemented across the entire nation. He is a credentialled Type I Incident Commander (IC) and along with countless high-profile incidents he served as the Deputy IC for the Space Shuttle Columbia Recovery mission. In 2020, Paul was inducted into the Hall of Legends, Legacies, and Leaders at the National Fire Heritage Center. Additionally, he retired as a Lieutenant Colonel with over 28 years in the Texas Army National Guard and U.S. Army Reserves.

Not to be overshadowed, Patrick Hughes has over 40 years of fire service experience and has been appointed on separate occasions by Governors of the State of Texas to serve as a State Fire Commissioner. He is a founding member of the Texas Commission on Fire Protection (TCFP) and the International Fire Service Accreditation Congress (IFSAC). He has been a leader for AHIMT development in Texas and the San Jacinto area. Patrick is a U.S. Navy Vietnam veteran who served with distinction.

Foreword by Paul Hannemann

"Organizing Chaos" by Dr. Mark Chadwick is a very insightful book where the author has taken his education and experience to develop a book that can be used as a College Textbook or Desk Reference Manual for entry level or seasoned Emergency Managers. Mark has used his many lessons learned over the years to provide a reference to Emergency Managers to understand the complex field and make good decisions in their career. Unlike other authors that have written books on Disaster Management, Incident Management, or Emergency Management; he has reached back in history to provide the evolution of the topic. Disaster, Incident, and Emergency Management are not new subjects, but in fact have been around a long time. Chadwick looks at it since the beginning of the United States in the 1600s and how it has evolved into what we have today. Once you read his book, you realize that disasters and incidents did not just happen in recent times, but in fact have occurred throughout all times. Perhaps we referred to them utilizing different terminology, but they still occurred. There were different results because of the individuals and organizations that actually managed historic disasters and due to their knowledge and previous experiences. To that end in his book, Dr. Chadwick has provided various solutions along with his research and experiences. Certainly, his experiences will many times provide a smile as the reader may have had similar experiences with a different result. I had the great pleasure to be on many of the same incidents as Mark; some in the same location and others at different locations, but the same incident. Mark has been a practitioner of what he has written about in his book which again provides the credibility for it. Likewise, his book has provided a tremendous bibliography of the various laws that have been passed resulting from disasters that have occurred in the last 100 years. Many of these have taken lessons learned to develop them and obviously many have been revamped as a result of subsequent disasters and lessons learned from them.

Paul F. Hannemann

Foreword by Patrick Hughes

As I've been reviewing Dr. Mark Chadwick's very insightful book *"Organizing Chaos,"* I'm constantly reminded that this book would have been an extremely valuable resource as I began my own journey into the Emergency Management realm. Mark has done a remarkable job of gathering a vast amount of pertinent information and organizing it in a way that makes the book a must have in your work backpack so that you'll always have it available as a go-to resource during every emergency activation. Like Mark, I began working in Emergency Management several decades prior to the most defining event for Emergency Management - the terrorist attacks on 9/11/2001. One positive takeaway from that horrible event was the eventual establishment of the National Incident Management System (NIMS). My personal experience with Mark over the last 15 years has shown me that he's truly dedicated and very knowledgeable in all aspects of effectively dealing with any emergency. To that point, I've sought his opinion on serious situations I've faced to gain his insight and advice. The Emergency Management profession is extremely complex, requiring skillsets and experience from numerous Local, State and Federal governmental backgrounds. An effective Emergency Management Coordinator (EMC) must also be adept at personnel management, planning with a dose of energy and enthusiasm. Most importantly there must be a sincere desire to help people! Mark possesses all these traits – personnel management, planning, energetic, enthusiastic. Another important trait he possesses is his uncommon ability to teach people how to become an effective EMC. Dr. Mark Chadwick has accomplished exactly what the title infers, he's truly *"Organizing Chaos."*

Patrick Hughes

Biography of Paul F. Hannemann

 Paul F. Hannemann retired from the Texas A&M Forest Service in 2020 after 25 years of distinguished service managing fire protection for the 254 counties in Texas. In 1981, he began working for the State as a Contract Trainer and rose through the ranks in his career to become the first fulltime Regional Fire Coordinator in Texas, then Chief of Fire Operations, and ultimately the Department Head for the Incident Response Department. Paul served as the Incident Commander (IC) on Texas Forest Service's Lone Star State Type I Incident Management Team (IMT) for 15 years. Among countless deployments, he served as a Deputy IC on the National Aeronautics and Space Administration (NASA) Columbia Shuttle Recovery for 100 days in 2003 and received the NASA Public Service for Outstanding Service to the NASA Mission. Paul has been on the forefront of IMT development, serving as a Deputy IC on the State Emergency Response Team for the Texas Division of Emergency Management (TDEM), U.S. Fire Administration (USFA) Type III IMT Development Team, Lead Instructor for the National Fire Academy (NFA) All-Hazard IMT (AHIMT), Instructor for the Emergency Management Institute (EMI) Position-Specific courses, and instructor for FEMA's AHIMT Development Group. He has held a myriad of professional positions; including Chairman of a Task Force for planning Industrial Fires of State Significance in Texas, US Forest Service Region's Planning and Logistics Section and Command & General Staff Training Cadre, Texas Intrastate Fire Mutual System (TIF MAS) Oversight Committee, National Association of State Forester (NASF) Complex Incident Management Course, National Wildland Coordination Group (NWCG) Operations & Training Committee, NIMS-ICS Committee, L-580 Leadership Course Steering Committee, and Incident Management Organization Successions Planning project. Paul has received numerous awards; most notably in 2012 the Regents Fellows Service Award from the Texas A & M University System Board of Regents and in 2020 he was inducted as the 74th inductee in the Hall of Legends, Legacies and Leaders at the National Fire Heritage Center. Prior to service with the State of Texas, he retired at the rank of Lieutenant Colonel after serving 28 years in the Texas Army National Guard and US Army Reserves having received two Meritorious Service Medals for service during Desert Shield/Desert Storm.

Biography of Patrick Hughes, TEM

Patrick Hughes began his professional career in the U.S. Navy where he served 4 years aboard the U.S.S. Saratoga CV(A) 60 from 1971 to 1975 including a 10- month tour in Vietnam and 6 months in the Mediterranean Sea. After his military service, Patrick served the City of North Richland Hills, Texas Fire Department for more than 25 years and rising to the rank of Assistant Fire Chief. He also served for 2 years with Stewart & Stevenson as the Fire Apparatus Product Line Manager and an additional 2 years with the Houston Community College as a Fire Training Program Faculty Member. Continuing his lifetime of public service, Patrick has served with the City of Sugar Land, Texas Fire Department as 1 of 4 Assistant Fire Chiefs and Emergency Management Coordinator (EMC) for the past 15 years. He has served in numerous professional positions, including as the first Texas Commission on Fire Protection Standards & Education Testing Committee in 1988; 1st Vice President of the National Society of Executive Fire Officers from 1989 to 1992; appointed by Texas Governor William Clements as a State Fire Commissioner in 1990; re-appointed by Texas Governor Ann Richards as a State Fire Commissioner to the newly created Texas Commission on Fire Protection (TCFP) from 1992 to 1997; Texas representative and founding member of the International Fire Service Accreditation Congress (IFSAC) from 1990 to 1997; IFSAC Board of Governors from 1995 to 2000; San Jacinto (San Jac) All Hazards Incident Management Team (AHIMT) Team Lead from 2007 to present; Pecan Grove Volunteer Fire Department Board President 2013; and the Houston Community College Fire Protection Advisory Committee from 2007 to present where he currently serves as Committee Chair. Patrick has earned several professional credentials, to include the Master Fire Instructor III through TCFP, Fire Officer I through TCFP, Master Fire Inspector through TCFP; Master Fire Fighter through TCFP; and Certified Texas Emergency Manager (TEM) through the Emergency Management Association of Texas (EMAT). For academic education, he has been awarded a Bachelor's degree from Columbia Southern University in Fire Administration and he completed the National Fire Academy Executive Fire Officer Program 1988 to 1992.

This page is intentionally left blank.

Acknowledgements

First, and most importantly, I want to thank my amazing wife, Becky, who has encouraged me throughout the writing of this book. She has been by my side every day supporting me as I have toiled away at writing and re-writing through the midst of the COVID-19 pandemic. Becky aided me by reading sections and providing her valued insight on editing. Without her love and support, I would never have begun, much less finished, writing "Organized Chaos!"

I want to offer my sincere gratitude to Paul Hannemann and Patrick Hughes, two amazing Emergency Managers whom I have been blessed to know and to work with on occasion. Paul and Patrick took valuable time to review this book and to provide their insight. Having professionals on their level to even agree to look over my work is an honor and having their words of encouragement in the Foreword fills is a major accomplishment in it's own right.

I have been fortunate to work alongside of some truly wonderful Emergency Managers in Texas, none more so than Kyle Coleman. I first met Kyle when I was in civilian law enforcement in 1990 and then had the privilege of coming to work for him in Bexar County in 2012 where he served as Emergency Management Coordinator (EMC). Kyle encouraged me to continually reach beyond myself and to build my knowledge and skills. He was not only my boss, Kyle was my closest friend. Sadly, Kyle passed from this world due to COVID complications on July 14, 2020.

Many peers in Texas I have worked with have encouraged me as an exercise developer, instructor, and Emergency Manager. The list of peers I would like to thank include Jeff Fincke, EMC Kendall County; Charlie Waller, EMC Uvalde County; Ray Kalio, EMC Frio County; Keith Lutz, EMC Medina County; and David Prasifka, EMC Atascosa County who also passed away from COVID complications in 2020. Each of these Emergency Managers has provided me with opportunities to excel and to become the Emergency Manager I am today.

This page is intentionally left blank.

Introduction

On September 11, 2001, Emergency Management was thrust into the spotlight not only in the United States, but all across the globe when New York City and Washington, D.C. came under attack from terrorists. In short succession, in the years that followed, other cataclysmic man-made and natural disasters again saw Emergency Managers highlighted in the national and international media. These incidents led some to mistakenly speculate that Emergency Management was either a new or emerging career field. This has led to a discordant amount of misinformation being espoused by the uninformed or inexperienced. However, nothing could be further from the truth in regards to Emergency Management.

The field and profession of Emergency Management is one which is long-standing and well established, as is proven in the documented annals of history in our great nation and the histories of the world. Disasters and emergencies are nothing new on any continent and reaching at length into antiquity there are recorded instances of disaster occurring where those responding set out to organize the ensuing chaos and incrementally improving upon response techniques and skills. For as long as there have been disasters in the world, there have been those men and women who have labored to pick up the pieces and restore our societies.

When I set out to write this book, it was with a couple of simple goals in mind: (1) to share the true chronicles of the Emergency Management profession and (2) to provide the next generation of Emergency Managers with a comprehensive understanding of the depth and breadth of the Emergency Management field. To that end, this text will have a recurring theme of delving into history and peering into the volumes of material that substantiate the work of Emergency Managers. History provides us with a window through which we can glimpse the failures and successes of the past and the progressive development of Emergency Management over the centuries. By analyzing the mistakes of yesterday and yesteryear we can avoid devastating pitfalls today and in the future.

Aside from the mere compilation of over a thousand hours of research, I speak from a lifetime of experience and training. I have worked in emergency response for more than 36 years. While on active duty in the U.S. Air Force Security Police, I responded to my first large scale disaster during the Central Missouri floods of 1986.[1] Since that time, I have served in hundreds of emergency and disaster responses for incidents in several States in roles with the military, civilian law enforcement, faith-based disaster response, as an employee of the American Red Cross, and in local government Emergency Management. Just a few of the catastrophic disasters I responded to include: 2005 Hurricanes Katrina and Rita; 2007 Tornadoes in Eagle Pass, TX; 2008 Hurricanes Gustav and Ike; 2013 Fertilizer Plant Explosion in West, TX; 2017 Hurricane Harvey; 2020 to 2021 COVID-19; and the 2021 Texas Winter Storm Uri.

During my career as a professional Emergency Manager, I have earned the Certified Emergency Manager (CEM), Certified Texas Emergency Manager (TEM), and Master Military Emergency Management Specialist credentials along with numerous associated credentials. Additionally, I have earned instructor certifications through Federal and State agencies to teach a myriad of Emergency Management courses, written a multitude of professional courses and workshops, developed countless exercises for dozens of jurisdictions, and managed an Emergency Management internship program for more than nine years.

I chose the title *"Organizing Chaos"* because that is a concise description of the job of Emergency Managers. The Cambridge Dictionary defines chaos as "a state of total confusion with no order."[2] That definition is an accurate depiction of what experience has taught me to expect immediately following a disaster. By the conclusion of this text, I believe you will agree that this is an accurate title. I want to express my gratitude for your interest in the field of Emergency Management and I hope you will find this book to be beneficial in your endeavors.

---

[1] (Historic Flood Events in the Missouri River Basin, 1986)
[2] (Chaos, n.d.)

Chapter 1: Historical Foundations of Emergency Management

Defining Emergency Management

When beginning to introduce a topic, we should always start by defining the topic we are seeking to describe. FEMA provides the following definition: *"Emergency Management is the managerial function charged with creating the framework within which communities reduce vulnerability to hazards and cope with disasters."*[3] In my opinion, this technical definition does not paint the full picture of what Emergency Management encompasses. By describing Emergency Management as a "managerial function", the definition gives the impression that Emergency Management is simply accomplished within the walls of an office building of some sort. Certainly, there are portions of the work of Emergency Management that must be conducted within the confines of an office or emergency operations center (EOC), behind a desk, and with a computer. However, that is merely scratching the surface of work conducted by professional Emergency Managers.

In the text *"Introduction to Emergency Management, Fourth Edition,"* Emergency Management is defined as *"a discipline that deals with risk and risk avoidance."*[4] In this same work, the authors describe Emergency Management as a discipline that is broad and all-encompassing due to expanding and contracting to

---

[3] (Dr. B. Wayne Blanchard, CEM, September 11, 2007)
[4] (George D. Haddow, Jane A. Bullock, and Damon P. Coppola, 2011)

meet the needs of the various incidents and leadership styles. While this depiction reaches further than the definition offered by FEMA, it still falls short of expressing the breadth and width of Emergency Management. Yes, risk and risk management are considerations for Emergency Managers. However, there is so much more to Emergency Management than the risk management equation of **"risk = threat x vulnerability x consequences."**

Emergency Management entails so much more than the tidy work conducted inside of a spotless office, and it revolves more around "coordination" than simple "management." Professional Emergency Managers know that the work of coordinating response and recovery operations can require rolling up our sleeves and getting dirty in environments that are less than hospitable. That is the problem with disasters; they are filled with destruction and the lives of people that are shattered. The job of Emergency Managers is to pick up the pieces and trying to safeguard the people and their way of life after emergencies and disasters.

Think it through; fires, floods, hurricanes, and tornadoes leave a swath of destruction in their path. Businesses, homes, and people are lost in that devastation. In the wake of catastrophic disasters all that we cherish, know, and love can be lost. Emergency Managers are the people who stand in that path as sentinels to protect our way of life. As I constantly remind those I teach, "Technology is not the answer and technology is not your friend." In the aftermath of a disaster, the first things to stop working are communications, electricity, water, and wastewater systems. Without those, you have no internet, no connectivity, and all of your electronic equipment is useless. When all of our glorious technology fails, Emergency Managers still have to do our job. That is why I tell people who are interested in becoming Emergency Managers that if they cannot do this job with a Big Chief tablet (for those too young to know, that is a paper tablet used to learn how to write by children years ago) and a number 2 pencil, they need to do something else. In other words, you have to be able to go "old school" and use nothing more than pencil and paper when all else fails. After a major disaster the public does not care that you do not have working technology, they just want all of the bad things to go away. Emergency Managers do not have the luxury of working only when our electronic gadgets are working. Emergency Management is not about the toys we have to do the job; it is about the people doing the job.

The reality is that Emergency Management is dynamic and entails all of the actions involved in coordinating and organizing the efforts in planning for, preparing for, responding to, recovering from, and mitigating the impact of disasters upon our society. In every class I teach on the topic, I simplify my definition to describing Emergency Management as "Organizing Chaos." Disasters and

> … Emergency Management is dynamic and entails all of the actions involved in coordinating and organizing the efforts in planning for, preparing for, responding to, recovering from, and mitigating the impact of disasters upon our society.

emergencies are inherently fraught with chaos and confusion. When Emergency Managers arrive on-scene, our task is to attempt to get our arms around that chaos and to incrementally begin restoring some sense of normalcy. The umbrella of Emergency Management is inclusive of all the response disciplines of emergency medical service, firefighting, law enforcement, public works, public health, and the volunteer and private sector.

Getting into the History

History is a prism through which Emergency Managers can view what has occurred in the past and it allows us to evaluate the documented facts relating to Emergency Management. The truth of the matter is that we find history littered with various citations of Emergency Management and responder discipline development. What the reader will find is the footprint left in the sands of time that illustrate the historical existence and development of Emergency Management over centuries.

In his 1905 publication of *"Reason in Common Sense,"* the Spanish-American philosopher George Santayana penned the phrase "Those who cannot remember the past are condemned to repeat it."[5] During a speech before the British parliament in 1948 Winston Churchill paraphrased Santayana when he said, "Those who do not learn history are doomed to repeat it." The lesson holds true for Emergency Managers as well. When I look back over the past several years, I cannot even count the number of times when I read articles and white papers espousing how Emergency Management was something new on the horizon. Instead of spouting innuendos, allow me to lead us down memory lane where we can learn from history about the roots of our noble profession. By no means is this a complete listing of every legislative or executive action on Emergency Management in U.S. History, rather, this is a representative sampling.

Important Dates in the Historical Development of Emergency Management

Going back as far as 21 BC we find that the Roman Emperor Augustus is cited as having instituted the *vigiles*, which means "watchmen of the city", to conduct firefighting in Rome.[6] The *vigiles* were comprised of freedmen and officers from the Roman army that were organized to fight fires arising throughout Rome and to arrest suspicious people encountered on the streets at night. The city of Rome was divided into 14 zones; each of which was assigned personnel and equipment to fight fires. The patrolling of the *vigiles* at night led to the concept of keeping a vigil. The annals of Roman history provide us with evidence of coordination and organization of responders to safeguard the citizens over 2,000 years ago.

Moving into the history of the United States (U.S.), Captain James Smith is credited in January of 1608 for having utilized a group of colonists to fight a fire that ravaged provisions and lodgings.[7] The development of this firefighting capability

---

[5] (Santayana, 1905)

[6] (Municipal Reforms of Augustus, n.d.)

[7] (Hashagan, n.d.)

---

arose from the ashes of the fire that devastated Jamestown, Virginia that destroyed most of the belongings and homes of the colonists. The loss of shelter, coupled with a devastatingly brutal winter, resulted in the death of over half of the settlers. While it is unrealistic to claim any success of this early American firefighting group, we must understand that some of our greatest achievements throughout time have come on the heels of failure. What we learn from Jamestown is that a lack of adequate management of response capability will only lead to fatal outcomes.

In the early colonial years, firefighting was conducted with community members and buckets responding to fires in their neighborhoods. In 1647, New Amsterdam (southern tip of Manhattan Island) developed a fire warden system with personnel patrolling streets during the night for fire hazards.[8] The four original fire wardens appointed by the governor of New Amsterdam, Peter Stuyvesant, were Adrian Geyser, Thomas Hall, Martin Krieger, and George Woolsey. Ordinances were developed empowering the fire wardens to inspect chimneys in homes and to issue fines for violations of the fire codes requiring chimneys to be swept to prevent fires. The fines were used to fund purchasing fire-fighting equipment. Thus, over 300 years ago in America, we have the beginnings of laws enacted to maintain public safety and empower officials to organize and coordinate emergency response.

In 1736, Benjamin Franklin is credited with co-founding the first American volunteer fire brigade, the "Union Fire Company," in Philadelphia and soon after other colonies followed his lead by forming their own volunteer fire brigades.[9] Union Fire Company was also known as the "Bucket Brigade" which was the manner by which they fought fires. Franklin's volunteer fire company was structured similar to that of the Boston Mutual Fire Societies. The difference between the two organizations is that Franklin's fire company served to protect their entire society where Boston's fire societies served only their membership. Here we have the next step forward in formalizing emergency response efforts within a jurisdiction by establishing a designated public safety system.

---

[8] (Thomas Hall, n.d.)
[9] (Union Fire Company, n.d.)

The ***Congressional Act of 1803*** is documented as the first Federal legislative act providing for disaster relief to a local community in the history of the United States.[10] A fire that devastated Portsmouth, New Hampshire in December 1802 was the incident leading to this historical act. The United States had only existed for 27 years at this time and the fire, which destroyed massive portions of the seaport in Portsmouth, threatened national commerce. Congress suspended the payments for bonds for several months to provide the much-needed aid to the merchants who had suffered severely from this fire. Literally, the United States was in its infancy when the concept of Federal assistance to State and Local governments was born.

Following the Civil War, the American Red Cross was founded in 1881 and received its first congressional charter in 1900 to provide disaster relief. The congressional charter was renewed in 1905 and the current version was adopted in 2007.[11] Clara Barton became inspired by the Swiss global Red Cross during a visit to Europe at the close of the Civil War. Initially, the mission in America was to provide for those who were injured in the war, however, that has grown to encompass domestic and international disaster relief. The American Red Cross has blossomed over the past 140 years to the point of now maintaining a veritable army of volunteers trained and poised to respond to aid the public in times of disasters. The birth of public-private partnership for disaster response can clearly be seen in the establishment and advancement of the American Red Cross.

On August 29, 1916, Congress created the Council of National Defense (CND) before entering into World War I. State Defense Councils were established and by November of 1918, those State Defense Councils comprised 182,000 people.[12] This executive branch committee was assigned to categorize and inventory national resources and report findings to Woodrow Wilson, President of the United States. The Council was charged with coordinating across industries engaged in resource production to enhance national security and public welfare. Critical and scarce

---

[10] (FEMA, History of FEMA, n.d.)
[11] (A Brief History of the American Red Cross, n.d.)
[12] (Harris, 1975)

---

resources were allocated between civilian and military sectors. Critical resource allocation is a major component of Emergency Management during response and recovery operations around the globe. As secondary accomplishment of the Council of National Defense was improvement of mobilizing massive numbers of the civilian population. Catastrophic disasters demand mobilization of critical resources to meet the needs of securing our society and are a bedrock of Emergency Management.

On September 8, 1939, *Executive Order 8248* established the Office of Emergency Management (OEM) as a component of the Executive Office of the President.[13] President Franklin Roosevelt reorganized the Executive Office of the President under this order and created the OEM as a unit responsible for reporting to the President in the event of a natural disaster or national emergency and to serve as a framework for managing such incidents. The structure allowed that the administration and facilities of the OEM would only be activated and become an integral component of the President's administration in times of emergencies that might seriously threaten the United States. You might consider this a failsafe option that was only to be utilized in times of great need in the nation.

By *Executive Order 8757*, on May 20, 1941, President Roosevelt created the Office of Civil Defense (OCD) within the Office for Emergency Management. The OCD was authorized to coordinate the actions to ensure the defense of civilians between Federal, State, and Local governments. To accomplish these lofty goals, State and Local defense councils were established, plans were developed to protect people and property, and auxiliaries were recruited and trained to provide effective response for strengthening national defense. Nine OCD regions were created in Boston, New York, Baltimore, Atlanta, Cleveland, Chicago, Omaha, Dallas, and San Francisco. The OCD developed the Civil Defense logo (blue circle surrounding a white triangle with the letters C and D in a bright red hue) which would endure through 2006.[14]

---

[13] (Harris, 1975)
[14] (Harris, 1975)

Preparing the citizens of the Nation and our States through training and preparedness drills was a central focus throughout the era of the Cold War in the 1980's which has transitioned to our current Emergency Management training.

Public Law 253: National Security Act of 1947 was approved on July 26, 1947, under the *Unification Act* that established the National Security Resources Board.[15] The Board was charged with advising the President during times of war on the mobilization of manpower, resources, and the scientific concerns of the Department of Defense. The statutory mission of the Board included: (1) developing policies regarding civilian and industrial mobilization, (2) effective utilization of resources for civilian and military purposes, (3) policies to unify Federal agencies and departments involved in the transportation of supplies for civilian or military use, (4) the establishment of adequate critical and strategic resources and conservation, and (5) potential strategic relocation of economic, government, industry, and services to maintain continual operation of National security activities. One certainty during any type of disaster is that there are never enough resources at the beginning and the unique nature of disasters demands rapid response with limited or scarce resources.

"In 1950, Congress passed the *Federal Disaster Relief Act (Public Law 81-875)* also known as the *Disaster Relief Act of 1950*, authorizing the President to provide supplementary Federal assistance when a Governor requested help and the President approved the request by declaring a major disaster."[16] The Disaster Relief Act of 1950 authorized disaster relief funding to States and Local jurisdictions on a case-by-case basis that required an individual enactment of law by Congress for each disaster requiring Federal financial aid. This was actually an improvement over the preceding 150 years, from 1803 to 1947, during which some 128 separate statutes were on the books concerning disaster relief.

---

[15] (The National Security Act of 1947 – July 26, 1947, 1947)
[16] (FEMA, Unit Three: Overview of Federal Disaster Assistance)

The Disaster Relief Act was amended on several occasions, including:

- In 1966, the Act was amended to include some recovery measures.
- The 1969 amendment expanded public and individual assistance.
- The 1970 amendment included temporary housing and debris removal.
- The 1974 amendment introduced emergency declarations and provided a robust program of preparedness.
- In 1988 the Disaster Relief Act was amended and renamed as the "Robert T. Stafford Disaster Relief and Emergency Assistance Act (Stafford Act) which authorized the President to declare an emergency for any incident requiring Federal assistance, defined a major disaster, established a 75% minimum level of Federal assistance, and provided for a 50/50 cost sharing on grants for hazard mitigation. The Stafford Act, which will be covered in depth in Chapter 7, has been a cornerstone for Emergency Management since it was instituted.

By *Executive Order 10186*, on December 1, 1950, President Harry Truman created the Federal Civil Defense Administration under the Office for Emergency Management.[17] The Administration's purpose was to enable and promote civil defense in cooperation between the Federal and State governments. The functions of the Administration encompassed: (1) developing Federal plans for civil defense in conjunction with the States and neighbor countries, (2) developing and standardizing civil defense measures, (3) dissemination of civil defense information with foreign governments, (4) conducting training for State and Local civil defense leaders, (5) encouraging States to establish mutual aid agreements or compacts to respond to emergencies which exceed the capabilities of Local governments, and (6) providing for civil defense communication. Still today, we have State mutual aid agreements and the Emergency Management Assistance Compact (EMAC) to facilitate emergency assistance across State jurisdictional boundaries.

---

[17] (Harris, 1975)

The National Security Resources Board produced the *"Blue Book"* in 1950 that outlined how civil defense should be implemented within every level of government.[18] This book received its nickname due to the cover being a blue background inscribed with the words "United States Civil Defense." A central premise of the Blue Book is that civil defense begins with individual self-protection, which is then extended to the community, Local government, State government, and finally the Federal government. Civil defense was organized with volunteers working in cooperation for a common good. These volunteers served as components of the United States Civil Defense Corps. Individuals were trained and expected to first take care of themselves and their families during emergencies. Personal responsibility was the core facet of civil defense; a concept which must continue to maintain resiliency today and into the future.

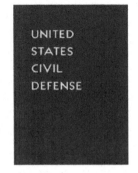

President Kennedy established the Office of Emergency Planning and Office of Civil Defense on July 20, 1961.[19] Admittedly, President Kennedy's primary concern was the threat of a nuclear strike upon the United States. However, by requiring an increase in building new emergency shelters and identifying existing facilities which could serves as shelters, this action began a process through which families and communities enhanced protection measures on a larger scale. Building shelters was only part of the mission of the Office of Emergency Planning; another goal was to exponentially increase public education efforts and methods for protection. Since 1961, individuals and communities have built shelters to protect against tornadoes, hurricanes, and even home invasions. Just stop and consider for a moment how each person taking actions to improve their own security has a positive impact upon the greater community protection.

In 1970, President Nixon renamed the Office of Civil Defense to the Defense Civil Preparedness Agency, and it took on the dual role of civil defense and

---

[18] (Civil Defense and Homeland Security: A Short History of National Preparedness, 2006)
[19] (Civil Defense, n.d.)

response to natural disasters.[20] While this may on face value seem to be a minor course correction, in reality, the adoption of the dual role model allowed States and Local governments to utilize civil defense funding for natural disaster preparedness. It is at this point that we begin to see the forming of a holistic view of preparedness. The impetus of this major change came from Governors applying pressure due to an increased opinion that separating civil defense and preparedness for emergencies was simply an outdated ideology. Thus, were lain the building blocks that would later lead to an "All Hazards" approach to emergencies that serves the interests of everyone in the nation today.

Due in part to the disaster of Three Mile Island, President Jimmy Carter established the Federal Emergency Management Agency (FEMA) on April 1, 1979.[21] Just a few days earlier, on March 28th, one of the Three Mile Island nuclear reactors near Middletown, Pennsylvania melted down resulting in the worst nuclear power accident in the history of the United States. Fortunately, only a small radioactive release arose from the accident and no noticeable impacts upon the health of workers, or the public were observed. However, the accidental meltdown was a revelation to officials at all levels of government. President Carter issued *Executive Order 12148* that consolidated numerous Federal agencies within the executive departments that had been assigned various portions of emergency preparedness into a single agency. Unifying the Federal efforts was only one of the major changes transpiring from this executive order. A secondary far-reaching component of this order was the establishment of FEMA as an "independent agency" not subject to Cabinet level interference. Since 1979, FEMA has served as the lead agency for all presidential declared disasters and continues to serve in that capacity.

Under *Public Law 107-296*, President George W. Bush established the Department of Homeland Security (DHS) on November 25, 2002.[22] Just one year

---

[20] (Defense Civil Preparedness Agency, 1972)

[21] (FEMA, FEMA History, 1979)

[22] (107th Congress, 2002)

prior to the founding of DHS, the United States suffered the worst terrorist attack on September 11, 2001. President Bush mandated that DHS would continually analyze threats, stand as guardians of our borders, provide protection for critical infrastructure industries, and lead coordination efforts for national emergencies. The Homeland Security Act of 2002 was the most widespread reorganization in the Federal government since the National Security Act of 1947. DHS was structured as an umbrella organization comprised of several Federal agencies, including FEMA, Federal Law Enforcement Training Center, Transportation Security Administration, U.S. Citizenship and Immigration Services, U.S. Coast Guard, U.S. Customs and Border Protection, U.S. Immigration and Customs Enforcement, and the U.S. Secret Service. DHS bolstered the national resolve to protect citizens against terrorism and has since aided in securing the populace in the face of natural disasters as well as terrorism.

On November 30, 2006, the old Civil Defense emblem was replaced with the Emergency Management (EM) logo.[23] This action was heralded as the death knell of the Civil Defense emblem, which had survived for 67 years as the beacon of emergency preparedness. The National Emergency Management Association, composed of State Emergency Managers, announced the replacement of the Civil Defense emblem and the Director of FEMA endorsed the decision. The developer, Mr. Morrie Goodman, explained that the new EM logo symbolized movement in the blue and gold sweeping arcs and that the three gold stars represented the levels of Local, State, and Federal government. Let me go on the record as saying there is nothing wrong with bringing a fresh image to the face of Emergency Management as long as we do not attempt to completely whitewash over what has come before. The old Civil Defense emblem served this country proudly for 67 years and we can all celebrate that heritage. Having lived through and served in the military during the Cold War and remembering the years of "duck and cover" Civil Defense training beginning in elementary school, I have an enduring respect for the work of civil

[23] (Dunlap, 2006)

defense. My personal hope is that the new EM logo might embody something with hope for a brighter future. Hopefully this logo be a beacon for the current Emergency Managers and for those aspiring to be the leaders of tomorrow.

On January 29, 2013, the *Sandy Recovery Improvement Act (SRIA)* was signed into law by President Obama. "In many ways, the passage of SRIA represents the most significant legislative change to the Federal Emergency Management Agency's (FEMA) substantive authorities since the enactment of the *Robert T. Stafford Disaster Relief and Emergency Assistance Act*."[24] Recommendations for nationwide changes included: greater flexibility for using Federal funds for Public Assistance, alternative procedures for debris removal, instituting a dispute resolution program, reimbursement for force account straight time, development of a national strategy to reduce the cost of future disasters, clarifying individual assistance, child care expenses, and a provision allowing Tribal governments to issue their own disaster declarations and request a Presidential declaration independent of the State or Local governments. While this sounds quite impressive, you have to fully comprehend the difficulty involved in maneuvering through the maze of Public Assistance (financial aid to State and Local governments) and Individual Assistance (financial aid to homeowners) following a major disaster. We will dive into the abyss of Federal Assistance in Chapter 7 covering the Stafford Act.

Building Blocks of Emergency Management Since 2003

To completely understand the current situation of Emergency Management in the United States, it is important to review the Federal mandates that have set the foundation. Ask any good contractor how to begin construction of a new building and they will explain how you first start by leveling and preparing the ground.

---

[24] (Sandy Recovery Improvement Act (SRIA) Fact Sheet, March 2014)

Follow that with erecting forms, digging piers and beams, adding an iron substructure, and then pouring and leveling concrete. Once you have the foundation in place, you can begin to assemble the designed edifice. After the terrorist attack on September 11, 2001, President George W. Bush was determined to take the existing foundational segments covered in the preceding historical paragraphs and lay the building blocks that strengthen Emergency Management. The plan was not to wipe away all that had proceeded, but rather to bring it all together into a national unified manner.

Homeland Security Presidential Directive (HSPD) 5: Management of Domestic Incidents

On February 28, 2003, President George W. Bush enacted *Homeland Security Presidential Directive 5* (HSPD 5) to address the management of domestic incidents. The policy set forth was "To prevent, prepare for, respond to, and recover from terrorist attacks, major disasters, and other emergencies, the United States shall establish a single, comprehensive approach to domestic incident management."[25] Up until this time, Emergency Management was conducted differently from jurisdiction to jurisdiction and little inter-agency coordination. Minimal coordination was fine on small incidents, however, on a catastrophic incident the lack of a single unified effort only adds to the chaos and confusion. Anyone who was alive on September 11, 2001, in the United States witnessed as first responders spent agonizing days on end trying to dig through the ashes and debris looking for survivors. What was also obvious, however, was the fact that there was tension amongst the various disciplines as they struggled to form some semblance of coordination. Even during the press briefings, there was confusion as to who was actually in charge. No one would argue that heroism was being exhibited for the world to witness. Even the hardest working responders, however, cannot overcome mismanagement and

---

[25] (Homeland Security Presidential Directive (HSPD) 5, February 28, 2003)

confusion. Our nation needed and deserved so much more in the face of the most destructive terrorist attacked on the civilian population. HSPD 5 was revolutionary in that it mandated the development of a comprehensive national incident management system. This directive became one of many sturdy building blocks in the strengthening of our national resolve to manage disasters.

Homeland Security Presidential Directive (HSPD) 7: Critical Infrastructure Identification, Prioritization, and Protection

Ten months later on December 17, 2003, President George W. Bush signed and released *Homeland Security Presidential Directive 7* (HSPD 7) to establish "a national policy for Federal departments and agencies to identify and prioritize United States critical infrastructure and key resources (CI/KR) and to protect them from terrorist attacks."[26] This term "critical infrastructure" was not a new way of describing something that had been a part of Emergency Management across the decades. HSPD 7 actually replaced *Presidential Decision Directive/NSC-62 Critical Infrastructure Protection* that was enacted on May 22, 1998. The term "critical infrastructure" has been the mechanism for describing those facilities, resources, and systems that are the most vital to the citizens of the United States. To that end, HSPD 7 designated Sector-Specific Agencies (SSAs) which possessed unique characteristics and models of operation regarding critical infrastructure. These agencies included the Department of Agriculture, Health & Human Services, Environmental Protection Agency, Department of Energy, Department of the Treasury, Department of the Interior, and the Department of Defense. HSPD 7 called for the development of a National Infrastructure Protection Plan (NIPP), to be address later in this text. What escapes the notice of most is that the vast majority of facilities and resources, which are classified as "critical infrastructure" in the United States, are privately owned. The owners of these facilities and resources may have to conform to guidelines

---

[26] (Homeland Security Presidential Policy (HSPD) 7, December 17, 2003)

established by Federal agencies, but private ownership prohibits any level of government from dictating complete control. That truth makes it even more necessary for all governmental agencies and private owners of CI/KR to work collaboratively to secure these facilities and resources.

On February 12, 2013, *Presidential Policy Directive (PPD) 21: Critical Infrastructure Security and Resilience* replaced HSPD 7. This directive cited three driving strategic imperatives to strengthen the CI/KR security and resilience: "(1) Refine and clarify functional relationships across the Federal Government to advance the national unity of effort to strengthen critical infrastructure security and resilience; (2) Enable effective information exchange by identifying baseline data and systems requirements for the Federal Government; and (3) Implement an integration and analysis function to inform planning and operations decisions regarding critical infrastructure."[27]

One of the reasons for sharing the documents and dates associated with CI/KR is to illustrate to the reader that the concept of protecting CI/KR was not something new. Rather, what we have seen over time is the progressive development and refinement of a nationwide approach. Prior to the institution of governmental oversight, the privately owned and operated CI/KR embraced industry standards for safety and protection. The vast majority of people do not realize that between 80% and 90% of all the CI/KR in the United States is privately owned. The birth of national plans for CI/KR protection served to bring all of the private sector stakeholders into a unifying effort under a single framework. The unity of effort objective is an expression of how we, as a Nation, are stronger and capable of attaining previously inconceivable achievements when we work together towards a common goal.

---

[27] (Presidential Policy Directive (PPD) 21, February 12, 2013)

Homeland Security Presidential Directive (HSPD) 8: National Preparedness

Also enacted on December 17, 2003, President George W. Bush signed *Homeland Security Presidential Directive 8* (HSPD 8) to strengthen the United States "by requiring a national domestic all-hazards preparedness goal" to enhance preparedness at the Federal, State, and Local levels of government.[28] The term "all-hazards" was defined within the directive as *those actions to prepare for acts of domestic terrorism, results of major disasters, and all other emergencies.* HSPD 8 served as a companion to HSPD 5 by establishing steps for improving coordination efforts in response to all types of incidents. Along with preventing, responding to, and recovering from all-hazards, the goal of HSPD 8 focused on promoting Federal assistance to State and Local governments in a more effective, efficient, and timely manner. To further highlight an emphasis on cooperation, HSPD 8 mandated engaging the private sector businesses and individual citizens in preparedness.

This signaled, not only a new age of coordination, but also a streamlined process. Considering that prior to the enactment of HSPD 8, individual jurisdictions and varying levels of government developed separate plans for the various potential incidents that were hazard dependent. In-depth plans were written to address the conceivable threats such as fires, flooding, hurricanes, tornadoes, and wildfires. The work alone in doing so was monumental and the proliferation of so many complex plans insured that only the planners truly knew what was contained within each plan. What HSPD 8 accomplished was to get responders at all levels to key in on those common tasks that must be completed regardless of the hazard. Tasks ranging from conducting a scene size-up to field operation processes are examples of common tasks. Now planners could write plans around those common tasks that must be accomplished at every scene; thus, the birth of the term "all-hazards" to state that these are the things we do for all hazardous incidents. Why was this so

---

[28] (Homeland Security Presidential Directive (HSPD) 8, December 17, 2003)

important? It is due to the fact that history has taught us that it is impossible to plan for every eventuality. However, we can plan to do the things that must always be done.

On March 3, 2011, President Barack Obama issued *Presidential Policy Directive 8* (PPD 8) that expanded HSPD 8 by aiming to strengthen the United States security and resilience in preparedness for "acts of terrorism, cyber-attacks, pandemics, and catastrophic natural disasters."[29] PPD 8 recognized that the preparedness of our nation was a shared responsibility across all levels of government, the private sector, and each individual citizen; coining the phrase "whole community." PPD 8 directed the identification of core capabilities in preparedness and five mission areas of prevention, protection, mitigation, response, and recovery. As a component of the National Preparedness Goal, PPD 8 set out to develop frameworks for each of the five mission areas to define just how the "whole community" works together. Each of the five frameworks will be analyzed later in this section of this book.

National Incident Management System (NIMS)

A shining outcome of HSPD 5: Management of Domestic Incidents was the development of the *National Incident Management System (NIMS)*, released on March 1, 2004, which "provides a consistent nationwide template to enable partners across the Nation to work together to prevent, protect against, respond to, recover from, and mitigate the effects of incidents, regardless of cause, size, location, or complexity." [30] It is important to note that NIMS is applicable to everyone: Federal, Tribal, State, and Local governments, private sector businesses, non-governmental

---

[29] (Presidential Policy Directive (PPD) 8, March 3, 2011)
[30] (FEMA, National Incident Management System, Third Edition, October 2017)

organizations (NGO), and volunteer organizations active in disasters (VOAD). NIMS doctrine is developed around the three major components of Resource Management, Command and Coordination, and Communications and Information Management. The Incident Command System (ICS), which had been in existence since 1974, is listed as one of the components of Command and Coordination. ICS will be covered in depth in later chapters. As a template, NIMS is adaptable for all incidents of any type, flexible to meet the needs of a specific incident, scalable depending upon the size of the given incident, and relies upon unity of effort. What NIMS did for Emergency Management was to bring everyone to an even playing field. Every agency from any organization or government was mandated to adopt NIMS if they played any part in disaster response. Imagine that… one set of rules! Now there was only one set of rules an individual had to learn to respond anywhere in the United States. Amazing!

National Response Plan (NRP)

Another major achievement coming out of HSPD 5: Management of Domestic Incidents is the creation of the *National Response Plan (NRP)* in 2004. The NRP replaced the *Federal Response Plan (FRP)*, which was released in 1992 to provide "the mechanism for coordinated delivery of Federal assistance and resources to augment efforts of State and Local governments overwhelmed by a major disaster or emergency."[31] The Department of Homeland Security initially released the concept of the NRP on September 30, 2003, and later released the finalized version in December of 2004. The NRP set out the process of managing an incident progressively. When a local jurisdiction exceeded its capability to respond with resources to meet the demands of an emergency or disaster; that jurisdiction would then request assistance from their respective county. When the county exceeded its capability, the county would then make a request to the State. Ultimately, if a State

---

[31] (Federal Response Plan, April 1992)

exceeded its capability, the State would then make a request for assistance to the Federal government. This insured a coordinated response between Local, State, and Federal levels of government. The NRP was updated on May 25, 2006, to incorporate best practices and lessons learned from responses to Hurricanes Katrina and Rita in 2005. Then on March 22, 2008, the NRP was replaced with the *National Response Framework (NRF)* that was subsequently included in the National Planning Frameworks developed based upon the requirements of Presidential Policy Directive (PPD) 8.

Many people did not realize that the NRP/NRF merely documented what was already in existence in Constitutional law at the Federal and State levels. The Tenth Amendment to the United States Constitution as a portion of the Bill of Rights and reads "The powers not delegated to the United States by the Constitution, nor prohibited by it to the states, are reserved to the states respectively, or to the people."[32] Additionally, within States, local jurisdictions retain rights granted to them under "Home Rule" or "Dillon's Rule," depending on the individual State Constitution. What the NRP/NRF accomplished was to basically recognize that all incidents begin and end locally. That simply means that it is the local jurisdiction maintains authority in all emergencies and disasters unlike the Hollywood depiction that the Federal government can merely swoop into a local jurisdiction and forcibly take control from the Local or State government. Now you can clearly see that it is a violation of Constitutional law for the Federal or State government to intervene in a local jurisdiction unless such jurisdiction makes a request for the aid through the issuance of a Local Disaster Declaration. Keep that in mind as you continue to study what is presented within this book.

---

[32] (Madison, December 15, 1791)

Post-Katrina Emergency Management Reform Act (PKEMRA)

In the wake of the myriad of challenges identified in the response and recovery operations for Hurricane Katrina in 2005, the *Post-Katrina Emergency Management Reform Act (PKEMRA)*, also referred to as the Post-Katrina Act, was enacted in 2006. "The act enhances FEMA's responsibilities and its autonomy within"[33] the Department of Homeland Security (DHS). The Post-Katrina Act went far beyond extending organizational and management changes to FEMA. This act addresses issues of emergency communications by requiring the development of the National Emergency Communications Plan, augmentation of catastrophic planning, revision of the National Response Framework (NRF), grants for State catastrophic planning, evacuation planning, emergency exercises, and emphasis on the unique needs of individuals with disabilities.

Many critics of the Federal government response have painted a picture for the uninformed that all of the failures attributed to the response and recovery for Hurricane Katrina lay at the feet of FEMA or the President. While that may make for attention grabbing sound bites, the truth of the matter is that failures existed at the Local, State, and Federal levels. Mayor of New Orleans, Ray Nagin, waited until August 28, 2005, less than 24 hours before Hurricane Katrina made landfall in Louisiana, to issue an evacuation order for the residents of his city. Look back to the previous section in this text under the National Response Plan (NRP) and pay attention to the progression that is required by law for how a local jurisdiction can obtain Federal response assets. First, the Mayor of a municipality or senior County official must issue a Local Disaster Declaration and then the Governor of the State must issue a State Disaster Declaration that is forwarded to FEMA for recommendation to the President of the United States to issue a Presidential Disaster Declaration. Those steps are required due to Constitutional law at the Federal and

---

[33] (Actions Taken to Implement the Post-Katrina Emergency Management Reform Act of 2006, November 21, 2008)

State levels. You cannot simply ignore Congressional law, even in the face of a catastrophic disaster. During the issuance of the evacuation order by Mayor Nagin, he advised that "authorities were setting up 10 refuges of last resort, including the city's Superdome, for people who were unable to get out."[34] Make sure that you fully understand the level of negligence that is revealed by the delayed order to evacuate. New Orleans at the time had approximately 485,000 people, the city is below sea level, and it resides inside of levees to keep the seawaters from engulfing its citizens. Katrina had initially made landfall in Florida on August 25th as a Category 1 hurricane and then emerged on August 26th in the Gulf of Mexico where it rapidly intensified to a Category 5 hurricane before weakening to a Category 3 hurricane when it struck Louisiana and Mississippi on August 29, 2005. Mayor Nagin had over three full days to act, but he chose not to do so. By his inaction, Mayor Nagin prohibited Louisiana Governor Kathleen Blanco and President George W. Bush from being able to act. In fact, Governor Blanco admitted during the press release documented in The Washington Post that President Bush had called urging the issuance of an evacuation order prior to the mayor doing what should have been done days before the press briefing.

The difference between what I can attest to and what many authors have written is that I was deployed attached to the Texas National Guard under the command of Brigadier General Eddy Spurgin as a member of Joint Task Force Lone Star. I did not digest reports and rely upon what others have offered to form my analysis; I was in the middle of it all. Our convoy pulled into New Orleans less than 48 hours after landfall and what we found was as close to an apocalypse as I can imagine. All told, I was deployed and involved with the response to Hurricane Katrina and Hurricane Rita for 68 days. Therefore, what I have to share is not merely opinion, but rather, firsthand experience. There was no organized assistance by the City of New Orleans. Instead, it was sheer pandemonium. Thousands of people, many without transportation, were left to their own devices to care for themselves during and in the aftermath of Hurricane Katrina. Those within the Superdome and

---

[34] (Branigin, 2005)

---

the New Orleans Convention Center were without any basic necessities. People throughout the region were trapped on rooftops, inside of buildings, and stranded wherever they could find some high ground. There was a complete collapse of the local government, and the State government was utterly overwhelmed. I offer this insight to encourage those who are reading this material to fully understand that there was plenty of fault at all levels, but the cascading failures began at the local level. Do not fall prey to rhetoric and assume that because someone speaks or writes about Katrina that they are doing so with expertise.

I am deeply passionate about what occurred during Hurricane Katrina and when I speak or write about those incidents, I do so from firsthand experience. I have heard many people claim to have been in New Orleans during Katrina, but I cannot vouch for their claims, and I have not viewed the evidence of their claim. I could not have been everywhere all of the time and it is possible for someone to have been involved that I did not meet. However, those of us who were there for an extended period of time crossed paths often. My own time in New Orleans, Louisiana, and East Texas is more than well documented. For my personal achievements during Hurricane Katrina, I was awarded the following military honors: (1) Texas Outstanding Service Medal for "Exemplary Service," (2) Texas Humanitarian Service Medial for "Selfless Service," (3) Louisiana Emergency Service Medal, (4) Texas Governor's Unit Citation for "Extraordinary Meritorious Conduct," and (5) the Texas Adjutant General's Individual Award for "Distinguished Meritorious Achievement." I always tell my interns and students, "Never be afraid to prove yourself to others." I live by that philosophy and stand ready to prove myself.

National Infrastructure Protection Plan (NIPP)

The *National Infrastructure Protection Plan (NIPP)* was established in 2006 with the goal to: "Build a safer, more secure, and more resilient America by enhancing protection of the Nation's CI/KR to prevent, deter, neutralize, or mitigate the effects of deliberate efforts by terrorists to destroy, incapacitate, or exploit them; and to strengthen national preparedness, timely response, and rapid recovery in the event of an attack, natural disaster, or other emergency."[35] In addition to the Sector-Specific Agencies (SSAs), the NIPP identified the sixteen (16) critical infrastructure sectors of Chemical, Commercial Facilities; Communications; Critical Manufacturing; Dams, Defense Industrial Base; Emergency Services; Energy; Financial Services; Food & Agriculture; Government Facilities; Healthcare & Public Health; Information Technology; Nuclear Reactors, Materials, and Waste; Transportation Systems; and Water & Wastewater Systems Sectors. These 16 sectors were deemed to be so vital to Americans that impairment of their operation or destruction could debilitate the economy and security of our Nation. The NIPP was intended to create a single unifying structure for CI/KR protection. As with all other Federal directives and guidelines to this point, the NIPP stressed planning, partnership, and information sharing. As Emergency Managers, we have to fully understand the complexities created due to the private ownership of CI/KR because those issues will drive our planning considerations.

National Planning Frameworks

As previously mentioned, *Presidential Policy Directive 8* (PPD) 8 required the development of frameworks for each of the five mission areas of Response, Prevention, Protection, Mitigation, and Disaster Recovery. As a component of the National Preparedness System, the intent of developing the frameworks was to outline the involvement of the "whole community" in relation to the mission areas. The progression of Emergency Management over the decades and centuries is like what is evidenced in nature with the smoothing of the rough edges of a boulder as it is shaped over time by erosion, wind, and water. Over a protracted period of time, the rough edges of the boulder are minutely eroded away slowly and ultimately

---

[35] (FEMA, National Infrastructure Protection Plan (NIPP), 2006)

revealing a smooth surface. Emergency Management is no different; throughout the centuries, the concept of Emergency Management has been refined and sculpted and it will continue to do so in response to our ever-changing society. Each of the National Planning Frameworks builds upon the structures of Emergency Management that have been in existence in our Nation for quite some time. Thirty-two Core Capabilities, or examples of work, have been established along with the five mission areas. Basically, core capabilities are examples of the types of activities associated with the mission areas. The underlying theme for the Frameworks for the five mission areas of Response, Prevention, Protection, Mitigation, and Disaster Recovery is engaging the "whole community." It goes towards the old adage – "Many hands make the work light."

National Response Framework (NRF)

As articulated previously, the FRP/NRP/NRF had already been in place for 28 years at the time that PPD 8: National Preparedness was issued. The NRP/NRF was designed with the intention of aligning "key roles and responsibilities across the Nation."[36] The Fourth Edition of the NRF released on October 28, 2019, streamlined the 2016 Edition and expanded upon integrating the government and private sectors in response efforts. It is at this point that the conceptualization of the seven "community lifelines" of Safety & Security, Food/Water/Shelter, Health & Medical, Energy, Communications, Transportation, and Hazardous Materials were introduced. The 2019 NRF identified the community lifelines as primary services enabling continued operation of critical business and government functions, which are essential to the community as a whole. The lifelines are representative of the basic services our citizens rely upon for the safety and stability in their day-to-day lives. The community lifelines were linked to the core capabilities that may be assessed, built upon, or validated in preparedness and response operations. As a mission area, *response is inclusive of the actions, which are necessitated to save*

---

[36] (FEMA, National Response Framework, Fourth Edition, October 28, 2019)

lives, protect the environment and property, and provide for basic human needs in the immediate aftermath of a disaster or emergency incident. This newest version of the NRF concentrated on disasters and emergencies which negatively impinge the life of the individual citizen and how we, as Emergency Managers, must take that into account in all that we work towards.

Below are the core capabilities, examples of work, associated with the response mission area:

- Planning
- Public Information and Warning
- Operational Coordination
- Critical Transportation
- Environmental Response/Health and Safety
- Fatality Management Services
- Fire Management and Suppression
- Logistics and Supply Chain Management
- Infrastructure Systems
- Mass Care Services
- Mass Search and Rescue Operations
- On-Scene Security, Protection, and Law Enforcement
- Operational Communications
- Public Health, Healthcare, and Medical Services
- Situational Assessment

National Disaster Recovery Framework (NDRF)

The *National Disaster Recovery Framework (NDRF)* was first released in September of 2011 and the Second Edition came out in June of 2016. The "NDRF describes principles, processes, and capabilities essential for all communities to more effectively manage and enable recover following an incident of any size or scale."[37] Within the NDRF, the concept of recovery is far greater than merely repairing the damages caused by disasters and emergencies. A fundamental understanding of recovery is that it ***entails everything that can possibly be accomplished to attempt to restore a community back to some sense of normality.*** Restoration has to circle around cultural concerns, economic influences, infrastructure protection, physical security, and social needs to achieve any level of recovery. In every disaster of every shape and size, communities will require resources to recover. Catastrophic disasters will call for wide ranging resources, while less expansive disasters may necessitate fewer resource needs. In any incident, Emergency Managers will be challenged to pick up the pieces of society and attempt to put them back together like a giant jigsaw puzzle. Ages ago, we have learned the lesson that it is impossible to make a community whole by returning it back to its original state. Emergency Managers have moved beyond speaking of returning to normal and, instead, we refer to attaining a "new normal" because inevitably things will be different.

Below are the core capabilities associated with the disaster recovery mission area:

- Planning
- Public Information and Warning
- Operational Coordination
- Economic Recovery
- Health and Social Services
- Housing
- Infrastructure Systems
- Natural and Cultural Resources

---

[37] (FEMA, National Disaster Recovery Framework, Second Edition, June 2016)

National Prevention Framework

The first edition of the *National Prevention Framework* was released in May of 2013 and updated in June of 2016. ***Prevention focuses on terrorism or human-caused incidents because we do not possess the ability to prevent acts of terrorism.*** "This Framework provides guidance to leaders and practitioners at all levels of government; private sector and nonprofit sector partners; and individuals to prevent, avoid or stop a threatened or actual act of terrorism."[38] The National Prevention Framework is applicable to leaders in all levels of government, private and nonprofit sector, communities, and individuals working together to prevent acts of terrorism. Reporting of suspicious behavior or potential terrorism by the public and partnering with the private sector and law enforcement, is one manner in which the National Prevention Framework embraced the "whole community" concept. This represents the continued refinement of Emergency Management by broadening the scope of work to recognize how prevention of terrorism is a responsibility of every single man, woman, and child in America. Initiatives, such as ***"See Something – Say Something,"*** across the nation have encouraged individuals to report anything out of the ordinary to the authorities in hopes that we can prevent acts of foreign or domestic terrorism from disrupting our lives. To complement the 911 system, toll free phone numbers, mobile applications, and websites have been dedicated to allowing the public to make anonymous reports of suspicious activity. Prevention is quite often the most difficult nut to crack for Emergency Managers because most people in the public are resistant to engaging in prevention or preparedness activities until their lives have been affected by an emergency or disaster.

Below are the core capabilities associated with the prevention mission area:
- Planning
- Public Information and Warning
- Operational Coordination
- Forensics and Attribution

---

[38] (FEMA, National Prevention Framework, May 2013)

- Intelligence and Information Sharing
- Interdiction and Disruption
- Screening, Search, and Detection

National Mitigation Framework

The First Edition of the *National Mitigation Framework* was released in May of 2013 and the Second Edition was released in June of 2016. The Mitigation Framework defines mitigation as *"risk management action taken to avoid, reduce, or transfer those risks."*[39] The actions of mitigation involve reducing loss of life and damages to property as a consequence of a disaster. Mitigation encompasses the classic equation stating "risk = threat x vulnerability x consequences." Threat is seen in the countless types of disasters, which may befall our society; vulnerability is viewed in the weaknesses attributed to our communities and systems; and finally, the consequences are the potential loss of life, damage to property, and disruption of the basic needs for the existence of humanity. Through the reduction of disaster impact, mitigation supports both the prevention and protection mission areas illustrating how even though the mission areas are separate in one sense, they are integral components of a greater whole. Moreover, mitigation weaves together prevention and protection, improves response, and speeds along recovery. Mitigation can be accomplished through building codes and ordinances, construction projects, floodplain management, property acquisition, public outreach, relocation, and training. Interdisciplinary coordination is the Emergency Managers' primary mechanism for bringing about effective mitigation.

Below are the core capabilities associated with the mitigation mission area:
- Planning
- Public Information and Warning
- Operational Coordination

[39] (FEMA, National Mitigation Framework, Second Edition, June 2016)

- Community Resilience
- Long-Term Vulnerability Reduction
- Risk and Disaster Resilience Assessment
- Threats and Hazards Identification

National Protection Framework

The *National Protection Framework* was originally released on October 29, 2014 and was updated and re-released in June of 2016. "This Framework describes the core capabilities, roles and responsibilities, and network of coordinating structures that facilitate the protection of individuals, communities, and the Nation."[40] The Protection Framework highlights those capabilities designed to insure our national security against natural or manmade disasters and acts of terrorism. This Framework established a strategy and doctrine for building, sustaining, and delivering the core capabilities of Protection. The National Protection Framework is a single document outlining a model for interdisciplinary Protection coordination. Again, we see the "whole community" concept at play in bringing together all of our governmental leaders, private and non-governmental sectors, and every individual in the United States. In the field of Emergency Management, we recognize that collaboration in relation to protection is facilitated by partnerships at all levels, operational coordination, and established principles and systems.

Below are the core capabilities associated with the protection mission area:
- Planning
- Public Information and Warning
- Operational Coordination
- Access Control and Identity Verification
- Cybersecurity

---

[40] (FEMA, National Protection Framework, Second Edition, June 2016)

- Intelligence and Information Sharing
- Interdiction and Disruption
- Physical Protective Measures
- Risk Management for Protection Programs and Activities
- Screening, Search, and Detection
- Supply Chain Integrity and Security

Emergency Management through the Years

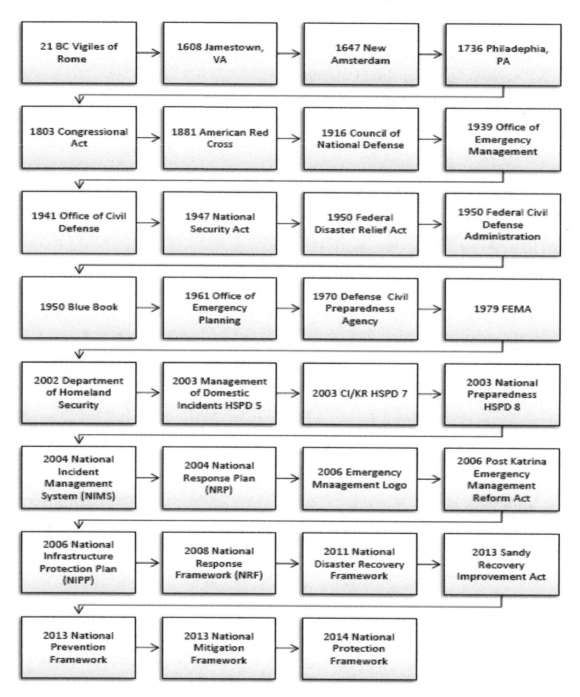

Table 1: Emergency Management Development (Ron Griffis)

In Chapter 1, we have covered historical documentation and development along with a review of 13 separate Federal mandate building blocks, which form the foundation of Emergency Management. Each of these directives, documents, plans, and frameworks have been enacted through the executive and/or legislative branches of the United States. Like a master craftsman building a stonewall, Emergency Managers set these foundational building blocks to erect a strong and durable system for managing disasters across our nation. Application, practice, and study aid us in gaining the needed proficiency to safeguard our citizens and communities.

Chapter 1 Summary

Key Terms (Alphabetical Order)

All-Hazards
Community Lifelines
Critical Infrastructure/Key Resources (CI/KR)
Emergency Management
Individual Assistance
Mitigation
Preparedness
Prevention
Public Assistance
Recovery
Response
Risk Management
Risk Management Equation
Whole Community

Historical Development of Emergency Management

In Chapter 1, we covered the time period of 21 BC to present day, over 2,000 years of history. I very well could have pulled out historical documentation of emergency response and planning which predated 21 BC, however, I felt going back 2,000 years was sufficient to make the point of the vast history of the field of Emergency Management. I also wanted to place the majority of my emphasis on the American development of Emergency Management and to view how we have shaped and molded this field since the founding of our Great Nation.

Building Blocks of Emergency Management

The building blocks are the Federal mandates comprised within Emergency Management. Each builds upon the best practices identified throughout U.S. history. Most of these building blocks were created to address critical issues experienced due to catastrophic disasters.

Homeland Security Presidential Directive (HSPD) 5: Management of Domestic Incidents

Homeland Security Presidential Directive (HSPD) 7: Critical Infrastructure Identification, Prioritization, and Protection

Homeland Security Presidential Directive (HSPD) 8: National Preparedness

National Incident Management System (NIMS)

National Response Plan (NRP)

Post-Katrina Emergency Management Reform Act (PKEMRA)

National Infrastructure Protection Plan (NIPP)

National Planning Frameworks

    National Response Framework (NRF)

    National Disaster Recovery Framework (NDRF)

    National Prevention Framework

    National Mitigation Framework

    National Protection Framework

In the next chapter, you will learn about how disaster management and incident command has evolved in the United States.

Chapter 2: The Evolution of Disaster Management and Incident Command

As we transition from Chapter 1 and the historical foundations of Emergency Management, we will revisit American history as we contemplate how disaster management and incident command has evolved since the colonization of our nation. Much of what we learn in Emergency Management has a founding in history because it is defined and re-defined through lessons learned and the application of best practices. Today we have luxuries, which were undreamt in the majority of the past four centuries and, at the same time, the challenges we face are far more complex. Therefore, for the modern person to comprehend how we have come to where we are in Emergency Management, we must study the struggles and challenges faced by our American ancestors.

Disaster Management in the United States from the Founding of the Nation

An elementary concept we must grasp when it comes to managing disasters is the dominant factor is that we are managing resources to meet the demands of the incident. FEMA defines a *resource* as *"Personnel and major items of equipment, supplies, and facilities available or potentially available for assignment to incident operations and for which status is maintained."*[41] Furthermore, the term *"equipment" is inclusive of aircraft, boats, heavy machinery, tools, and vehicles."*

---

[41] (FEMA, FEMA Glossary, n.d.)

Some of the Emergency Managers who have been around for a while refer to resources as "guts and gears and everything in between." By stepping back and peering into the past, our eyes are opened to the revelation that the early colonist and those who built this great nation over time had truly little in the way of resources as compared to what we have today. The colonists had to be resourceful and that is something we have inherited for them because in many disasters we have to be resourceful.

United States Management of Disasters in the 1600s

In general, historians refer to the history of the United States as beginning with the founding of the "Original 13 Colonies" which were established between the years of 1607 to 1776. However, since we are studying disasters in America, I feel that we at least need to mention the Roanoake Colony founded by Sir Walter Raleigh, which was comprised of 91 men, 17 women, and 9 children on the island of Roanoake in 1587. The reason for mentioning this first English colony in America is that the settlement mysteriously vanished by 1590 with no evidence of what happened to those colonists. Consideration of the Roanoake Colony is important because some unknown disaster occurred. It is not unreasonable to assume that the demise of the colony was at least partly due to a lack of their ability to respond to and manage the unknown incident based upon limited resources.

Transitioning to the period of the establishment of Jamestown on May 14, 1607, the early years for the original 100 colonists were fraught with tremendous hardships. A fateful fire was identified in Chapter 1, which occurred in Jamestown in January 1608, less than a year into the life of the Jamestown Colony. It was during this fire, which ravaged the provisions and lodgings of the colonists, that Captain James Smith is recorded as having organized an ad hoc group to respond to and battle the fire and possibly marks the first attempt of disaster management in the U.S. Making matters worse on the colonists, illnesses of typhoid and dysentery were common due to contamination of drinking water with human waste and seawater.

Which illustrates an utter lack of understanding of personal hygiene affecting public health in the early 1600s. The following two years would prove to be far harsher and taxing upon this fledgling colony. The winter of 1609 brought a bitter freezing cold to an unprepared colony; this period from the end of 1609 to the beginning of 1610 is referred to as the "Starving Time." George Percy served as the president of the colony during the "Starving Time" when over 400 colonists died leaving a total of some 60 survivors and he documented the disaster in the annals of history. Starving colonists were executed for stealing food from the colony provisions and early into the winter the people began eating the horses, dogs, cats, mice, fish, snakes and even the leather soles of their boots. Percy wrote his account *A True Relation* in which he recorded "And now famine beginning to look ghastly and pale in every face that nothing was spared to maintain life and to do those things which seem incredible as to dig up dead corpses out of graves and to eat them, and some have licked up the blood which has fallen from their weak fellows."[42] Yes, out of desperation, the colonists resorted to gruesome cannibalism to survive. Ironically, the ship arriving in the Jamestown harbor in September of 1610 was named the *Blessing*. These new arrivals found less than one-fifth of the original population of the Jamestown Colony in a state of precarious existence.

Why was a single fire and a bitterly cold winter so detrimental to the colony? The answer is – they had no resources with which to provide for the safety and security of the colony to endure those incidents. When those colonists stepped off of the boats and onto the shores of America, there were no homes and they had only the provisions and tools that they carried in their hands and on their backs. Every major resource they would need to survive, they had to craft or scrounge for themselves. There was no lumber to build homes, no nails, no crops, and no protection. For early colonists to have a home, they had to chop trees and cut logs because there were no milled boards to erect lodgings. Each family had to plant their own crops, fish, hunt, and trap to have a meal to eat. Government buildings and systems did not exist and would take generations to be fully established. Therefore,

---

[42] (Percy, 1624)

when it came to disasters and emergencies, there were no resources available to manage the incidents. Whether through individual determination or sheer dumb luck, a small percentage of these colonists were able to endure the hardships.

Subsequent arrivals of new colonists over time were slowly able to construct a semblance of livelihood and a foundation upon which to build our Nation. Yet, the challenges grew as the population began to blossom. The indigenous Native tribes and the colonists were constantly embroiled in conflict as the colonists began to expand into Native lands and consume natural resources. In 1622, the Powhatan tribe attacked the Jamestown Colony killing between 350 to 400 colonists in response to encroachments upon their lands. Those conflicts continued to fester over the next five decades, which led to the Bacon Rebellion in 1676 when Nathaniel Bacon took up arms against Governor William Berkeley in response to Native American uprisings. Bacon charged the Governor with corruption, drove Berkeley from the capital, and set fire to Jamestown on September 19, 1676. Less than one year later, Bacon died due to failing health brought on by dysentery in October of 1677. The final insult came in 1698 when the Jamestown central statehouse was burned to the ground resulting in moving the capital to the Middle Plantation (now Williamsburg) and utter abandonment of Jamestown in 1699.

From our review of the 1600s, Emergency Managers come face-to-face with the reality of the consequences when resources are scarce or completely unavailable to respond to protect lives and property. With few resources, no infrastructure, and only a vague governing system, the colonists had little to sustain themselves. Disasters were not so much as managed as they were survived – or not during the 1600s. The lessons learned by the colonists were brutal and must never be marginalized.

United States Management of Disasters in the 1700s

By the dawning of the 1700s in America, only ten out of thirteen founding colonies were in existence: Virginia (1607), New Hampshire (1629), Maryland (1632), Connecticut (1636), Rhode Island (1663), Delaware (1664), New Jersey (1664), New York (1664), Pennsylvania (1681), and Massachusetts (1691). Homes and buildings were springing up more in the populated regions, farming was taking more of a foothold, and government was continuing to be instituted during expansion. In the southern colonies, great plantations came into existence alongside of the single-family farms. Shipbuilding was a growing enterprise in the northern colonies. Water powered sawmills were erected in most towns, which provided ready access to lumber for building. Transportation, though, was extremely limited to either travel by foot, horseback, wagon, or boat where possible. Infrastructure roads were, more often than not, little more than dirt paths dotting the countryside. Yet, by 1775, over 2.5 million people had migrated to the shores of America. A Federal government system was finally beginning to take root within the nation. The Declaration of Independence was written in 1776, the Constitution of the United States was ratified in 1788 and the first Presidential election was held from December 15, 1788, to January 10, 1789. At the close of the 1700s, there were a total of 16 States which had been admitted into the United States (in order of year admitted): Delaware, Pennsylvania, New Jersey, Georgia, Connecticut, Massachusetts, Maryland, South Carolina, New Hampshire, Virginia, New York, North Carolina, Rhode Island, Vermont, Kentucky, and Tennessee.

The 1700s were also replete with wars on several fronts for the American colonies. At the forefront of the battles for this Colonial era, the Revolutionary War for independence from British rule spanned the years of 1775 to 1783. In the midst of the Revolutionary War, American colonists also struggled through wars with Native American tribes as settlers spread into the frontiers into tribal lands. Immediately following the war for independence, the newly formed American government had to contend with Shay's Rebellion in Massachusetts over taxation and citizen debt from 1786 to 1787, the Whiskey Rebellion in Pennsylvania over the taxation on whiskey from 1791 to 1794, and the Fries Rebellion in Pennsylvania over the taxation of Dutch farmers from 1799 to 1800.

An over-abundance of natural disasters during the 1700s further complicated the lives of these early Americans. Below is a selection of some of the disasters, which created added challenges during the formative years of the United States:

1. The "Great Snow" of 1717 resulting from four consecutive storms over 11 days dropping between 3 to 5 feet of snow on New England, which killed over a thousand sheep and numerous cattle, and horses.
2. Plagues of caterpillars descending upon Virginia in 1728 and 1729.
3. Charleston's "Great Fire" of 1740 causing over 250,000 pounds British Sterling in damages.
4. Back-to-back hurricanes pummeling Charleston and the surrounding plantations in September of 1752.
5. Earthquakes in 1755.
6. Boston's "Great Fire" of 1760, which incinerated more than 340 buildings and caused over 53,000 pounds British Sterling in damages.
7. The "Great Fresh" catastrophic flood in May of 1771 along the James River in Virginia. "Dozens of people and hundreds of cattle drowned and thousands of hogsheads (equivalent to 1,000 pounds per hogshead) of tobacco washed away from storehouses along the river."[43]
8. A hurricane, which viciously lashed the Leeward Islands in 1772.
9. The "Great Hurricane" of 1780, which ravaged the Caribbean from October 9th to the 15th. "The resulting casualties of the storm were on the order of 20,000 to 22,000 people on the islands and at sea. There are no reliable estimates of the financial damage, but the economies of the islands struck took decades to recover."[44]

Pause to consider the magnitude of challenges faced by early Americans in this time period. Added to the challenges, we must grasp the truth that colonists

---

[43] (Mulcahy, February 2018)
[44] (235th Anniversary of the Great Hurricane of 1780, October 13, 2015)

were still extremely limited in their capability to respond to disasters. Chapter 1 of this text documented how Benjamin Franklin is credited in the U.S. with establishing the first volunteer fire department in Pennsylvania in 1736. However, the amount of time required to respond to even a simple disaster was much different than we are accustomed to today. Volunteers responding to fires in this time had to do so on foot or horseback, a wagon may have needed to be hitched, water resources were monumentally scarce, bucket brigades may have to be formed, and the operation of wagon mounted pumps where available in very few cities. When it came to sea or water rescues, the process was much more tedious as boats were powered manually by rowing or with sails relying upon wind currents. Oftentimes, it was far less hazardous to those responding to wait for survivors and the deceased to make their way to shore on their own where they could then be tended. Much needed resources were becoming somewhat more available, yet the capability of the resources to be able to be rapidly deployed was non-existent for the most part. While the progression of disaster management moved at a snail's pace in the 1700s, it was moving forward and that forward momentum would set up the United States for massive growth and resource developments on all fronts in the years to come in disaster management.

United States Management of Disasters in the 1800s

The United States experienced rapid growth during the era of the 1800s. From 1803 to 1896 an additional 29 States were admitted to the Union bringing the total to 45 States (in order of year admitted): Ohio, Louisiana, Indiana, Mississippi, Illinois, Alabama, Maine, Missouri, Arkansas, Michigan, Florida, Texas, Iowa, Wisconsin, California, Minnesota, Oregon, Kansas, West Virginia, Nevada, Nebraska, Colorado, North Dakota, South Dakota, Montana, Washington, Idaho, Wyoming, and Utah. While there were some advancements in industry in the first two-thirds of the century; it was during the decades following the Civil War, which are regarded as establishing the U.S. as an industrial giant in the world. The generations born prior to the 1870s witnessed a sweeping revolution of industry and technology. Society and the way of life changed rapidly in the lifetimes of the U.S. citizenry. "Industrial growth transformed American society. It produced a new class of wealthy industrialists and a prosperous middle class. It also produced a vastly expanded blue collar working class."[45] Below you will find a sampling of some of the radical changes to the lives of Americans during the 19th Century:

1. Lighting sources transitioned from candles and kerosene lamps to electric light bulbs.
2. Transportation evolved from travel by foot, horse, and boat to steam powered locomotives, cable cars, electric trolleys, combustion engine automobiles, subways, and steamer ships crossing the Atlantic.
3. Communication by pony express and telegraph gave way to the invention of the telephone making it possible to communicate over great distances in a relatively short amount of time.
4. The agricultural community gave way to a burgeoning industrial society.
5. Millions of Americans would migrate from the rural setting to blossoming cities.
6. The quiet and peaceful rural setting was replaced with air pollution, constant noise, sanitation and health problems, slum or tenement housing, and the building of skyscrapers.
7. In the first half of the 19th Century, the Nation saw wagon trains to the West and in the later half railways and automobiles dotted the landscape.

The 1800s proved to be a prolific time period of wars including over 25 wars with Native American tribes, the War of 1812, Texas Revolution (1835 – 1836), Mexican American War (1846 – 1848), Civil War (1861 – 1865), Spanish American War (1898), and the Philippine American War (1899 – 1902). The proliferation of wars with Native American tribes was due to the Federal government driving the natives from the southeastern portion of the United States to allow for American settlements. Many government officials initially set out to "civilize" the Native American tribes through religious conversion, encouraging education of the English

---

[45] (Weiser-Alexander, 2018)

language, and adoption of European-style customs. Most tribes rejected the teachings of the American settlers and conflicts broke out as the two cultures overlapped. As a result, State governments joined with the Federal government in driving the Native Americans out of the southern region. In 1830, Andrew Jackson "signed the Indian Removal Act, which gave the federal government the power to exchange Native-held land in the cotton kingdom east of the Mississippi for land to the west, in the "Indian colonization zone" that the United States had acquired as part of the Louisiana Purchase. This "Indian Territory" was located in present-day Oklahoma."[46] Between 1831 and 1850, thousands of Creeks, Choctaw, and Cherokee were driven from their lands and forced to march more than 1,200 miles to Indian Territory (Oklahoma). In 1838, President Martin Van Buren ordered General Winfield Scott and 7,000 American soldiers to herd the Native Americans at gunpoint. Along the way, thousands of Native Americans died from cholera, dysentery, exposure, starvation, typhus, and Whooping cough. That fatal march is referred to as the "Trail of Tears" and it stands as a blemish upon American history. You may be asking, "What does that have to do with disaster management?" You have to look at it from the viewpoint of moving thousands of people with few belongings from their home to another location. During disasters, we may be called upon to relocate or evacuate large numbers of people. While the forced relocation of Native tribes is quite different from an evacuation, we can learn about the issues of communicable diseases, emotional and mental stresses, and personal safety related to evacuations from those relocations.

In the midst of all of the other chaos, the United States suffered a number of catastrophic disasters during the era of the 19th Century. On December 16, 1811, the first of three major earthquakes registering between 7.5 and 7.7 struck with an epicenter near New Madrid, Missouri. The second and smallest of the three earthquakes occurred on January 23, 1812. The third earthquake, on February 7, 1812, equaled or exceeded the December quake. "There were thousands

---

[46] (Trail of Tears, 2020)

of aftershocks, of which 1,874 were large enough to be felt in Louisville, Kentucky, about 190 miles (300 km) away. The number of lives lost from the earthquakes remains unknown; however, scholars note that the number was probably not great, because the region had only a sparse rural population."[47] The New Madrid earthquakes are confirmed as the strongest earthquakes recorded in North America east of the Rocky Mountains. The New Madrid Seismic Zone (NMSZ), named after the epicenter of these quakes, spans an eight State region across Alabama, Arkansas, Illinois, Indiana, Kentucky, Mississippi, Missouri, and Tennessee. While the region was a sparsely populated rural setting in 1812, today several million people inhabit the area. "Were these earthquakes to occur today, their effects would be considered catastrophic, directly affecting several million people across eight states and indirectly affecting millions of others."[48] Shifting forward in time, in 2006 the Central United States Earthquake Consortium (CUSEC) began the New Madrid Seismic Zone (NMSZ) Catastrophic Planning Project. The New Madrid earthquakes are a perfect example of why Emergency Managers must be knowledgeable of the historic disasters, which have befallen our nation because they may occur again.

In 1871, the Great Chicago Fire "burned from October 8 to October 10, 1871, and destroyed thousands of buildings, killed an estimated 300 people and caused an estimated $200 million in damages."[49] It is estimated that over 100,000 people were left homeless, and 17,000 structures were destroyed. You may have heard the legend that Catherine O'Leary's cow started the fire by kicking over a lantern in her barn. Speculating on the cause is irrelevant since there is no way to determine the veracity of such claims. What is important to note is that a second fire broke out on the same day in Peshtigo, Wisconsin, which killed 1,000 people and burned until October 10, 1871, when it was finally brought under control in part due to a rainstorm that aided the firefighting efforts. Why were these fires so destructive? It is because of flammable building materials and firefighting equipment, which was not adequate to fight fires of this scale. In less than two decades following the Great Chicago Fire,

---

[47] (Rafferty, 2010)
[48] (New Madrid Seismic Zone Catastrophic Planning Project, n.d.)
[49] (Chicago Fire of 1871, 2018)

the city had almost doubled in population, modern high-rise structures dotted the skyline, and the economy and public transportation were booming. The Chicago Fire Department Training Academy today is located on the site where this horrific fire started in 1871 and serves as a testament of that fateful fire.

On May 31, 1889, an earthen dam built in the 1840s on the Conemaugh River collapsed and created a flood which killed over 2,000 people 14 miles downstream in Johnstown, Pennsylvania. At the time, this was the largest earthen dam in the United States at a size of 900 feet wide and 72 feet high. The dam had originally been built from dirt and rock to create the largest man-made lake of this era, Lake Conemaugh, and an extensive canal system to transport goods. As trains and the railways began carrying the majority of the goods across this region, the dam was neglected and no longer maintained. Steady rains across the area and a logjam of debris in the spillway spelled disaster. "An engineer at the dam saw warning signs of an impending disaster and rode a horse to the village of South Fork to warn the residents. However, the telegraph lines were down, and the warning did not reach Johnstown. At 3:10 p.m., the dam collapsed, causing a roar that could be heard for miles."[50] As was pointed out in Chapter 1, Clara Barton founded the American Red Cross in May of 1881 and the Johnstown Flood marked one of the first major disaster relief missions undertaken by the private volunteer agency.

Even though nearly 200 years have passed since some of these disasters, we are still dealing with some of these same issues. Natural disasters of communicable disease, flood, fire, and the like are constant concerns for the modern Emergency Manager. From the disasters of the 1800s, we learn that larger and more complex disasters demand the implementation of advanced planning, better building standards, resources capable of handling massive incidents, mobilization of community volunteers, and training for responders to better manage the incidents. The nation was growing rapidly during the 19th Century and that rapid expansion brought new challenges along with hope for facing what might lay ahead. Innovation and invention were bringing technologies to bear which have served as a

---

[50] (Johnstown Flood of 1889, 2020)

springboard to achieve greater heights for humankind. A monumental leap forward for disaster management was borne in engaging the community in disaster management which has paved the way for our concept today of "Whole Community."

United States Management of Disasters in the 1900s

From 1907 to 1959, the last five States were admitted to the U.S. bringing the total to the current 50 States: Oklahoma (1907), New Mexico (1912), Arizona (1912), Alaska (1959), and Hawaii (1959). Where the later portion of the 1800s ushered in an industrial revolution, the 1900s were filled with unprecedented technological advancements in the United States. Leaps and bounds were prevalent in communications, computers, defense, flight, space flight, and transportation technology. Sadly, many of our technological advancements coincided with some of the most devastating wars in global history and more than a few regional conflicts.

1. Between the opening of the 20th Century and 1924, the United States engaged in at least 10 more wars with Native American tribes.
2. The United States and Mexico fought the Border War from 1910 to 1919
3. World War I from 1914 to 1918
4. World War II from 1939 to 1945
5. Cold War from 1947 to 1991
6. Korean War from 1950 to 1953
7. Vietnam War from 1959 to 1975
8. Gulf War from 1990 to 1991

The 20th Century was also the era, which was laden with terrorist acts, carried out on U.S. soil. Ask the average citizen when the first terrorist bombing of the 20th Century was carried out within the Nation, and most would cite the late 1990s or early 2000s. However, in truth, the first terrorist bombing in New York was carried out shortly after 12:00 pm in downtown Manhattan on the corner of Wall and Broad Street just outside of the J.P. Morgan Building on September 16, 1920. At the time of the explosion, the sidewalks of Manhattan were filled with brokers, clerks, and receptionists on their way to lunch. The source of the explosion was a horse drawn cart loaded with roughly 100 pounds of the high explosive Trinitrotoluene (TNT) and 500 pounds of fragmented sash weights for shrapnel. The resulting blast killed 39 people, injured more than 300, flipped nearby automobiles, shattered thousands of windows over a half-mile radius, and caused financial damages in the millions of dollars. "The noise was heard throughout Lower Manhattan and across the East River in Brooklyn. The smoke-filled streets were covered with a layer of shattered glass, debris from the damaged buildings, and bodies."[51] Seven decades later the City of New York endured the first, World Trade Center bombing in February of 1993, which killed seven people and injured over 1,000. Just over two years later, Timothy McVeigh committed the worst act of domestic terrorism in the history of the U.S. when he bombed the Alfred P. Murrah Federal Building in downtown Oklahoma City on April 19, 1995. McVeigh loaded a Ryder truck with ammonium nitrate, diesel, and other chemicals to create the massive explosion, which rocked Oklahoma City shortly after 9:00 a.m. "Within moments, the surrounding area looked like a war zone. A third of the building had been reduced to rubble, with many floors flattened like pancakes. Dozens of cars were incinerated, and more than 300 nearby buildings were damaged or destroyed."[52]

The 20th Century was also plagued with catastrophic disasters, which were complicated with high population densities in the respective areas of impact. For the sake of brevity, we will review three of the natural disasters to strike the United States in the 1900s and list others afterwards. The first disaster befalling this era is the deadliest natural disaster in U.S. history, which occurred when Galveston, Texas was decimated on September 8, 1900, as a category four hurricane made landfall. With storm winds surpassing 135 miles per hour, more than 3,600 buildings were destroyed in its path. "Estimates of the death toll range from 6,000 to 12,000, according to the National Oceanic and Atmospheric Association (NOAA)."[53]

---

[51] (Kiriakova, n.d.)
[52] (Oklahoma City Bombing, n.d.)
[53] (Little, 2019)

At the time, hurricane prediction science was far less advanced than current capabilities. The second disaster presented in the 1900s, which we will consider, is the 1918 Spanish Influenza Pandemic. This strain of influenza spread worldwide from 1918 to 1919. Some 500 million people, approximately one-third of the global population, is estimated to have been infected with the virus. "The number of deaths was estimated to be at least 50 million worldwide with about 675,000 occurring in the United States."[54] Similar to COVID-19 in 2020, there was no vaccine at the time of the Spanish Influenza outbreak and non-pharmaceutical measures focused on personal hygiene, isolation, limiting public gatherings, and quarantine. The third disaster we will address is the cataclysmic eruption of Mount Saint Helens in Skamania County, Washington on May 18, 1980, which is recorded as the worst volcanic disaster in the United States. The eruption cost the lives of 57 people and caused far-reaching issues. "A high-speed blast leveled millions of trees and ripped soil from bedrock. The eruption fed a towering plume of ash for more than nine hours, and winds carried the ash hundreds of miles away. Lahars (volcanic mudflows) carried large boulders and logs, which destroyed forests, bridges, roads and buildings."[55] The site of the eruption became a laboratory for studying volcanic activity and has led to many advancements in volcanology and eruption prediction. Other complex disasters experienced in the 1900s include:

1. Scofield Mine Explosion in May of 1900
2. San Francisco Earthquake in April of 1906
3. The Great Mississippi Flood in April of 1927
4. The Dust Bowl in the 1930s which is also referred to as the "Dirty Thirties"
5. Three Mile Island in March of 1979 (previously mentioned in Chapter 1)
6. Wreck of the Exxon Valdez in March of 1989
7. Oklahoma F5 Tornado in May of 1999

On the positive side, the 20th Century set a blazing pace for technological advancements that would represent profound improvements for disaster management. Over the course of the next hundred years, the Nation witnessed as

---

[54] (1918 Pandemic (H1N1 virus), n.d.)
[55] (Mount St. Helens 1980 Eruption Changed the Future of Volcanology, 2020)

telephone communications advancements were rapidly changing. The age of the telephone moved beyond the years of relatively few telephones existing in a community, to landlines in most homes, and finally to cellular phones owned by the vast majority of Americans. Computer technology started at a slow pace with the invention of the "Turing Machine" by Alan Turing in 1936, which became the central concept for the modern computer. While the introduction of the personal computer after the advent of the microprocessor in 1971 began a chain of inventions, which fill our society today. Cellphones, tablets, laptops, watches, defense technology, and more all have a lineage coming from the microprocessor. The aircraft industry has benefitted greatly from micro technology as well and has grown far beyond those first days of flying. On December 17, 1903 "Near Kitty Hawk, North Carolina, Orville and Wilbur Wright make the first successful flight in history of a self-propelled, heavier-than-air aircraft."[56] Since the days of the old bi-planes, we have seen the invention of the helicopter and first turbojet in 1939, the first intercontinental commercial flight in 1939, breaking of the sound barrier in 1947, launching of the first U.S. satellite "Explorer I" in 1958, manned sub-orbital space flight in 1961, landing the first man on the moon in 1969, and the launching of the space shuttle program in 1981. Similarly, transportation has astronomically advanced since Henry Ford began the first assembly line manufacturing his automobile on December 1, 1913. When comparing the speeds of the early 1900s vehicles to those at the end of the century, it is like comparing a snail to a cheetah. The top end speed of a 1913 vehicle was between 40 to 45 miles per hour. Today, we have vehicles rolling off of assembly lines capable of easily traveling at 100 to 200 mph, which does not even come close to the high-performance racing Indy cars with top speeds up to 240 miles per hour. The capacity, fuel, performance, safety, size, and shape of automobiles currently on the market varies widely.

---

[56] (First Airplane Flies, 2019)

In 400 years, this nation has come a long way since those early days when there were not enough resources to secure the safety of 91 men, 17 women, and 9 children on the island of Roanoake. The United States Census Population Clock estimates the U.S. population on October 21, 2020, as more than 330,479,604 and advises there is one birth every 8 seconds. In our founding years, we struggled due to rapid growth and a limited capability to provide the resources needed to manage large-scale disasters. Manpower and the vital equipment were scarce and lacking. Incrementally through the past four centuries, American ingenuity has been spurred along by necessity. This Nation has seen more than its fair share of hardships and, yet, we have continued to push the boundaries of development. The continuation of the Global War on Terrorism since September 11, 2001, with combat on multiple fronts in the Middle East has also served as an impetus to technological achievements. Only time will tell of the technological marvels we will see come from the 21st Century. Infrastructure systems exist today because of the downfalls we have faced in the past. No longer do you have to navigate by using a sextant to chart the stars because we have technology, we have launched amongst the stars to guide using the Global Positioning System (GPS) from our cellphones, laptops, tablets, vehicles, and even our watches. The industrial achievements in this era set the cornerstones for building the vast infrastructure we rely upon in our everyday lives. For disaster management, we learned some difficult lessons and established best practices to guide us through catastrophic incidents. Cars, trucks, heavy equipment, boats, planes, and unmanned aircraft are available making the management of disasters today much more successful. Computers, connectivity, and technology systems provide capabilities, which allow us to manage disasters, which would appear to be magical to our ancestors. However, I caution, it is not the technology and toys we have that make us capable – it is the people, Emergency Managers, and our knowledge, which make us capable when faced with challenges. Chaos abounds in disasters and knowledge can win the day! When we apply our time to learning from the past, we make ourselves better prepared to deal with the unknown disasters of tomorrow. It is because of our growth over the past four centuries that today we have the capability and capacity to rapidly respond to and manage catastrophic disasters.

Establishment of the Incident Command System (ICS)

Many have wrongly assumed that the *Incident Command System (ICS)* was developed after the terrorist attacks of September 11, 2001. The truth of the matter, however, is that ICS has been in existence since the 1970s, which we will get to later in this section. Before we get too far ahead of ourselves, it would be best to identify ICS and how it is utilized. The Incident Command System (ICS) is defined by FEMA as *"A standardized on-scene Emergency Management construct specifically designed to provide an integrated organizational structure that reflects the complexity and demands of single or multiple incidents, without being hindered by jurisdictional boundaries."*[57] The beauty of ICS is that it is applicable to and can be utilized for any incident or event of any size or duration. Which leads right to defining both an incident and an event. The textbook definition of *an incident is "An occurrence, natural or human-caused, that requires a response to protect life or property."*[58] While *an event is defined as a planned activity such as a concert, fair, parade, private or public gathering, sporting competition, or exercise.* The key difference between an incident and an event is that incidents occur at any time and require response without the benefit of pre-planning, whereas events allow us time to pre-plan. In this section of Chapter 2 we will look at how the Incident Command System (ICS) has blossomed from a mere concept, primarily attributed to fighting wildland fires, to a nationally implemented system to manage all types of incidents and events within the United States.

The Military Model of the Early 1900s

When we look back to our history following World War I, you can see how the fire service and law enforcement embraced a military command structure. This

---

[57] (FEMA, FEMA Glossary, n.d.)
[58] (FEMA, FEMA Glossary, n.d.)

is heavily due in part to the service members returning after the war instituting a familiar rank structure in emergency services. Officer and sergeant ranks were conferred upon those in leadership to create an orderly chain of command. Some variations were melded into the mix creating a quasi-military rank structure; however, the basis was something, which was familiar to the majority of the population of the U.S. The military model enabled the public, as well as other emergency service personnel, to be able to quickly distinguish the senior leadership at a glance. Internally, the military model provided an orderly mechanism for personnel to be able to refer issues upward to progressive levels of supervision and it allowed issues to be managed at the lowest possible level. For single department or single jurisdiction incidents, the military model functioned exceptionally well. However, when multiple departments worked a single incident, the possibility could arise where equal ranking officers from different agencies would be managing the same scene. In most cases, the confusion could be managed through mutual cooperation. To the public, however, it may have been a bit more frustrating to determine who was in charge and misunderstandings could exist even on the best-managed incidents. The weakness of the military model is seen in that it was driven by the orders of a leader, or leaders, basing actions upon experience without much in the way of a thought through plan. This model was more geared towards the "take that hill" concept than one of strategies and tactics to achieve objectives.

The Large Fire Organization (LFO) Model from the 1940s to 1980s

Much like the Military Model, the *Large Fire Organization (LFO)* model grew from service members returning home from World War II and incorporating applied military command and control tactics learned during the war to wildland fires. As a prime example, in 1956 the United States Department of Agriculture (USDA) Forest Service conducted "the first practical airplane tanker airdrop of water and chemicals on a forest fire. Many of the airplanes were converted World War II bombers, now with their bomb bay doors full of borate and other mixtures rather than bombs."[59] Repurposing surplus military equipment, implementation of military battlefield strategies and tactics, in addition to an orderly rank structure flowed out of the lessons learned in combat over the next four decades. Catastrophic disasters have many similarities to the chaos and destruction of war because the loss of life and devastation of property is a reality. Improvements in military tactics from World War II, Korean War, Vietnam War, and the Cold War would all trickle into management of disasters as military members applied their battlefield skills back home in the face of man-made and natural disasters. "As an incident management system, LFO was capable of expanding to incorporate multiple agencies, but its downfall was it lacked a strong central coordinating mechanism. This was one of the shortcomings exposed during the 1970 fire season."[60] In the military, there is always a central commanding headquarters to provide high-level guidance for units deployed in the field to insure common and inter-related goals are being achieved. That guiding focal point was the missing piece of the puzzle in LFO. Nowhere was the lack of a centralized management more evident than the devastating Southern California fire season of the 1970s. "At the time, the sky was full of giant smoke columns and fire apparatus were passing each other on their way to incidents, with some going north as others headed south. Individual Command Posts and fire camps were established by multiple agencies for the same incident. Response resource availabilities reached critically low levels."[61] Over 13 days, these fires claimed the lives of 13 people, destroyed more than 700 homes and structures, burned over half a million acres, and caused over $234 million in damages. The U.S. Forest Service and partner fire agencies from across Southern California conducted an after-action review to examine incident management of these fires and found that the origins of the confusion were based upon differing terminology, organizational structures, procedures, and competition for critical resources. In short, each agency had its own "play book" that varied from lesser to greater extents than those of other agencies. This, in turn, led to the organization of the interagency group named

---

[59] (Gerald W. Williams, April 2005)
[60] (History of ICS, n.d.)
[61] (History of ICS, n.d.)

---

the *Firefighting Resources of Southern California Organized for Potential Emergencies* or FIRESCOPE, which set out to accomplish two main goals for managing wildland fires: (1) development of a Multiagency Coordination System (MACS) and (2) creation of a unifying Incident Command System (ICS).

During this same time period, "the Phoenix Fire Department developed the Fire Ground Command System (FGC) which potentially set up for two competing incident management systems. The concepts of FGC were similar to FIRESCOPE ICS, but there were differences in terminology and in organizational structure. The FGC system was developed for structural firefighting and was designed for operations of 25 or fewer companies."[62] Several attempts were made to blend FIRESCOPE ICS and FGC, including the National Fire Protection Association (NFPA) issuance of NFPA 1561 in 1987 titled the *Standard on Fire Department Incident Management System*. In 1990, the National Fire Service Incident Management (IMS) Consortium was created to evaluate the development of a single command system. Leaders from FIRESCOPE and the Phoenix Fire Department served as representatives of the consortium. One of the consortiums' greatest outcomes was an agreement to develop operational protocols within ICS to form a common system. In 1993, the consortium published a document titled *Model Procedures Guide for Structural Firefighting* and FIRESCOPE incorporated the IMS model enabling responders to effectively apply ICS in any region of the country. NFPA, who had adopted FIRESCOPE in 1980, subsequently incorporated the IMS Consortium model into its own academy training.

The *National Interagency Incident Management System (NIIMS)*, sometimes referred to as the "two-eyed NIIMS," was accepted by Federal and State wildland fire agencies in 1981. NIIMS incorporated both the Large Fire Organization (LFO) and Incident Command System (ICS) to include management of "national disasters such as terrorist bombings, floods, hurricanes, and earthquakes, and local situations in which several jurisdictions are involved, such as tornadoes, major aircraft

---

[62] (FEMA, NIMS and the Incident Command System, n.d.)

accidents, and hazardous material spills"[63] to be managed more efficiently. NIIMS would become the basis for the National Incident Management System (NIMS), introduced in Chapter 1. The "two-eyed NIIMS" was comprised of five major components; foremost of which was ICS. It is between the 1970s to the early 2000s that we begin to see how all of the ideas would meld together and form what we currently understand as the Incident Command System (ICS). In 1983, only two years after NIIMS began to be accepted by Federal and State wildland fire agencies, FEMA adopted the use of ICS at the National Fire Academy (NFA). All of the growing pains of the past now set the stage for bringing about the implementation of an incident management system, which could be standardized across the Nation for all types of hazards, rather than specific to structural, and wildland firefighting.

Institutionalizing ICS from the 1970s to Present Day

The transition, over the next three decades, was shaped by catastrophic incidents pushing the nation forward from an Incident Command System (ICS) primarily for the fire service to a system, which is applicable to *"All Hazards," which describes human-caused, natural, or technological incidents warranting actions intended to protect lives, property, environment, and safeguard basic human needs*. Simply put, "All Hazards" means any type of incident of any shape, size, or complexity. We have seen up to this point how FIRESCOPE, the Phoenix FGC, and even the "two-eyed NIIMS" focused on wildland and structural fires. Admittedly, fires comprise the bulk of the disastrous incidents, which occur on any given day in the United States. However, a broad spectrum of disasters occur aside from fires and those incidents must be managed as well to prevent ensuing chaos in our society. It is unfathomable to have separate incident management systems for the different types of disasters and emergencies experienced.

---

[63] (National Interagency Incident Management System , 2004)

The first major incident propelling ICS along the path towards an "All Hazards" approach was the Exxon Valdez Oil Spill, which happened on March 24, 1989, when the oil tanker *Exxon Valdez* spilled roughly 11 million gallons of crude oil in Alaska's Prince William Sound. "The Exxon Valdez oil slick covered 1,300 miles of coastline and killed hundreds of thousands of seabirds, otters, seals and whales."[64] It is estimated that the Exxon Valdez Oil Spill killed over 250 bald eagles, 250,000 birds, 300 seals, and 22 killer whales. The salmon and herring industry completely collapsed in the region as a result of the impact of the oil on the ecological system. The spill was caused when the Exxon Valdez struck the Bligh Reef resulting in a gash to the ship's hull. At the time, the Exxon Valdez Oil Spill was recorded as the single largest oil spill in U.S. territorial waters. Response attempts to contain the spill were a massive failure. The oil slick spread across the waters uninhibited for months and eventually would coat nearly 1,300 miles of a once pristine coastline. More than 11,000 Alaskan residents, responders, and Exxon employees labored for months attempting to conduct clean up, recovery, and restoration. As recently as 2001, over half of the 91 beach sites in the area tested found oil contamination. The economic impact was crushing on the Alaskan communities as fishermen went bankrupt, shoreline communities suffered untold losses, and an overall estimate of the total in economic loss is projected to be in excess of $2.8 billion. An outcome of the Exxon Valdez Oil Spill was an expansion of the National Contingency Plan (NCP), "the federal government's blueprint for responding to both oil spills and hazardous substance releases."[65] The struggles to respond to the Exxon Valdez Oil Spill were complicated due to a lack of a cohesive incident management process. The agency with the primary jurisdiction in U.S. territorial waters is the United States Coast Guard (USCG) and they studied the failures in the response and scoured the Nation for a solution, which they found in the Incident Command System (ICS). On September 28, 1998, the USCG issued Commandant Instruction 3120.14 adopting "the use of the National Interagency

---

[64] (Exxon Valdez Oil Spill, 2018)
[65] (National Oil and Hazardous Substances Pollution Contingency Plan (NCP) Overview, n.d.)

Incident Management System (NIIMS) based Incident Command System (ICS)."[66] Since 1998, the U.S. Coast Guard has become the premier military component of the United States for the application of ICS. The Coast Guard ICS expertise was put to the test on April 20, 2010, when the *Deepwater Horizon* oil rig exploded in the Gulf of Mexico and gushed over 210,000,000 million gallons of crude oil over 87 days. Deepwater Horizon would dwarf the spill of the Exxon Valdez, becoming the worst oil spill in U.S. history. The USCG response was unprecedented and thanks to the National Contingency Plan (NCP) designating the Coast Guard as the authority to coordinate hazardous pollution incidents in U.S. coastal zones. The economic and environmental impact of the Deepwater Horizon incident cannot be understated, but the difference was this time there was an effective system in place to manage the incident.

Finally, we come to the incident cited by many as being a catalyst for institutionalizing ICS in America – the terrorist attacks of September 11, 2001. An entire generation has been born since that day and many have no concept of the magnitude of horror brought about by 19 militant Islamic terrorists. On this fateful day, the terrorists hijacked four commercial airplanes, flew two of the planes into the World Trade Center (WTC) twin towers in New York, flew a third into the Pentagon outside of Washington, D.C., and the fourth plane was crashed into a field in Shanksville, Pennsylvania. The first three airplanes struck their intended targets; however, the target of the fourth plane is unknown. The body count was staggering with some 2,996 people killed and nearly 10,000 injured. The death toll could have been much higher had not passengers and crew members of the fourth plane, United Flight 93, taken action to rebel against the 4 terrorists who had seized control of the plane. The American heroes of United Flight 93 thwarted the terrorists, attacked the cockpit, and brought the plane down in that rural field in Shanksville. Responders, military, non-governmental agencies, volunteer organizations, and private citizens poured into the impact areas to search for survivors, treat the injured, and start trying to bring order to chaos. Heroic achievements were accomplished in the days, weeks, and months to come, however, some of the

---

[66] (Commandant, United States Coast Guard, September 28, 1998)

tragedy was self-inflicted. *The 9/11 Commission Report* did not paint a flattering picture for incident management: "For a unified incident management system to succeed, each participant must have command and control of its own units and adequate internal communications. This was not always the case at the WTC on 9/11."[67] Fire, law enforcement, and other agencies failed to have a cohesive unified command center to provide command and control and critical information for decision-making was not shared with key stakeholders. As discussed in Chapter 1, this series of tragedies led President George W. Bush to issue Homeland Security Presidential Directive (HSPD) 5 to establish a single, comprehensive approach to domestic incident management system and HSPD 8 to implement a nationwide "All Hazards" incident management approach applicable to all levels of government. Those two Presidential Directives brought about the establishment of the *National Incident Management System (NIMS)* or "one-eyed NIMS" requiring the use of the Incident Command System (ICS) for "all levels of government, nongovernmental organizations (NGO), and the private sector to work together to prevent, protect against, mitigate, respond to, and recover from incidents."[68] While there are only a few differences between them, the "one-eyed NIMS" replaced the "two-eyed NIIMS" in March 2004; a major change was the shift from being fire centric to "All Hazards." The process of institutionalizing ICS nationwide flowed from HSPD 5, which states "Beginning in Fiscal Year 2005, Federal departments and agencies shall make adoption of the NIMS a requirement, to the extent permitted by law, for providing Federal preparedness assistance through grants, contracts, or other activities."[69] Grant eligibility and jurisdictional emergency operations plans were tied to NIMS Compliance, which entails complying with NIMS training requirements for all responders, "adoption and use of the Incident Command System (ICS), a plain language requirement, the inventorying and typing of resources, and more."[70] What that means is that each jurisdiction was required to officially adopt, through a State

---

[67] (9/11 Commission, July 22, 2004)
[68] (FEMA, National Incident Management System, Third Edition, October 2017)
[69] (Homeland Security Presidential Directive (HSPD) 5, February 28, 2003)
[70] (FEMA, NIMS Training Program FAQs, October 3, 2011)

or Local law, and use NIMS ICS. That is where the "carrot and the stick" comes into play for NIMS Compliance. By that, I am referring to the use of a "carrot" as a means to lure jurisdictions into adopting ICS by pointing out that by doing so they will then be eligible for Federal grant money. The backside of the adoption of ICS is in the "stick" with which a jurisdiction can be punished by not being eligible for grants, not being eligible for reimbursement during major disasters, and the jurisdiction plans would not be accepted if the jurisdiction was found not to have adopted using ICS. These were all measures to prevent jurisdictions from "pencil whipping" or stating on paper that they were complying, while in reality they never practiced and applied ICS during disasters and emergencies.

When we look back on what has transpired since the 1970s to institutionalize an Incident Command System (ICS) within the United States, you begin to see how the entire process was molded by catastrophic disasters, which our Nation faced at several points. That is what is commonly referred to as "Lessons Learned" and, unfortunately, those lessons almost always come at great cost of lives and economic impact. Additionally, after a major disaster we develop an After-Action Report (AAR) to document what we set out to do, what we actually accomplished, what challenges were identified, and what actions should be adopted as "Best Practices" for future disasters. It is through this looking glass that we are continually evaluating and improving to meet the unknown challenges in the future. An evaluation had to occur after the fires in Southern California in the 1970s, after the Exxon Valdez Oil Spill in 1989, and after the terrorist attack of September 11, 2001. From each incident, we have been able to refine our processes, improve our training, and strengthen our capabilities and capacities. That is why I always tell people, "Emergency Management plans are written in sand and not chiseled in stone." We have to remain flexible and open to change as the challenges we face become more daunting.

Chapter 2 painted the picture that during the past 400 years have been filled with heartaches, growing pains, and tragedies as our Nation has struggled with taming a frontier and building America. However, along with every hardship, we have experienced great achievements at all levels, and we have built a grand country. As Emergency Managers, we are going to face painful incidents in our careers, but we cannot allow those incidents to discourage us. We exist to bring order into chaos and to be an unseen force providing safety and security to our loved ones, family, friends, neighbors, and the rest of our communities. Today we have an Incident Command System (ICS) for all types of incidents and all that goes along with it because of our forebears who endured destruction and mayhem but grew from those trying times to go on to accomplish greatness. Those who serve as Emergency Managers and those who will come after us have inherited a legacy of perseverance and fortitude.

Chapter 2 Summary

Key Terms (Alphabetical Order)

After Action Report (AAR)
Best Practices
Event
Fire Ground Command System (FGC)
Firefighting Resources of Southern California Organized for Potential
Emergencies (FIRESCOPE)
Global Positioning System (GPS)
Incident
Large Fire Organization (LFO)
Lessons Learned
Military Model
National Interagency Incident Management System (NIIMS)

Management of Disasters in the United States through the Centuries

In Chapter 2, we have sifted through 400 years of crises and advancements, which have formed the United States. Manmade and natural disasters, industrial and technological achievements, and a plethora of wars have dotted our history and changed the methods we employ in disaster management. Concepts birthed in tragedy have grown to fruition and our resilience has risen in spite of the catastrophes endured. Below is a list of the selected disasters, which were covered in this chapter:

1600s: Founding Struggles

Roanoake Colony 1587
The "Starving Time"
New Arrivals
Conflict with Native American Tribes and Settlers
The Bacon Rebellion
Survival Mode

1700s: Expansion of a New Nation

Colonial Establishment
Revolutionary War 1775 to 1783
Frontier Wars with Native American Tribes
Shay's Rebellion 1786 to 1787
Whiskey Rebellion 1791 to 1794
Fries Rebellion 1799 to 1800
Pestilence 1728 to 1729
Charleston "Great Fire" of 1740
Charleston Hurricane of 1752
Earthquakes of 1755
Boston's "Great Fire" of 1760
The "Great Fresh" of 1771
Leeward Island Hurricane of 1772
Caribbean "Great Hurricane" of 1780
From 13 Colonies to 16 States
Establishment of a Disaster Management Foothold

1800s: Growing Pains and Industrial Revolution

U.S. nearly tripled in Number of States
Wars with Native American Tribes
War of 1812
Texas Revolutionary War 1835 to 1836
Mexican – American War 1846 to 1848

Civil War 1861 to 1865

Spanish – American War 1898

Philippine – American War 1899 to 1902

New Madrid Earthquakes 1811 to 1812

Trail of Tears 1831 to 1850

Great Chicago Fire of 1871

Johnstown Flood of 1889

Complex Demands of Catastrophic Disasters

Mobilization of Community Volunteers

1900s: Wars, Terrorism, and Technological Advancement

Wars with Native American tribes

Galveston Hurricane 1900

Scofield Mine Explosion in May of 1900

San Francisco Earthquake in April of 1906

United States and Mexico Border War from 1910 to 1919

World War I from 1914 to 1918

Spanish Influenza Pandemic 1918

Terrorist Attacks 1920, 1993, and 1995

The Great Mississippi Flood in April of 1927

Dust Bowl of the 1930s

World War II from 1939 to 1945

Cold War from 1947 to 1991

Korean War from 1950 to 1953

Vietnam War from 1959 to 1975

Three Mile Island in March of 1979

Eruption of Mount St. Helens 1980

Wreck of the Exxon Valdez in March of 1989

Gulf War from 1990 to 1991

Oklahoma F5 Tornado in May of 1999

Dawning of a National instituted Incident Command System (ICS)

The second half of Chapter 2 focused on how ICS was initially envisioned and how it grew to become institutionalized throughout the Nation. Driven by the needs of ever increasingly complex incidents, the United States grappled with developing a systematic approach to protecting lives, property, and the environment in light of major disasters. The three major progressive attempts to carry out this enormous goal are catalogued below:

Military Model of the Early 1900s

The influence of military members returning from World War I.

Large Fire Organization (LFO) from the 1940s to 1980s

Implementing military command and control measures shaped by World War II, Korean War, Vietnam War, and the Cold War.
1970s Southern California Fires
National Interagency Incident Management System (NIIMS)

Incident Command System from the 1970s to Present

Firefighting Resources of Southern California Organized for Potential Emergencies (FIRESCOPE)
Fire Ground Command System (FGC)
Exxon Valdez

In the next chapter, you will learn about the characteristics and application of the Incident Command System (ICS).

Chapter 3: The Incident Command System (ICS) From Theory to Practice

In the preceding chapter, we studied disaster management development and institutionalizing the Incident Command System (ICS) within the United States. It has been a long road to get to where we are and there have been tremendous bumps along the way. Continuing our forward momentum, we must now turn our attention to understanding how ICS functions. Before jumping in with both feet, I want to encourage the readers to take advantage of the ICS training provided by FEMA online (https://training.fema.gov/is/crslist.aspx) and in the classroom setting. There is a vast array of free training provided by FEMA, which is required for Emergency Managers, and you can also check with the local or State Emergency Management in your area for other training opportunities. Now, moving onward and upward, we will study ICS from the foundational characteristics, organizational structures and facilities, and round it off with an overview of the Incident Action Plan (IAP) process.

Foundations of the Incident Command System (ICS)

As was articulated in Chapter 2, the foundations of ICS stretch back over the past 50 years of American history. The groundwork was accomplished in the wake of adversity and tragedy time and time again. Much like the mythology of the phoenix, ICS has risen from the ashes and devastation of incidents across the United States. When we have experienced calamity and tackled challenges pushing the boundaries of the capabilities of our Nation, we may have stumbled on occasion, however, we have continually persevered. Confronting and analyzing identified deficiencies is a painful process, which brings about productive growth and adds value to both personal and professional development. ICS has benefitted from this process, as it has been refined and expanded from being fire centric to an "All Hazards" approach.

ICS: A Component of the National Incident Management System (NIMS)

Recall from Chapter 1 that in 2004 the *National Incident Management System (NIMS)* was released to provide a consistent nationwide template to enable partners from across the United States to work together effectively on any disaster regardless of cause, size, location, or complexity. Such a lofty goal does not come easily, nor is it simplistic in nature. Within the covers of the NIMS document, we find three main components, which were identified as critical elements to achieve what had been set forth in this system: (1) Resource Management, (2) Command and Coordination, and (3) Communications and Information Management. Of the three components, the Incident Command System (ICS) is a sub-component of Command and Coordination. Along with ICS, Emergency Operations Centers (EOCs), Multiagency Coordination (MAC) Groups, and the Joint Information System (JIS) round out the element of Command and Coordination. Historically, we have seen that ICS predated the formation of NIMS by thirty years and had been slightly modified over that time period. At the point of the release of NIMS, we now see that ICS has not only been incorporated into this national guidance, but it has become a major segment of the larger whole.

Fourteen NIMS Characteristics adopted into ICS

Resulting from the intermingling of NIMS and ICS, a homogeneous byproduct was created. Take, for example, that NIMS is expressed as being comprised of fourteen foundational characteristics and, after 2004, ICS is presented as adopting these very same characteristics. Separate from this co-mingling, NIMS and ICS each are strong pillars of the construct of Emergency Management. However, through the amalgamation of the two, we end up with a single process reinforced system in which both parts uphold each other. There is a symmetry I truly hope you will not overlook in what was accomplished. Even in the process of developing a template to enable agencies to work together, we have systems, which are now being designed to "work together" like the cogs of a gear. Often times when you hear Emergency Managers speak of NIMS or ICS; the two terms are used synonymously simply because the two are inseparable. That point must be clear before I launch into describing the fourteen foundational characteristics adopted by ICS. Individually, we will analyze these characteristics and consider their meaning within ICS and NIMS.

1. **Common Terminology**

   Throughout our study of the history of disasters, we have seen findings where differences in terminology are cited as an issue negatively affecting operations. To address those instances, NIMS set out a requirement for all agencies working on disasters to do so using "common terminology." Easy, no problem, right? No, it is not quite so simple. Partially this was driven by the use of "10 Codes" on radio communications by emergency medical services, firefighters, and law enforcement because each had their own set of "10 Codes" and they were not the same. From jurisdiction to jurisdiction within the United States, agencies would adopt and modify "10 Codes" to the point where those used by law enforcement in one area did not match the codes used by other law enforcement agencies a few short miles down the road. The terminology issue was one far more encompassing than just the codes used on radios when speaking to dispatch. The naming terminology for pieces of equipment, facilities, position titles, work assignments, and so forth also varied widely between agencies. People from different agencies could be standing in the same room and discussing an operation and be utterly misunderstood. When we step back from the situation and think, it is not difficult to understand how this can transpire. Pronunciation and names of "things" are different from State to State, culture to culture, and region to region. What NIMS was requiring through the "common terminology" characteristic was for responders across disciplines to learn a new language. That is why I express to students and groups I am addressing about Emergency Management that our "common terminology" requirement is an oxymoron because it is not referring to language, which is common to the rest of the world; it is referring to our own agreed upon language. So, as responders from all disciplines are trained on ICS, they are indoctrinated with our language and, thereby, making it common to us. The nomenclature for positions, facilities, equipment, and actions is established in NIMS and ICS. Everyone, regardless of their type of agency, is mandated to use the specified terminology. That is particularly important for people entering into a responder or Emergency Manager field because you will have to learn this language and not deviate from it.

2. Management by Objectives

This is a process through which an Incident Commander establishes objectives for the work to be accomplished during a single *operational period, which is "The period of time scheduled for execution of a given set of tactical actions as specified in the Incident Action Plan."*[71] An operational period is basically a work shift; typically, 8 to 12 hours. What is important for the reader to comprehend is that the identified objectives are intended to be completed within the given operational period. The objectives are utilized then to identify strategies and tactics to accomplish the objective. It is a systematic approach to aid in the development of work assignments and plans. The specific objectives developed provide benchmarks to measure performance, apply corrective measures, and establish subsequent objectives. The entire concept of managing by objectives is to insure a well thought out plan is formulated and to avoid disorganized mismanagement. Once objectives have been developed, all

---

[71] (NWCG, n.d.)

personnel on the incident are notified of the objectives through the produced Incident Action Plan (IAP) for the specified operational period.

3. **Manageable Span of Control**

Managerial leadership for disasters and emergencies is unlike business organizational management where a single manager may supervise dozens of people. As disasters grow and expand; so too grows the number of personnel working on the incident and the burden of adequately providing leadership can become onerous. Decades of experience have proven that a single person is only capable of effectively supervising a limited number of people in the midst of the consuming chaos in disaster response. The framers of ICS ultimately agreed that a limitation must be placed upon the number of personnel supervised by each leader. Therefore, it was determined that the manageable span of control for all supervisors would be limited to 3 to 7 and the optimum being five people. The whole idea of a manageable span of control is to prevent any one supervisor from being overwhelmed by the demands of those assigned to them. Anyone who has ever worked in a chaotic environment knows that it does not take much to create a logjam in leadership. Just one critical issue can monopolize the time of a supervisor and prevent that person from being able to adequately provide the leadership needed for others in their team. The limitation of a manageable span of control reinforces effective leadership by instituting a centralized leadership, which is supported by subordinate supervisors.

4. **Comprehensive Resource Management**

Resource management is a vital and complex task in coordinating disaster response. To assure that the right resource is procured for work assignments, within ICS, resources are classified by "Type" and "Kind." *Type describes "the size, capability, and staffing qualifications"*[72] of a resource and *kind describes what a resource is (for example: police officer,*

---

[72] (FEMA, ICS for Single Resource and Initial Action Incidents, Student Manual, October 2013)

firefighter, paramedic, etc...). Every resource has a type and a kind to be able to better assure that the resources ordered will be capable of performing the required job. Managing resources for disasters encompasses identifying requirements, ordering and acquiring, mobilizing, tracking and reporting, demobilizing, and finally reimbursing and restocking the needed resources. From the outside, resource management may not appear all that daunting. However, the fact is that as you go beyond mere hundreds of resources to thousands or tens of thousands of resources on a single incident, all of which must be tracked from the beginning to the end, the process becomes convoluted. Adding to the confusion, resources will be moved frequently from one work location to another to address the requirements of the incident. In addition, at any time throughout the process, you need to be able to quickly identify where the given resource is located. When it comes to personnel resources, you have to be able to rapidly locate a person who is working on an incident. Imagine, if you will, that a responder working on an incident has a family emergency where a loved one is critically injured or ill. If you cannot quickly locate that worker and demobilize them to be with their family, it is highly possible that they will experience the loss of the loved one and not have the opportunity to be there with their family. Equipment must also be able to be tracked at all times to make certain that we can get it back to where it belongs at the conclusion of the incident. When you lose a piece of equipment on the operation, it becomes expensive because you will then have to replace that piece of equipment, which will result in an expenditure of funds due to negligence. If that happens too often, you will probably end up looking for a new job. From the minute that a resource is deployed for an operation to the minute it is returned to where it belongs, we are responsible for its condition. When we fail to effectively manage resources, we can easily end up creating long lasting problems with our partners because they may choose not to allow us to utilize their resources in the future due to concerns that their resource will be damaged.

5. **Establishment and Transfer of Command**

In ICS, the question of how to determine who is in charge has been answered in a simplified manner. The first responder on-scene becomes the initial Incident Commander (IC). Thereafter, command may be transferred when a more qualified responder arrives on-scene. Take a search and rescue operation for example; the initial responder may be a police officer. That officer becomes the initial incident commander and will establish command and notify dispatch where command has been established, which will be communicated to all personnel heading to the incident. As additional responders arrive on-scene, a Search and Rescue team leader may arrive at which point the initial incident commander may transfer command. At some point in an operation, the IC should be the most qualified person on-scene to manage the specific hazard. For example, the IC for a hazmat scene should be a hazmat technician, for a crime scene it should be a law enforcement officer, and so forth. Throughout the cycle of an incident, command will be transferred at the end of each operational period and as the incident expands or contracts. One important point to clarify is that higher ranking does not translate to being more qualified; or as we commonly say, "In ICS – Rank means nothing!" That is not to say that you cannot have someone who is a high-ranking responder to be in the IC position. It is just that rank is not the determining factor as to whether someone is the highest qualified person for the incident.

6. **Chain of Command and Unity of Command**

Chain of command "is an orderly line of authority and reporting relationships within the ranks of the organization, with lower levels subordinate to, and connected to, higher levels."[73] Each person must know who they work for and who is in charge of the various elements of the operation. As was discussed in Chapter 2, responders established a quasi-

---

[73] (FEMA, Intermediate Incident Command System for Expanding Incidents, ICS 300, April 2019)

military organization after returning home from World War I and that continues today. Interwoven into the chain of command in ICS is the concept of *"Unity of Command," which is a simple way of stating that each person working on the disaster has only one supervisor.* By having a single supervisor, responders do not have to deal with the issue of being pulled in more than one direction by multiple supervisors issuing conflicting orders. Within the chain of command, communication from leadership is described as either "Formal Communication" or "Informal Communication." Supervisors use *formal communication to issue work assignments, order resources, and providing progress reports. Informal communication, on the other hand, serves the purpose of exchanging information on an incident,* such as the Food Unit Leader asking the Operations Section Chief for the number of personnel working on an incident to be able to order meals. Unity of command and designations of formal and informal communication uphold the chain of command and support the personnel assigned to work the incident. When responders know, who they work for and how they will receive work assignments, confusion is limited, and the entire operation is enhanced.

7. **Dispatch/Deployment**

What is vital to understand about the dispatch and/or deployment characteristic of ICS is that no one should ever "self-dispatch" or show up on their own without being requested by the incident. Those resources, personnel or equipment, which show up without a request are typically returned immediately. Why??? Because you are responsible financially for every resource received on an incident and you have no idea what you are getting when you did not vet the resource during the ordering process. It was not uncommon, in the past, for some agencies to self-dispatch every broken-down piece of equipment they had to an incident hoping that some unsuspecting individual might accept them so that later they could have the equipment repaired while on the incident when they broke down. As far as for personnel, you do not have time to verify the credentials of personnel who just show up without being requested and if you put someone to work who is not qualified you will be responsible for everything they do. To eliminate disreputable practices and reception of non-qualified personnel, dispatch or deployment of resources was instituted along with inspection of resources before putting any resource to work.

8. **Modular Organization**

As we get into the organization chart, modular organization will become more evident. Being modular means that we fill only the positions, which are needed on an incident. Just because a position exists on the organization chart does not necessitate filling that position. What will become more and more obvious as you progress in studying Emergency Management is that every decision has a financial burden attached to it. ICS aids organizations with financial responsibility by allowing the IC to determine if a position is needed and to fill or not fill positions based upon need. When you consider that on average most disasters do not qualify for reimbursement, it is incumbent upon Emergency Managers to limit costs and to eliminate financial waste because the local jurisdiction will withstand the worst of the financial cost. When incidents are mismanaged and financial irresponsibility occurs, a resulting effect may be that due to jurisdictional budget concerns local services may have to be cut and personnel may lose their jobs due to poor fiscal management.

9. **Incident Action Planning**

Later within this chapter, we will cover the Development of Incident Action Plans (IAPs) in depth. For brevity's sake at this point, an IAP is a plan, which spans a single operational period and the objectives to be accomplished during that time. Fortunately, the IAP process has been simplified through the use of standardized forms and procedures.

10. **Incident Facilities and Locations**

Under the "Common Terminology" characteristic above, it was stated that ICS has specific naming for positions, facilities, and equipment and those names do not change from one jurisdiction to another. The facilities most often cited include the Incident Command Post (ICP), Staging Area, Base,

Camp, and Heli-Base or Heli-Spot. The ICP is the location from which the Incident Commander and Command Staff will manage an incident. The ICP is normally setup at a safe location near the site of the incident and there is only one ICP per incident, no matter how many agencies are assisting. "A staging area can be any location in which personnel, supplies, and equipment await assignment."[74] All personnel and equipment waiting to be assigned will be staged and ready to rapidly respond as directed by leadership. A base is the main location where resources not assigned are allowed a rest cycle. Resources on a rest cycle, out of service due to maintenance issues, or awaiting to be demobilized will be relocated to a base. Similarly, multiple camps might exist on a large operation to allow resources to have a place to rest or be out of service without having to travel long distances back to the base. Continuing our review of incident facilities, a heli-base is a permanent helicopter landing area such as those pre-identified and marked at a hospital. On the other hand, a heli-spot is a temporary helicopter landing area, which may be on a highway, or any flat area of ground to be able to land and load patients requiring emergency air ambulance transport or for other urgent needs to land a helicopter outside of a heli-base. The names of these facilities will be the same in any area of the U.S. and the common naming aids responders to be able to better communicate. It is incumbent for personnel entering the field of Emergency Management to learn the names of these facilities and utilize the correct terminology. When a person uses the wrong terminology for resources or facilities, it is a red flag for experienced personnel because it indicates that the speaker may have little experience and, therefore, may result in a lack of trust.

11. Integrated Communications

Simply stated, integrated communications mean that there is a single coordinated communications plan, which covers the radio frequencies or

---

[74] (FEMA, Intermediate Incident Command System for Expanding Incidents, ICS 300, April 2019)

channels and types of systems being utilized by all responders. Going back for hundreds of years, communication has been the number one problem area identified on almost every incident. The issue with communications can be caused by the inability to communicate across incompatible radio frequencies, areas with no radio tower coverage, and with personnel who refuse to communicate. Through the concept of integrated communications, these issues began to be addressed as a plan to communicate was mandated through NIMS and ICS.

12. Unified Command

As incidents increase in size and complexity, it is possible to have multiple departments from a single jurisdiction, multiple agencies across jurisdictional boundaries, and agencies from a mixture of Local, State, and Federal jurisdictions working together. Through a *unified command (UC),* *"agencies work together through the designated members of the Unified Command, often the senior person from agencies/disciplines participating in the Unified Command, to establish a common set of objectives and strategies and a single IAP."*[75] This is a fancy way of saying, "Everyone is working together as a single team." More will be covered in the Incident Complexity section within this chapter.

13. Accountability

Accountability is fairly straightforward; it is knowing the location and condition of the personnel assigned to you on an incident at any given moment. At no time should a supervisor lose track of anyone assigned to work for them during a disaster or emergency response. Leaders in the fire service refer to this practice as Personnel Accountability Reporting (PAR) and that practice has been adopted into ICS. Through accountability, we can ascertain if responders are missing and requiring emergency rescue at a moments' notice. Failure to maintain an accurate accountability can result in lives lost and that is never acceptable.

---

[75] (FEMA, Intermediate Incident Command System for Expanding Incidents, ICS 300, April 2019)

14. Information and Intelligence Management

When we refer to "Intelligence" in ICS, we are generally speaking about verified information having a law enforcement value. Through the Intelligence/Investigation element in ICS, a Fusion Center or other law enforcement entity, will process raw information which is gathered, verified, evaluated, and formed it into actionable intelligence. Especially on law enforcement operations, information must be analyzed, and intelligence must be generated. Once actionable intelligence is compiled it can then be shared with those having a "need to know" to be able to safely manage the incident. However, what must be understood is that not everyone has a need to know and to maintain its value intelligence must be shared under controlled conditions.

Organization of the Incident Command System (ICS)

Following our examination of the fourteen foundational characteristics, we move directly into scrutinizing the ICS organization. This is the point where the ICS leadership positions, roles, and responsibilities come into play. So far, the position of the Incident Commander (IC) is the single role, which has been presented. However, the IC is one of the many positions within ICS you will need to understand. In the preceding section, you were introduced to the concept of modular organization, which was explained as filling only the positions needed. To be able to fully comprehend how the positions are filled as needed, you will first need to know what the various positions are and how they relate to each other within the organization. How can you understand the whole of the ICS structure without a basis of knowledge of the individual positions? The answer is you cannot! However, the beauty of ICS is that once you learn these position titles, roles, and responsibilities – you will know the organization for ICS in any jurisdiction anywhere within the United States.

Leadership Roles and Responsibilities within ICS

Fortunately, the ICS organization is fairly straightforward and easy to learn. There are three main levels within the ICS organization: (1) the Incident Command position, (2) Command Staff, and (3) General Staff. We will progressively build upon comprehension of the organization one level at a time. For catastrophic incidents, the ICS organization may become complex, however, if you know the basics you can function on the most complicated incidents. Do not become overwhelmed by the totality of the organization; break it down level by level and the intimidation of ICS will fade into the sunset.

Starting right at the top of the ICS organization, the role of the *Incident Commander* is that this is *the person who has the overall responsibility for the incident, sets the objectives, and manages the Command and General Staff*. "In ICS, and especially in larger incidents, the Incident Commander manages the organization and not the incident."[76] Additionally, the IC is responsible for:

- Receiving a delegation of authority or letter of intent from the jurisdiction
- Ensuring incident safety is the highest priority
- <u>Filling the necessary positions</u> and establishing incident facilities; the IC is responsible for determining which positions need to be filled
- Approving resource requests, press releases, and the Incident Action Plan (IAP)
- Approving strategies and tactics to meet the incident objectives
- Ordering demobilization of equipment and personnel
- Ensuring after-action reviews are conducted at the conclusion of the incident

The next level in the ICS organization is the Command Staff, which is comprised of the Public Information Officer (PIO), Safety Officer (SOFR), and Liaison Officer (LOFR). "The Command Staff is assigned to carry out staff functions

---

[76] (FEMA, ICS Organizational Structure and Elements, March 2018)

needed to support the Incident Commander."[77] On each incident, the IC will determine which Command Staff positions need to be filled. These personnel report directly to the IC and are assigned to manage the following specific activities:

1. **Public Information Officer (PIO):** "The PIO is responsible for communicating with the public, media, and/or coordinating with other agencies, as necessary, with incident related information requirements."[78] One important note is that all press releases prepared by the PIO must be approved by the IC before release. Additionally, the PIO may conduct or assist with press briefings, monitor social media, and participate in the planning meeting. It cannot be overstated how much a professionally trained PIO is invaluable in relating to the media and community and serves as a representative to the IC.

2. **Safety Officer (SOFR):** The SOFR "monitors incident or event operations and advises the Incident Commander on all matters relating to incident health and safety of emergency responder personnel. The Safety Officer has emergency authority to stop and/or prevent unsafe acts during incident operations."[79] Safety officers identify and determine mitigations for hazards, prepare the Safety Message, review the Medical Plan, and participate in the planning meeting. The SOFR is the only staff member, other than the IC, who is authorized to call a complete halt of all operations due to life safety issues.

3. **Liaison Officer (LOFR):** The LOFR "is the point of contact for representatives of other governmental departments and agencies that are not members of Unified Command, non-governmental organizations, and/or the private entities."[80] LOFRs directly coordinate with the representatives of assisting agencies and keep the IC advised on potential inter-agency concerns or issues. On any incident response, assisting

---

[77] (FEMA, ICS Organizational Structure and Elements, March 2018)
[78] (FEMA, Basic Guidance for Public Information Officers (PIOs), November 2007)
[79] (FEMA, Position Qualifications for Operational Coordination: Safety Officer, October 2012)
[80] (FEMA, Position Qualifications for Operational Coordination: Liaison Officer, October 2012)

agency personnel almost always want a few minutes of time to speak with the IC. However, it nearly always ends up being much longer than a few minutes. The LOFR becomes the staff member who will interact with the assisting agencies and free up the IC to be able to effectively lead without distraction.

The third level of the ICS organization is the General Staff who are responsible for the functional elements of the incident command structure. "The General Staff consists of the Operations, Planning, Logistics, and Finance/Administration Section Chiefs."[81] For some incidents, the General Staff may also include an Intelligence/Investigation function, however, that function may be established as a Command Staff position, its own General Staff Section Chief, or as a subcomponent under the Operations or Planning Sections. Again, it is the ICs responsibility to assign people to the positions, which need to be filled for the incident. Below we will examine each of the sections:

1. **Operations Section Chief (OSC):** "The Operations Section Chief is responsible for managing all tactical operations at an incident."[82] Tactics are those work assignments carried out by the various disciplines of emergency medical service (EMS), firefighting, law enforcement, public health, public works, and so on. The OSC manages each of the disciplines organized under the Operations Section, which may include Branch Managers, Division Supervisors, Group Supervisors, Taskforce Leaders, Strike Team Leaders, or Single Resources. The easy way to remember it is that the OSC manages all of the supervisors working in the field, which is referred to as the *"tactics" or specific tasks to achieve strategies and objectives.*

2. **Planning Section Chief (PSC):** The PSC is responsible for collecting all incident information and documentation, providing input to the IC, compiling incident status, and developing all situation reports and plans for an incident. The PSC manages the Planning Section personnel, which

---

[81] (FEMA, April 2019)

[82] (FEMA, ICS Organizational Structure and Elements, March 2018)

may include The Situation, Resource, Documentation, and Demobilization Unit Leaders as well as Technical experts and Forward Observers. The Planning Section "collects situation and resources status information, evaluates it, and processes the information for use in developing action plans."[83] The Planning Section maintains all of the copies of incident paperwork in a master file, which will be turned over to the local jurisdiction at the conclusion of the incident.

3. **Logistics Section Chief (LSC):** The LSC manages all of the supplies and services, with the exception of air operations, which are required to meet the demands of an incident. The LSC manages the Logistics Section personnel, which may include The Support Branch Director who supervises the Supply, Facilities, and Ground Support Unit Leaders; and the Service Branch Director who manages the Communications, Medical, and Food Unit Leaders. The Logistics Section orders, acquires, inspects, places into service, and ultimately demobilizes the resources on an incident.

4. **Finance/Administration Section Chief (F/ASC):** The F/ASC "is responsible for all financial, administrative, and cost analysis aspects of an incident."[84] The F/ASC manages the Finance Section personnel, which may include The Time Unit, Procurement Unit, Compensation/Claims Unit, and Cost Unit Leaders. The Finance Section pays for all of the incident associated costs for contracts, supplies, services, equipment, and personnel.

What has been presented in this chapter, to this point, is the basic foundation for the ICS organization. Certainly, during catastrophic incidents, the ICS organization may become convoluted. However, no matter how large the incident becomes, the three levels of Incident Command, Command Staff, and General Staff will always be represented. Those entering the field of Emergency Management will

---

[83] (FEMA, ICS Organizational Structure and Elements, March 2018)

[84] (FEMA, Resource Typing Definition for the National Qualification Sytem: Finance/Administration Section Chief, September 2017)

be required to complete numerous ICS courses, which will cover the organization in greater detail. For familiarization, the information provided here is designed to offer a beginning level of comprehension. Understanding the construction of the ICS organization will be beneficial in building the vital relationships with the first responders and senior leadership on an incident. The following graphic representation shows the basic ICS Organization Chart depicting the three levels.

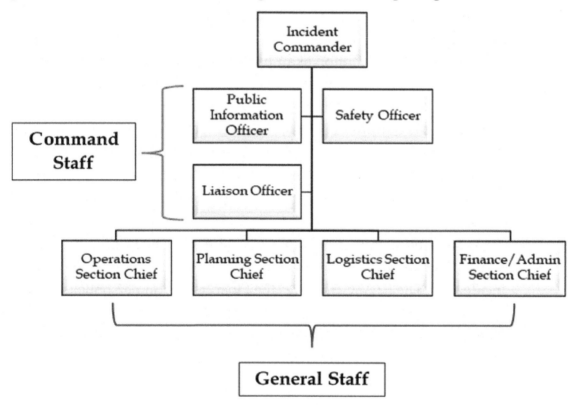

Figure 1: ICS Organization Chart (FEMA)

Influence of Incident Complexity upon the ICS Structure

"The *National Qualification System* defines *Incident Complexity as the Incident criteria determined by the level of difficulty, severity, or overall resistance faced by incident management or support personnel while trying to manage or support an incident to a successful conclusion or to manage one type of incident or event compared to another type.*"[85] A myriad of inter-related factors determine incident complexity; such as the area impacted, jurisdictional boundaries, organization structure, political concerns, strategies, tactics, and weather. Somewhat similar to resource typing, ICS has typed incident complexity on a five-point scale where a Type 5 incident is the least complex and a Type 1 incident is the most complex (see Table 2). Each incident type has been referenced along with the corresponding criteria and examples of incidents, which would qualify for the specified type.

Type	Incident Complexity
1	National Level Incident • The most complex type of incident; will require deployment of Local, State, and National resources to effectively manage the incident; examples include catastrophic hurricanes, blizzards, or terrorist incidents. • Type 1 incidents typically last weeks, months, and longer. • The number of personnel working the incident is likely to exceed 1,000 people.
2	National Level Incident • This type of incident may require deployment of Local, State, and National resources; examples include massive fires, floods, tornadoes, or hurricanes crossing State boundaries. • Type 2 incidents typically last weeks, months, and longer. • The number of personnel working the incident is typically 200 to 500 people.
3	State Level/Large Metropolitan Area Incident • This type of incident may include localized flooding, large brush/wildfires, tornadoes, or widespread HazMat incidents. • Type 3 incidents typically last several days to weeks.

---

[85] (FEMA, Incident Complexity and Type, March 2018)

	• All or most of the Command and General Staff positions may be filled.
4	**Local Incident** • This type of incident may include small HazMat incidents, small brush/wildfires, small flooding incidents, or commercial fires. • Type 4 incidents typically last 12 to 24 hours. • This incident may be managed by a task force or strike team with several resources.
5	**Local Incident** • The least complex type of incident; examples include Motor vehicle accidents, law enforcement traffic stops, residential fires, or emergency medical service (EMS) calls. • Type 5 incidents typically lasts less than 2 to 4 hours. • This incident may be managed by 2 to 10 people.
Table 2: Incident Complexity (Chadwick)	

We are just beginning to break ground on the influence of "complexity" upon the ICS organizational structure. Up to this point, we have delineated between the five types of incidents, but that only scratches the surface. Aside from the type of incident, you also have to understand how the Incident Command position may be organized differently and be more challenging from one disaster to another. The least complex incidents, Type 5 incidents, are relatively easy to manage and are generally organized as a Single command which means that there is a single person assigned as the Incident Commander. However, as an incident becomes more complex, the command position may be structured in a variety of formats.

When incidents cross-jurisdictional boundaries or entail numerous departments within a single jurisdiction; it could become necessary to organize the IC position as a Unified Command. My simplified definition of Unified Command is "Teamwork." Remember this; as incidents become more complex there will be more agencies, departments, and jurisdictions working together. Unified Command allows us to work together without the hassle of one or more of the entities being overlooked and eliminates the competition for scarce resources. In this teamwork effort, the Command position can be set up by having one qualified representative from each of the agencies having jurisdiction to serve as Unified Commanders; preferably not more than 3 to 4 because it becomes cumbersome and more difficult to manage. Within themselves, the Unified Commanders will select a single person to by the spokesperson for the UC to promote "Speaking with one voice." The spokesperson may alternate over time and depending upon the incident. The key to UC is that the Unified Commanders work together to establish a common set of objectives covering all of the areas of concern. When I am teaching ICS, I always stress that the only thing that changes between a Single Command and Unified Command is that you have multiple people working together in the Command position. There will still only be a single set of objectives and shared personnel and facilities such as a single ICP. Let us look at some examples for utilizing a UC:

1. **Multiple Agencies within a Single Jurisdiction:** When an incident in a single jurisdiction expands to include numerous personnel from multiple disciplines, it may be prudent to form a UC. In this case you may have Law Enforcement, Fire, EMS, and others working together on a major incident and it is determined that a UC will be formed with a qualified representative from each discipline. Remember, however, that our list of response disciplines is not limited to the common first responder agencies. A UC within a single jurisdiction may include representatives from any of the agencies, departments, and offices of that jurisdiction.

2. **Multiple Jurisdictions:** When an incident crosses jurisdictional boundaries, it is always best to establish a UC to ensure the concerns from all jurisdictions are addressed. Fires, floods, hazmat, hurricanes, tornadoes, etc… do not stop at the city and county line. Each jurisdiction may have divergent views of what is most important based upon community and political pressures. UC can be utilized to address these issues in a cooperative manner and strengthen regional partnerships.

3. **Multiple Agencies in Multiple Jurisdictions:** "This type of Unified Command would be established for complex incidents where the State* and Federal government agencies have jurisdiction"[86] in conjunction with the Local government. There are countless incidents, which may

---

[86] (FEMA, Intermediate Incident Command System for Expanding Incidents, ICS 300, April 2019)

necessitate Local, State, and Federal governments to work collaboratively on an incident. In those instances where multiple levels of government must collaborate, UC provides a mechanism to be able to do so effectively and efficiently.

Incidents are comprised of a multitude of issues, layered on top of each other, which may further complicate response and recovery efforts. One fact that is easily overlooked is that all incidents are a culmination of multiple incidents or what is referred to as the "Incidents within an Incident." Consider how a single car collision can be composed of many incidents: (1) vehicle tire fails resulting in a blow out, (2) driver loses control and veers off the edge of the road, (3) driver overcorrects jerking the steering wheel as a fear reaction, (4) the forward momentum of the vehicle is interrupted with the tires turning at an angle and catching purchase on the edge of the road and grass, (5) rapid change to vehicle direction causes the vehicle to roll, (6) uncontrolled roll send the vehicle into a gas station along the roadway, (7) vehicle strikes gas pump spilling fuel on surrounding surfaces, (8) vehicle strikes supporting column for awning over gas pumps causing the awning to fall on people and vehicles beneath it, (9) driver of out of control vehicle is entrapped and unconscious, (10) patrons at gas station are injured by awning, (11) fuel is ignited by sparking electric lines from lighting in the awning, and (12) the fuel catches on fire. Explaining it in this manner allows us to begin to express how every incident is a combination of multiple incidents each of which is a problem on its own. The same is true for all incidents and Emergency Managers must be aware of the nature of incidents within an incident. Part of what we need to be able to do is to think outside of the box and in our minds to be playing the "what if" game to be proactive rather than reactive to incidents. For example, if we are experiencing heavy rains in the region. "What If" – roadways are impassable, homes are flooded, motorists and residents require swift water rescue, water systems are flooded causing the city water supply to become tainted, and on and on. Experience based upon past emergencies and disasters will aid us to be proactive and to be wary of additional incidents arising from a single incident.

We can also add to our concerns the possibility of an "Incident Complex," which is not the same as "Incident Complexity." These are separate terms with quite different meanings. Incident Complexity, shown above, refers to the classification of the 5 incident types. Whereas *an "Incident Complex" is "Two or more distinct incidents in the same general area that, by management action, are managed under a single incident commander or unified command in order to improve efficiency and simplify incident management processes."*[87] It is not uncommon for two or more non-related incidents to occur at the same time in close proximity to each other. A large commercial fire can break out at the same time as a massive hazmat spill happens within a couple of miles of each other. Each incident will require critical resources and you can easily face a reality where the two incidents are competing over the very same resources. In such cases, it may be determined that an Area Command (AC) should be established. *"Area Command is an organization that oversees the management of multiple incidents or oversees the management of a very large or evolving situation with multiple ICS organizations."*[88] Area Command has some of the same types of components as Incident Command, but AC has a much smaller footprint and a narrow purpose. For staff in AC, there is the Command position, Public Information Officer, Liaison Officer, Planning Section Chief, and Logistics Section Chief. Area Command exists strictly to aid in coordination between the incidents and to facilitate effective deployment of critical resources. The Area Commander oversees the AC Staff and the Incident Commanders for the individual incidents. The primary purpose for establishing AC is to manage allocation and re-allocation of the critical resources.

The last element of incident complexity I will address is the dreaded *"Cascading Incident" in which a single catastrophic incident is plagued with secondary incidents occurring in rapid succession in a relatively short amount of time.* This is what some people describe as the "domino effect" where one thing happens triggering another, that triggers something else, and the race is on. The best example I have to illustrate a cascading incident is the Wedgwood Senior Adult

---

[87] (NWCG Glossary - Incident Complex, n.d.)
[88] (FEMA, April 2019)

Apartment high-rise fire I responded to on December 28, 2014, in Castle Hills, Texas. I wrote a workshop I have presented at several professional conferences based upon this incident. The day began by receiving a call dispatching me to this fire at 5:40 am. Some background to help you understand what would later prove to complicate the incident is that this facility is an eleven-story apartment building housing over 200 senior adults between 70 and 102 years of age. The Wedgwood is an independent living facility, which does not provide any type of medical care; it is simply an apartment complex for the elderly. The weather played an initial factor, as it was approximately 30 degrees outside with a heavy mist. When I arrived on-scene, I was facing utter chaos. Residents had been pulled from their rooms expediently to save their lives and they were milling around in the parking lot and adjacent area wearing nothing more than pajamas, nightgowns, and in most cases no shoes. Because of the need to rapidly evacuate them from the building, the majority had no canes, scooters, walkers, wheelchairs, or any other type of durable medical equipment. They also did not have their eyeglasses, hearing aids, false teeth, purses or wallets, money or credit/debit cards, identification cards, and medications or prescriptions. The most important task to accomplish immediately was to try to get these senior adults out of the inclement weather conditions, so, we ordered transit buses to temporarily provide some protection. Fire apparatus were parked closely around the building, which prevented us from getting the buses closer than 200 feet to people who were evacuated. Without their canes, scooters, walkers, and wheelchairs; we had to move them one at a time across the parking lot to the awaiting buses. At this point, I had one job – to keep these senior citizens alive! The first lady I escorted was in her 80s and dressed in a cotton nightgown which was drenched from the heavy mist. As I was holding and stabilizing her to walk her to the bus, I asked if she had been checked out by a paramedic. Her response chilled me to the bones when through labored breathing she said she had not and that she had a heart condition. I immediately began a head-to-toe physical assessment, as we were moving towards the bus. When I glanced at her feet, I saw that they were purple in color. I asked her if her feet were bothering her, and she replied that she did not know because she could not feel them. And that was just the first of over 200 senior adults to finally get out of the weather. Firefighters extinguished the fire in a couple of hours, but I would work that incident response for the next 22 days. Five elderly people died in the building from the fire and two more died later: one at the hospital and one in a hotel. Below I will list some of the cascading elements of this response:

- Unified command was not initially established by fire and law enforcement
- Because of a lack of unified command, not all agencies were able to communicate on-scene
- No perimeter security had been established
- Elderly people were roaming around exposed to the inclement elements
- No initial coordination had been established for evacuation and sheltering
- No initial family reunification had been established
- Some residents were being staged in the first-floor lobby of the burning building while fire suppression operations were on-going
- Apartment management was advising family member to come to the first-floor lobby and pick up their elderly family members during fire suppression
- Apartment management was not tracking who had been picked up or how to contact them
- Buses could not get close to the building which forced the elderly to have to be aided individually to the awaiting buses
- Many of the elderly could not walk onto the buses and had to be lifted manually
- Lack of adequate clothing or resources to protect the elderly from exposure
- Last minute changes on the location of a temporary shelter
- Mobility issues after being transported due to lack of durable medical equipment
- The elderly needed life sustaining medications and had no money, prescriptions, medications, identification, of insurance cards

These are just a few of the issues we faced on the Wedgwood fire. The workshop I wrote based upon this fire is titled *"Cascading Challenges within a Single Incident."*[89] I present this as a two-hour case study on cascading incidents and how they are an Emergency Manger's worst nightmare. The key points of that workshop are: (1) Cascading challenges are a myriad of incidents happening one on top of another too fast to be able to respond, (2) When you are in the midst of cascading challenges it is easy to become overwhelmed, and (3) Ultimately, the only way to work through cascading challenges is to take them one issue at a time and keep moving forward. This is the reality of what we deal with as Emergency Managers. We do not just work in a cozy office, writing reports and plans, and separated from the hardships and hazards associated with disasters and emergencies. No, Emergency Managers make decisions and take actions where people's lives are on the line. The cascading incident is something we fear, but we must be prepared to manage. I hope you never have to deal with a cascading incident; however, I constantly remind people "Hope is not a plan!" We have to proactively plan and prepare ourselves for the eventuality of handling the vast array of influences, which impact incident command.

Planning Functions within the Incident Command System (ICS)

As we switch our focus to studying planning functions within ICS, it is important to state upfront that Incident Action Plans (IAPs) are tactical plans and are not the same as Emergency Operation Plans (EOPs) which will be covered in Chapter 6. Tactical plans are the plans we develop in response to a given emergency or disaster. The processes of incident action planning and development of IAPs are a central fixture to managing incidents. "The incident action planning process helps synchronize operations and ensure that they support incident objectives."[90] In this

---

[89] (Chadwick, Cascading Challenges within a Single Incident, 2014)
[90] (FEMA, Incident Action Planning Process, March 2018)

section, we will review the variety of FEMA forms utilized during initial response, the planning cycle, and development of IAPs. Every Emergency Manger must be familiar with the planning functions and how to write the infamous IAP. What will be presented here is an overview. I encourage you to complete classroom ICS training including the *ICS-300 Intermediate Incident Command System (ICS)* for Expanding Incidents and *ICS-400 Advanced Incident Command System (ICS)* courses and to build proficiency in the planning process.

Initial Response and the Planning Cycle

During the initial response to an incident, an Incident Commander (IC) will likely be facing a chaotic scene, limited situational awareness, and an urgent need to develop an initial plan with incomplete information. "As the incident management effort evolves, additional lead time, staff, information systems, and technologies enable more detailed planning and cataloging of events and lessons learned."[91] A statement I use to describe the gravity of the situation in initial response is "Time is Our Enemy!" You never have enough time, you cannot make more time, and time keeps ticking away and slipping through our fingers as we are diligently struggling to bring the incident under control. The very nature of incident response demands Emergency Managers and responders to make rapid decisions. You cannot succeed in this field if you are the type of person who needs an exorbitant amount of time to decide; or, what is referred to as **"analysis paralysis" where a person is frozen in analyzing a situation and cannot formulate a decision.** The ICS provides us with a planning process and standardized plan format to aid all involved from the beginning to the end of an incident in a timely manner.

Sorting out what is most important is simplified through the use of the ICS Incident Priorities as mandated by FEMA. These priorities are the same, regardless, for any incident anywhere in the United States. In order of importance, the priorities are: (1) Save Lives, (2) Protect property and the environment, (3) Stabilize the

---

[91] (FEMA, Incident Action Planning Process, March 2018)

incident, and (4) Provide for basic human needs. These priorities set a starting point no matter the shape, size, or complexity of an incident. This is vital when we are faced with a catastrophic cascading incident because when chaos abounds, we go back to the basics and work the priorities beginning with saving lives. We employ the priorities in the development of our objectives, strategies, and tactics comprising the basis of our incident action planning.

FEMA has adopted many best practices, which have been defined and refined over decades of emergency response. This brings us to addressing the planning phases of an incident: (1) Initial Response Phase, (2) Multiple Operational Period Phase, and (3) the Recovery Phase. I have a set of "trick questions" I use when teaching ICS to get the attention of students. I always preface the question by admitting upfront that it is in fact a trick question. When teaching the initial response phase, I ask the following trick question – "How many times do you initially respond to an incident?" You would be surprised at the number of times I am greeted with blank stares as people are trying to reason through the question. The answer is simple – "You respond one time initially!" That is important as we move forward and begin to present the planning cycle. There are specific and different planning actions, which are required during the initial response phase as opposed to the other planning phases. As we look into the actions of the planning phases, you will be introduced to several "meetings." While they are meetings, they are not the typical business or board meetings, which may last an hour or more at a time. No, the meetings we will consider are kept short because "time is our enemy" and, therefore, kept to 15 to 30 minutes in length. Let us take each of the planning phases separately to enumerate the tasks to be completed for each:

1. **Initial Response Phase**
   - An incident occurs
   - Notification of the incident goes out to responders/Emergency Managers
   - Initial response units are dispatched to scene
   - A scene size-up is conducted (How big is big – How bad is bad?)
   - Responders/Emergency Managers brief the Agency Administrator or Elected Official on the incident

- Complete the FEMA form ICS-201 Incident Briefing; a 4-page form which includes a map, safety briefing, current objectives, list of times and actions taken, organization chart, and assigned resources.
- Conduct an Initial Unified Command (UC) Meeting if using a UC
- IC/UC sets the initial incident objectives
- IC/UC conducts the initial strategy meeting

2. **Multiple Operational Period Phase** (This phase is only for incidents which are not completed in the initial response phase)
   - Incident Commander (IC)/Unified Commanders (UC) develop or update the objectives to be included on the FEMA form ICS-202 Incident Objectives. "After the initial operational period, the IC/UC reviews the incident objectives and may validate them, modify them, or develop new objectives."[92]
   - Conduct a Strategy Meeting or Command and General Staff Meeting if necessary
   - Prepare to conduct the Tactics Meeting by beginning the FEMA forms ICS-215 Operational Planning Worksheet and ICS-215A Incident Action Plan Safety Analysis
   - Conduct the Tactics Meeting and complete the ICS-215 and ICS-215A
   - Prepare to conduct the Planning Meeting by completing the FEMA forms ICS-203 Organizational Assignment List, ICS-204 Assignment List (one for each discipline), ICS-205 Incident Radio Communications Plan, ICS-206 Medical Plan, and ICS-208 Safety Message
   - Conduct the Planning Meeting
   - Incident Action Plan (IAP) preparation and approval
   - Conduct an Operational Period Briefing
   - Begin the next Operational Period; execute plan and assess progress
   - Start the multiple operational period phase all over again as the incident continues

---

[92] (FEMA, Incident Action Planning Process, March 2018)

Before I present the actions of the Recovery phase, there are tasks, which are completed during the multiple operational period phase throughout the incident: Development of a Demobilization Plan, Demobilizing resources no longer required as the incident downsizes, Transferring Command, Conducting an Agency Administrator Closeout Meeting and Team Closeout Meeting, and Conduct an After-Action Report (AAR).

3. **Recovery Phase** (When we are trying to return society to some sense of normality)

   - *Recovery* is defined by FEMA as encompassing *"both short-term and long-term efforts for the rebuilding and revitalization of affected communities.* Examples: Short-term recovery focuses on crisis counseling and restoration of lifelines such as water and electric supply, and critical facilities. Long-term recovery includes more permanent rebuilding."[93]

   - Emergency Managers begin planning for recovery long before we respond to an incident, and this will be covered in Chapter 6 under strategic planning.

   - Recovery is where Emergency Managers engage *"Whole Community" partners (governmental, non-governmental, private, and volunteer sector, and individual citizens) in the work of building the "new normal"* as presented in Chapter 1.

   - There is no way to pre-determine how long the recovery phase will last; the larger the catastrophic incident the longer recovery will take, and it could last weeks, months, or years.

   - Recovery overlaps with response; there is no definitive separation between the two phases.

FEMA developed the *Planning "P"* as a graphic illustration of the Initial Response and Multiple Operational Period phases (see Figure 2). I modified the

---

[93] (FEMA, FEMA Glossary, n.d.)

FEMA graphic to indicate which FEMA forms are completed at the appropriate time in the planning process. The graphic is read from the bottom (referred to as the leg of the "P") and then up and around clockwise. The leg of the "P" corresponds to the Initial Response; remember, you only accomplish those actions one time. If an incident goes beyond a single operational period, you enter into the top portion of the "P" at the development of objectives. All of this will begin to make more sense as we progress through the next section on developing IAPs.

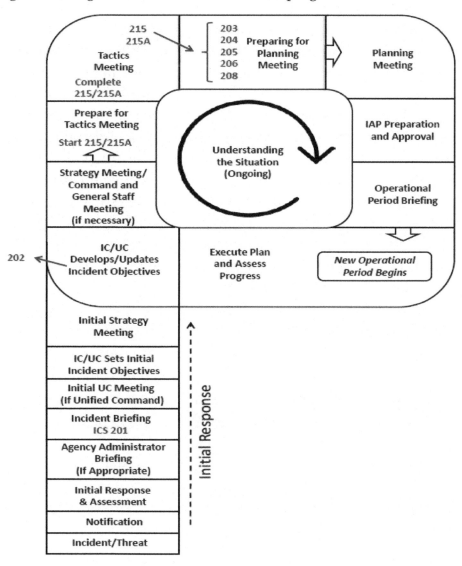

Figure 2: Planning "P" (FEMA; modified by Chadwick & Hannemann)

Development of Incident Action Plans (IAPs)

Writing IAPs can seem quite daunting when you look at the plethora of FEMA forms and the hundreds of blocks to be completed. Another source of confusion is understanding that we write IAPs to cover the objectives to be completed for the next operational period. Look back at the Planning "P" for a moment. During the Initial Response, we will complete the ICS-201 Incident Briefing to record our initial actions. Then, if the incident is going to continue into additional operational periods, we will begin developing an IAP for the personnel who will relieve us at the end of our shift or operational period. That will provide the on-coming personnel with a plan of action to be completed during their shift and they will prepare an IAP for the personnel who will relieve them at the end of their operational period. This is why in ICS we say, "We are always planning for the next operational period." The best advice I can give anyone on learning how to write IAPs is to first take the *ICS-300 Intermediate ICS for Expanding Incidents* class and then shadow, or work alongside of someone who is experienced, to gain proficiency. Over the twelve years that I have been teaching ICS, I have developed a step-by-step process, which has aided thousands of responders to learn how to write IAPs. I will share that process along with pointers on writing IAPs in this section.

Incident Action Plan (IAP) Process

1. Identify the Problems & Issues: The number one mistake people make is that they do not pause to list the problems they are facing, and they attempt a "Shotgun Approach" and hoping to hit the target. That leads to mismanagement because you begin trying to apply solutions without having analyzed the problem. Listing the big picture problems, not the little details, only takes a few minutes. Consider a flood incident for example, the problems might be listed as: Impassible roadways, flooded residential areas requiring evacuation, need to establish shelters, debris removal on blocked roadways impeding emergency vehicles, utility disruption, traffic control/perimeter control, high water rescues, and medical triage/treatment/transport (TTT).

2. Prioritize the Problems & Issues: The next step is to prioritize the problems, which is accomplished using the Incident Priorities. Once you

have prioritized the problems, you can now put them in order of importance and write objectives to address each problem. As a reminder, the Incident Priorities[94] are:

- Save lives
- Protect property and the environment
- Stabilize the incident
- Provide for basic human needs

3. Develop Incident Objectives to address the Problems & Issues: At this juncture, we will write "SMART" Objectives.[95]

- **S**pecific – The wording must be precise and unambiguous in describing the objective.
- **M**easurable – The design and statement of objectives should make it possible to conduct a final accounting as to whether objectives were achieved.
- **A**ction Oriented – The objective must have an action verb that describes the expected accomplishments.
- **R**ealistic – Objectives must be achievable with the resources that the agency (and assisting agencies) can allocate to the incident, even though it may take several Operational Periods to accomplish them.
- **T**ime Sensitive – The timeframe for planned completion should be specified (if applicable).

4. Record the Objectives on an ICS-201 (for Initial Response) or ICS-202 (as part of the Incident Action Plan – IAP for Multiple Operational Periods)
5. Complete the FEMA form ICS-215 Operational Planning Worksheet
6. Complete the FEMA form ICS-215A Incident Safety Analysis
7. Conduct a Tactics Meeting utilizing the ICS-215 & ICS-215A
8. Prepare IAP documentation

---

[94] (FEMA, Intermediate Incident Command System for Expanding Incidents, ICS 300, April 2019)

[95] (FEMA, Intermediate Incident Command System for Expanding Incidents, ICS 300, April 2019)

- Cover Page – FEMA does not provide a cover page form; the cover page will include at a minimum: Name of the Incident, Operational Period, and Jurisdiction (where the incident occurred).
- Complete the FEMA form ICS-202
- Complete the FEMA form ICS-203
- Complete the FEMA forms ICS-204's – you will have one for each discipline (Firefighters, Emergency Medical Services, Law Enforcement, Public Works, Public Health, etc...) working the incident.
- Complete the FEMA form ICS-205
- Complete the FEMA form ICS-206
- Complete the FEMA form ICS-208
- Add in supplemental information, including Weather Forecast, Situation Unit Map, or other information.

9. Conduct a Planning Meeting to go over the completed forms
10. Conduct an IAP Approval: Command and General Staff will agree to support the plan and the Incident Commander (IC) will approve the plan as presented.
11. Produce copies of the IAP: You will need a copy for each of the on-coming staff (IC, Command and General Staff, and Supervisors) for the next operational period.
12. Conduct an Operational Period Briefing: Go over the IAP prepared with the personnel relieving you.

The question always arises "Do you always have to write an IAP for every incident?" The simple answer is – No, a written IAP is not always required. On a single operational period incident (does not exceed 8 to 12 hours) you can complete the 4-page ICS-201 Incident Briefing or any agency report which documents the information recorded on an ICS-201. One of the practices we have developed on fast moving incidents is to utilize our large white response vehicles as a tool to capture information. Let me state emphatically that to use this method you must only use Wet Erase Markers ONLY. Dry erase and permanent markers can permanently stain the paint and could land you in hot water with your supervisor. Wet erase markers, available at any office supply, will not smudge and can easily be washed off at a car wash. What we do when we respond is to use the hood or other large portions of the vehicle to quickly draw a map, list some safety concerns, write our initial objectives, draw our organization chart, and list the resources on-scene and ordered. Then we step back and take a photo of each section with our cellphone. We can then print the photos, staple them together, and file them as our incident briefing. Amazing; and all done without the aid of complicated technology systems in a relatively short of amount of time. Do not forget – "Technology is not our friend!" because post disaster many times cellphone systems, phone lines, and connectivity do not work, and you still need to accomplish the job at hand.

There are some general guidelines as to when a written IAP is required. "The **Comprehensive Environmental Response, Compensation, and Liability Act (CERCLA)**, commonly known as *Superfund*" enacted by the U.S. Congress on December 11, 1980, and amended in 1986, requires documentation for hazardous materials (HazMat) spills. Additionally, State environmental agencies may also require documentation. An IAP provides excellent documentation for HazMat incidents. Typically, an IAP should be written when you are dealing with an incident, which exceeds a single operational period. In addition, agency specific policies may also dictate that IAPs are required for specific incidents. More importantly, an IAP should be written to document our due diligence for most incidents. In the ICS world, we teach, "If it isn't written down, you can't prove it." What that means is when you are subpoenaed for a lawsuit for a response you managed for an incident; you must be able to show documentation of the actions taken. Many a lawsuit has been dismissed or won because a jurisdiction provided exceptional documentation.

The other issue that can come up from time to time is when you have multiple agencies writing IAPs for a single incident and that should not happen. There should only be one official IAP per incident and it should be maintained by or for the *Authority Having Jurisdiction (AHJ) which is the jurisdiction having the legal authority over the location where the incident occurred*. A jurisdiction is a City, County, State, Tribal, or the Federal government. Non-governmental, private sector, faith-based, and volunteer agencies should not have a separate IAP because they are not statutory jurisdictions. All agencies working an incident should be recorded on the official IAP with the AHJ. When you have multiple IAPs, it creates confusion and vital information may be missed in the official IAP. A single IAP is developed for single command and unified command incidents. In the case of unified command incidents, the official IAP will be shared with and cover all of the jurisdictions and assisting agencies.

With the proliferation of FEMA forms, it can be confusing, as to which forms are required at a minimum in an IAP. Some points to keep in mind are that the ICS-201 Incident Briefing, ICS-215 Operational Planning Worksheet and ICS-215A Incident Action Plan Safety Analysis are NOT part of the IAP. The ICS-201 is used to document an initial response. The ICS-215 and ICS-15A are planning documents used to aid in writing an IAP, but they are not included in the IAP. The ICS-215 and ICS-215A will be filed in the incident documentation by the Planning Section. FEMA lists the following forms comprising an IAP at a minimum:
- ICS-202
- ICS-203
- ICS-204s
- ICS-205
- ICS-206
- ICS-208

Additionally, an IAP should always include a cover page with at least the name of the incident, date, and operational period. A weather forecast, situation unit map identifying the incident location in relation to other incident facilities, and additional information pertinent to the incident should also be contained within the IAP. Maps are extremely important to provide overall situational awareness and to provide the location of incident facilities to all assigned personnel. The situation unit map may be a freehand sketch or, when possible, a digital map copied into the IAP. The situation unit map will provide the location of the incident along with the locations of all the incident facilities (ICP, Staging Area, Base, Camp, Heli-Base, Heli-Spot, and any other facilities). When preparing a situation unit map, utilize the correct standardized ICS map symbols. Below I am providing the basic map symbols utilized in preparing the situation unit map:

⊗ **Incident Location**

◥ **Incident Command Post**

Ⓢ **Staging Area**

Ⓑ **Base**

Ⓒ **Camp**

Ⓗ **Heli-Base**

● **Heli-Spot** (each Heli-Spot will be numbered to differentiate)
H-3

Not all potential facilities have a correlating standardized map symbol, such as the Joint Information Center (JIC) where the PIOs work, Media Staging, and shelters. On incidents where a non-standard facility is established, the Situation Unit Leader (SITL) will develop a symbol to include on the situation unit map. When preparing a map for an IAP, you should include a legend and provide descriptions of all symbols, standard and non-standard, to insure comprehension of the readers. This is the area where you would include any custom symbols used for identifying any other important facilities. Aside from incorporating symbology, situation unit maps should include the following elements to meet the STAND principle:[96]

Scale	One inch equals how many miles
Title	Title of the Incident and Location
Author	Who drew the map?
North Arrow	To orient the reader to the location
Date & Time	When was this map prepared?

---

[96] (Texas A&M Forest Service, July 2014)

In Chapter 3, we have covered a lot of ground regarding the Incident Command System (ICS). We looked at how ICS flows from NIMS and the adoption of the 14 foundational characteristics makes NIMS and ICS an integrated process. From the ICS organization, we studied the roles and responsibilities of leadership positions in Command, the Command Staff, and General Staff. That was rounded off with an overview of the planning cycle and development of Incident Action Plans (IAPs). As was stated from the beginning of this chapter, numerous courses are available to help you build your competency with ICS. The online FEMA classes are free and work through at your own pace, so, the only cost is the investment of your time. The classroom courses are easier to obtain in some regions than in others and, in most cases, are normally offered through local jurisdictions at no cost. I would encourage you to contact your local Office of Emergency Management (OEM) or Emergency Management Agency (EMA) for more information on the availability of this valued training.

Chapter 3 Summary

Key Terms (Alphabetical Order)

Accountability
Analysis Paralysis
Area Command
Authority Having Jurisdiction (AHJ)
Base
Camp
Cascading Incident
Chain of Command and Unity of Command
Command Staff
Common Terminology
Comprehensive Resource Management
Dispatch/Deployment
Emergency Management Agency (EMA)
Emergency Operation Plan (EOP)
Establishment and Transfer of Command
Finance/Administration Section Chief
Formal Communication
General Staff
Heli-Base
Heli-Spot
Incident Action Plan (IAP)
Incident Action Planning
Incident Command Post
Incident Complex
Incident Complexity
Incident Facilities and Locations
Incident Priorities
Initial Response Phase
Informal Communication
Information and Intelligence Management

Integrated Communications
Joint Information Center (JIC)
Joint Information System (JIS)
Kind
Liaison Officer
Logistics Section Chief
Manageable Span of Control
Management by Objectives
Modular Organization
Multiple Operational Period Phase
Operational Period
Operations Section Chief
Personnel Accountability Reporting (PAR)
Planning "P"
Planning Section Chief
Public Information Officer
Recovery Phase
Self-Dispatch
Situation Unit Map
Staging Area
Tactics
Type
Unified Command

Foundations of ICS

Within the foundations of ICS in Chapter 3, we have explored taking ICS from a theory and putting it into practice. The aspects of how NIMS and ICS are intertwined have been illuminated and expounded upon to provide greater understanding. The segments covered included ICS: A Component of NIMS and the Fourteen Foundational Characteristics of ICS. Understanding the foundations of ICS serves to advance our ability to appropriately utilize ICS in the disasters we will be called upon to manage.

Organization of ICS

Working through the ICS structure requires a firm knowledge of the organization, comprehension of the levels of leadership, and how complexity can alter the structure of leadership. Serving as an Emergency Manager demands complete familiarization with the ICS organization. You must fully grasp the Command, Command Staff, and General Staff positions. Furthermore, Emergency Managers must be able to readily recognize and categorize the five Incident Complexity Types and understand how complexity can require the implementation of a Unified Command or Area Command.

Planning Functions in ICS

A tremendous amount of information was crammed into the pages covering the planning cycle and development of IAPs. The cursory coverage of incident planning presents a fundamental process, which may be beneficial, but will require additional study, training, and practical application. It is highly recommended that you find a mentor in your local jurisdiction and obtain experience to write effective IAPs.

In the next chapter, you will learn about the National Preparedness Goal Mission Areas and the associated Core Capabilities.

Chapter 4: The National Preparedness Goal

Within the previous chapter, we investigated a step-by-step process of taking the Incident Command System (ICS) from a theory to an established practice. That trek has led us along a path of examining the foundations, organization, and planning functions in ICS. With each successive chapter, we will now begin a targeted approach of applying National planning guidance into localized Emergency Management operations. In Chapter 4, we will begin to peel back the layers of emergency operations plans (EOPs). An exhaustive knowledge of planning is a must for successful Emergency Managers. To continue building upon the foundation of information provided in the preceding chapters, we will explore the National Preparedness Goal and Comprehensive Planning Guides (CPGs) which provide the basis for Emergency Management strategic and operational plans.

Evolution of the National Preparedness Goal

Presidential Policy Directive 8 (PPD-8): National Preparedness, which was enacted in March of 2011 and covered in Chapter 1, directed the identification of core capabilities and mission areas to strengthen preparedness in the United States. One of the outcomes of PPD-8 is the *National Preparedness Goal*, released in September of 2011, is phrased as developing *"A secure and resilient Nation with the capabilities required across the whole community to prevent, protect against, mitigate, respond to, and recover from the threats and hazards that pose the greatest risk."*[97] Emergency Management continually evolves by building upon the

---

[97] (FEMA, National Preparedness Goal, September 2011)

foundations, which have been set in place for many decades, as evidenced in PPD-8 leading to this initiative. Within 4 years of the initial release, the National Preparedness Goal was updated, and the second edition was released in September of 2015 incorporating real world lessons learned from incidents and institution of best practices. A subtle, but important, language change is evident between the first and second editions upon close inspection. The first edition used the terminology "we will use", whereas the second edition states "We use an integrated, layered, and all-of-Nation approach as our foundation for building and sustaining core capabilities and preparing to deliver the effectively."[98] That shift shows that, as a Nation, we have moved beyond the stage of planning to use an all-of-Nation approach to actually using the approach by embracing the "whole community" to be prepared for the various types of disasters we experience. That is a huge accomplishment in a mere 4-year time span. Rolling out a nationwide program of this nature, covering each of the 50 States and the United States territories requires a herculean effort and coordination at the Local, State, Tribal, and Federal levels.

Composition of the National Preparedness Goal

Let us really analyze the way that the National Preparedness Goal, or the Goal for brevity's sake, is composed. It all flows from the central statement to achieve a "secure and resilient Nation." The first step towards achieving the Goal was to identify the mission areas, which encompass all of the work actions of Emergency Managers. The next step was to scrutinize the identified mission areas and deconstruct them to classify the capabilities required to accomplish the work of the mission areas and reach the Goal. The last step was to institutionalize the National Planning System "which supports the integration of planning across all levels of government and the whole community to provide and agile, flexible, and accessible delivery of the core capabilities."[99] The process was a complete reverse-

---

[98] (FEMA, National Preparedness Goal, Second Edition, September 2015)
[99] (FEMA, National Preparedness Goal, Second Edition, September 2015)

engineering feat to determine how our Nation could meet the Goal of security and resilience. When you go back through the history of Emergency Management and then slowly consider each major accomplishment, you will find that we are a career field that has flourished by first deciding where we want to go and then determine how to best get to the desired point. This is the hallmark of highly qualified Emergency Managers, to envision an end result and to then determine all of the minute details to get to that point. In that light, we will look at the mission areas, core capabilities, and the National Preparedness System, which have been established to achieve the Goal.

1. **Five Mission Areas:** As introduced in Chapter 1, the Five Mission Areas of prevention, protection, mitigation, response, and recovery describe the phases of work for Emergency Managers. This is the point where I emphasize to students and interns that Emergency Management is unlike most career fields. I explain that by stating, "If you are looking for a career field where you can rise to a level where you plateau and coast, you need to go somewhere else!" Emergency Managers are consummate multi-taskers working all five mission areas. It is also important to grasp the fact that Emergency Managers do not have the luxury of working only one mission area at a time. No, you can easily be working prevention efforts, setting in place protections, mitigating potential hazards, responding to specific disasters, and recovering from a separate disaster all at the same time. It is what I refer to as the vortex, which is continually spinning in Emergency Management. As Emergency Managers progress in their careers, they become responsible for more and more elements of the vortex and increase their daily jobs. Let us examine each of the mission areas individually:

    Vortex (Chadwick)

    *   **Prevention:** The National Prevention Framework defines prevention as the activities to *"avoid, prevent, or stop a*

threatened or actual act of terrorism."[100] The key difference for prevention efforts is that this mission area is explicitly focused on the threat of terrorism and not man-made or natural disasters. This distinction will become more evident later in this chapter when we begin studying strategic and operational plans.

- **Protection:** The National Protection Framework defines protection as the ability to *"secure the homeland against acts of terrorism and manmade or natural disasters."*[101] Protection efforts are applicable to manmade and natural disasters and acts of terrorism. Whereas prevention was specific to terrorism, protection is all encompassing for the threats and hazards we are called upon to address.

- **Mitigation:** The National Mitigation Framework defines mitigation as *"capabilities necessary to reduce loss of life and property by lessening the impact of disasters."*[102] Mitigation is all about recognizing that it is impossible to avert all manmade and natural disasters. Therefore, Emergency Managers must find ways to minimize or mitigate the risks inherent to our communities from disasters and emergencies.

- **Response:** The National Response Framework defines response as *"saving lives, stabilizing community lifelines, protecting property and the environment, and meeting basic human needs after an incident has occurred."*[103] Response entails all of the operations performed immediately in the aftermath of a disaster. This is the stage where Emergency Managers coordinate with all of the emergency response disciplines (firefighting, law enforcement, emergency medical, etc...) to meet operational objectives.

- **Recovery:** The National Disaster Recovery Framework defines recovery as *"the capabilities necessary to assist communities affected*

---

[100] (FEMA, National Prevention Framework, Second Edition, June 2016)
[101] (FEMA, National Protection Framework, Second Edition, June 2016)
[102] (FEMA, National Mitigation Framework, Second Edition, June 2016)
[103] (FEMA, National Response Framework, Fourth Edition, October 28, 2019)

by an incident to recover effectively."[104] As introduced in Chapter 1, recovery is the process whereby a local jurisdiction is attempting to return society to some sense of normality after a disaster. Emergency Managers do not refer to recovery as returning to normal, but rather to a "new normal" because it is impossible to return all of the elements of a community to pre-disaster levels.

Within the National Preparedness Goal, the Five Mission Areas are the big-picture endeavors which give Emergency Managers a target to remain focused before, during, and after disasters strike. However, what are the tasks required to meet a competent standard for performing the mission areas? That is where core capabilities come into play. I find that it is helpful to explain core capabilities as the examples of the types of tasks, which must be accomplished for each mission area. So, as we progress to considering core capabilities, keep in mind that these examples are meant to guide us along the path to effectively meet the standards of the mission areas.

2. **Core Capabilities (32):** On the next page, Table 3 will provide you with a visual representation of how the Five Mission Areas and the 32 Core Capabilities are inter-related. Some of the capabilities are specific to one or two mission areas and three are common to all five mission areas: (1) Planning, (2) Public Information and Warning, and (3) Operational Coordination. Planning is a task, which must be performed in prevention, protection, mitigation, response, and recovery. The same is true for keeping the public informed and for coordinating the operations for each mission area. Table 3, produced by FEMA, allows Emergency Managers to see the National Preparedness Goal in a holistic conceptualization. Using the Recovery mission area as an example for how to read this table, the Five Mission Areas are presented across the top of the table with columns beneath to ascribe the core capabilities applicable to each mission area.

---

[104] (FEMA, National Disaster Recovery Framework, Second Edition, June 2016)

Below Recovery, you will find that the three common core capabilities are the first to be listed. Continuing downward, you will see that the core capability of Infrastructure Systems is shared by Response and Recovery. Further, down, you will find that the core capabilities of Economic Recovery, Health and Social Services, Housing, and Natural and Cultural Resources are specific to Recovery. Emergency Managers may not perform all of the work entailed within the core capabilities; however, each core capability plays an integral role in how Emergency Managers plan and coordinate to successfully meet the mission areas and the Goal.

Prevention	Protection	Mitigation	Response	Recovery
Planning				
Public Information and Warning				
Operational Coordination				
Intelligence and Information Sharing		Community Resilience	Infrastructure Systems	
Interdiction and Disruption		Long-term Vulnerability Reduction	Critical Transportation	Economic Recovery
Screening, Search, and Detection			Environmental Response/Health and Safety	Health and Social Services
Forensics and Attribution	Access Control and Identity Verification	Risk and Disaster Resilience Assessment	Fatality Management Services	Housing
		Threats and Hazards Identification	Fire Management and Suppression	Natural and Cultural Resources
	Cybersecurity		Logistics and Supply Chain Management	
	Physical Protective Measures		Mass Care Services	
	Risk Management for Protection Programs and Activities		Mass Search and Rescue Operations	
	Supply Chain Integrity and Security		On-scene Security, Protection, and Law Enforcement	
			Operational Communications	
			Public Health, Healthcare, and Emergency Medical Services	
			Situational Assessment	

Table 3: Mission Areas and Core Capabilities (FEMA)

Architecture of the National Preparedness System

Moving on to the last step of the National Preparedness Goal, creating a *National Preparedness System*, we will look at the components of the system and how the system unifies other Federal guidance. The National Preparedness System builds upon additional Emergency Management guidance such as the Post-Katrina Emergency Management Reform Act and various other Federal regulations. "Through the implementation of the National Preparedness System, these efforts will be integrated to be more efficient and effective, supporting our Nation's ability to confront any threat or hazard."[105] Once again, we have the unifying theme seen throughout the history of Emergency Management where new developments are intentionally designed to fit into the overarching puzzle to enhance National security and resilience. Communities across the United States constantly face new developments and extremely complex incidents due to ever-increasing threats and hazards requiring the "whole community" to rally together to build, deliver, and sustain the core capabilities identified in the Goal. The National Preparedness System aids Emergency Managers to meet the challenges from new developments by outlining "an organized process for everyone in the whole community to move forward with their preparedness activities and achieve the National Preparedness Goal."[106] There are six parts to the National Preparedness System, which are individually explored below:

1. **Identifying and Assessing the Risk:** Before Emergency Managers can meticulously plan and prepare for disasters and emergencies; we must first understand the threats and hazards, which are unique to our given communities. Yes, not all communities are alike, and neither are all threats nor hazards common for all communities. Each region of the United States has threats and hazards which are both common to their given locations and unique from other regions. Take a coastal community as an example;

---

[105] (FEMA, National Preparedness System, November 2011)
[106] (FEMA, National Preparedness System, n.d.)

---

the region could have common threats and hazards associated with hurricanes and flooding. That same region may have a community with a large port system where gas and oil are transported by sea, which brings its own inherent unique threats and hazards. Emergency Managers must be familiar with the common and unique threats for their communities to adequately plan and prepare to safeguard the community. Later, in this chapter, we will study the Threat and Hazard Identification and Risk Assessment (THIRA), which provides "a common, consistent approach for identifying and assessing risks and associated impacts"[107] for jurisdictions. The beauty of this approach is that the information gathered through a targeted threat and hazard assessment can be utilized by Emergency Managers to build and sustain levels of preparedness within the Local, State, Tribal, and Federal government levels.

2. **Estimating Capability Requirements:** Once Emergency Managers have identified and assessed the risks, we can establish planning factors to ascertain desired outcomes for disasters and emergencies pertaining to the identified threats for our communities. The planning factors will aid in determining whether the community resources currently available are adequate to achieve the desired outcomes. Through honest examination, weaknesses and deficiencies can be discovered and addressed before tragedy strikes the community. Projected hazard outcomes can be pre-determined and provide a baseline for potential community-wide impacts.

3. **Building and Sustaining Capabilities:** Capability gaps can then be prioritized providing the groundwork for planning to take preemptive action to address the gaps and strengthen the community. "Working together, planners, government officials, and elected leaders can develop strategies to allocate resources effectively, as well as leverage available assistance to reduce risk."[108] This part of the National Preparedness

---

[107] (FEMA, National Preparedness System, November 2011)
[108] (FEMA, National Preparedness System, November 2011)

System highlights one of the bedrock axioms in Emergency Management – "None of us can handle every incident we may face alone!" Over and over again, the concept of partnership development to build resilience will be presented as you continue to study the field of Emergency Management. Partnership, resource acquisition, training, funding, and skills development can be mechanisms for building and sustaining capabilities.

4. **Planning to Deliver Capabilities:** After identifying risks, estimating impacts, and strengthening capabilities; Emergency Managers can then begin planning to address the inherent threats and hazards. This is where NIMS, ICS, National Frameworks, and the National Preparedness Goal meld into a cohesive strategy. Like the great archways of a Gothic cathedral, all of the elements are carefully lain in place with a central capstone anchoring preparedness for our communities. That is not to say that the work to achieve our planning and delivery objectives is going to be simple and pain-free. I use the following statement to express the ingrained difficulty in planning – "Plans are easy; however, the planning process is anything but easy!" The next portion of this chapter will open your eyes to just how complicated the planning process is for Emergency Mangers to develop good and solid emergency operations plans (EOPs).

5. **Validating Capabilities:** As plans are developed, Emergency Managers take on the task of evaluating the effectiveness of the plans. To determine whether or not a plan is effective will require exercising and testing the plan. An untested plan has little value because there are no metrics to ascertain if the objectives contained within the plan can be effectively carried out to protect a community. As I previously stated in Chapter 3, "Hope is not a plan." Never forget that the threats and hazards to a community are constantly changing. Business and housing development can result in a change to flooding as more and more hard surfaces and put in place, drainage is reduced, homes and businesses not previously in flood plains are encroached by human-caused flood zones, increased vehicle volume place a larger percentage of motorists within the new flood zones, and on and on throughout the spectrum of threats and

hazards for a community. Our ever-changing world demands Emergency Managers to constantly be vigilante to how the changes will affect our communities and, thereby, and necessitate alteration of existing plans following an honest period of validation.

6. **Reviewing and Updating:** "Changes in a community's exposure and sensitivity can and do occur, however, whether from evolving threats and hazards, aging infrastructure, shifts in population, or changes in the natural environment."[109] Emergency Managers need to implement a schedule to continually address evolving threats, changing capabilities, availability of resources, aging infrastructure, population migration, funding constraints, and alterations to the natural environment. Planning is a cycle, which revolves around the six parts of the National Preparedness System. Emergency Managers are never truly done when it comes to planning; we just move on to the next step and in the cycle.

Implementing a Comprehensive Emergency Management Planning Process

Before delving further into the planning process, let us begin by laying the foundation with a definition of the word *"comprehensive"* as the *"complete or nearly complete coverage of the elements of a given topic."* With that understanding, what we will accomplish in the second half of Chapter 4 is a broad perspective view of Emergency Management planning. The journey starts by acknowledging that there are three tiers of Emergency Management planning: (1) Strategic-level, (2) Operational-level, and (3) Tactical-level plans. The first two tiers are described as *"Deliberate Plans"* which are defined as *"plans to prevent, protect against, and mitigate the effects of, responding to, and recovering from threats or hazards."*[110]

---

[109] (FEMA, National Preparedness System, November 2011)
[110] (FEMA, National Prevention Framework, Second Edition, June 2016)

Tactical-level plans are Incident Action Plans (IAPs) which were covered in the preceding chapter. Therefore, we can concentrate on the first two tiers, which are described as follows:

- Strategic-level plans are contextual representations of the very high-level expectations for operational plans. Strategic plans will be all-hazards and capability based. Examples include National Wildland Fire Strategies, State Preparedness Plan, and Local Hazard Mitigation Plans.
- Operational-level plans chronicle the tasks and resources required to execute the strategic plans. Examples include State or Local Emergency Operations Plans (EOPs), Pre-Disaster Recovery Plans, and Non-Governmental Organization Plans.

Imagine for a moment that you are flying in an airplane looking down on the tiers of planning. Strategic plans would encompass what you can see from a 60,000-foot altitude, operational plans are the visibility you might have at a 30,000-foot level, and tactical plans are the details that can be seen at ground level. Emergency Managers commonly utilize the terminology of a 60,000- and 30,000-foot level view to relate to the level of detail. When we are discussing strategic plans, we expect an overview of concepts. At the operational level, we expect to be introduced to limited details on how operations are intended to be conducted. It is not until we get to tactical plans for specific disasters or emergencies that the majority details are added based upon the incident, location, and hazards. The bulk of the planning work for Emergency Managers will revolve around operational plans; therefore, the next section will concentrate on various operational plans.

Comprehensive Preparedness Guide (CPG) 101: Developing and Maintaining Emergency Operations Plans (EOPs)

Several times a year I receive questionnaires from students in Emergency Management degree programs and inevitably one of the questions will be "When was the last time your Emergency Operations Plan (EOP) was updated?" Since we are about to open the examination of EOPs, I want to provide you with some valuable insight. The very question makes it obvious that the person who developed the question does not understand EOPs because this is not a single plan, but rather numerous plans and there are mandates in place for updating and submitting plans for approval. All of this and more will be revealed as we delve into EOPs.

The *Comprehensive Preparedness Guide (CPG) 101: Developing and Maintaining Emergency Operations Plans* was released in November of 2010 to provide "Federal Emergency Management Agency (FEMA) guidance on the fundamentals of planning and developing emergency operations plans (EOPs)."[111] As the title of these plans indicates these are operational plans, which define the scope of Emergency Management, planning for a jurisdiction. An EOP assigns responsibilities, establishes lines of authority, describes lifesaving and property protection measures, identifies available resources, concept of operations (CONOPS) and may include mutual aid agreements with surrounding jurisdictions and agencies. CPG-101 acknowledges that there are several acceptable methods of EOP formats and briefly covers three of the common methods utilized: (1) Traditional Functional EOP Format, (2) Emergency Support Function (ESF) EOP Format, and the (3) Agency-/Department-Focused EOP Format. Some misperceptions exist and have been spread claiming that EOPs must conform to the ESF Format. However, CPG-101 makes it clear with the statement "None of these formats are mandatory to achieve NIMS compliance."[112] While the Federal government does not stipulate which format to use, some States do require the use of a prescribed format. Typically, States and Local jurisdictions require each plan maintained by Emergency Management to be updated and submitted for approval, or re-approval, every 5 years. In some States, the EOP is a protected document and not subject to release to the public because, should a plan get into the hands of someone with malevolent intentions, it could result in a catastrophic incident. Consult State statutes concerning Emergency Management plans to insure you have accurate information

---

[111] (FEMA, E/L0103 Planning: Emergency Operations, September 2016)
[112] (FEMA, Comprehensive Preparedness Guide (CPG) 101: Developing and Maintaining Emergency Operation Plans, November 2010)

for your jurisdiction. We will briefly explore each of the three formats to provide an overview of methods of structuring an EOP.

1. **Traditional Functional EOP Format:** From the 1990s up until recent years, the traditional structure was the most common format utilized by jurisdictions. There are three main sections of a Traditional Functional EOP: (1) Basic Plan, (2) Functional Supporting Annexes, and (3) Hazard-Specific Annexes or Appendices. Jurisdictions using the Traditional EOP Format may have between 25 to 30 individual plans comprising the EOP.

   - **Basic Plan:** This is a jurisdiction broad and generalized plan which will lay out the basic roles and responsibilities, explain the cycle for updating the plan, and it will normally contain some information which is required by law.

   - **Functional Supporting Annexes:** The functional annexes are individual plans which focus on Emergency Management operations. Annexes will include roles and responsibilities for partnering or assisting organizations, explain how operations are managed throughout the span of the incident, identify agencies or departments responsible for implementing the plan, and general strategies expected to be used during disasters and emergencies. Below is a table with a list of some, but not all, of the possible common types of Functional Annexes a jurisdiction may maintain:

Communications	Human Services	Resource Management
Direction & Control	Law Enforcement	Search & Rescue
Donations	Legal	Terrorism
Evacuation	Mass Care	Transportation
Firefighting	Public Information	Utilities
Hazard Mitigation	Public Works	Warning
HazMat	Radiological	
Health & Medical	Recovery	

Table 4: Functional Annex Examples (Chadwick)

   - **Hazard-Specific Annexes or Appendices:** The plans at this stage will highlight "the policies, situation, CONOPS, and responsibilities for particular hazards, threats, or incidents."[113] For instance, direction and control may be designated to a specific agency or department and definitive emergency response strategies may be outlined in these plans. From region to region, Hazard-Specific Annexes or Appendices could vary based upon the localized threats to the region. Some examples of these types of plans would be Hurricane Evacuation, Shelter Operations, and so forth.

2. **Emergency Support Function (ESF) EOP Format:** The ESF format began as a Federal level model and was the structure utilized in writing the National Response Framework (NRF) to "describe federal coordinating structures that group resources and capabilities into functional areas most frequently needed in a national response."[114] More and more States are moving to adopting the ESF format and prescribing or encouraging local jurisdictions to transition to the ESF format. This is another area where Emergency Managers should consult with their respective State to ensure the format utilized is the approved model. The ESF format will include a Basic Plan, ESF Annexes, Support Annexes, and Hazard-Specific Annexes. Jurisdictions using the ESF EOP Format may have between 30 to 35 individual plans comprising the EOP.

- **Basic Plan:** An ESF Format Basic Plan provides an overview of the Emergency Management system employed by a jurisdiction. Similar to the Tradition format, the ESF Basic Plan outlines capabilities, expected hazards, organizational structure, and roles and responsibilities. Lead agencies responsible for mission execution will be aligned with the ESF structure.

- **ESF Annexes:** Emergency Support Function (ESF) Annexes will generally identify an ESF coordinator along with the primary and support agencies assisting for the given function. "An ESF annex describes expected mission execution for each emergency phase and

---

[113] (FEMA, Comprehensive Preparedness Guide (CPG) 101: Developing and Maintaining Emergency Operation Plans, November 2010)
[114] (FEMA, National Response Framework, n.d.)

identifies tasks assigned to members of the ESF, including nongovernmental and private sector partners."[115] The table below provides the listing of ESFs:

ESF 1 Transportation	ESF 9 Search & Rescue
ESF 2 Communications	ESF 10 Oil & HazMat Response
ESF 3 Public Works & Engineering	ESF 11 Agriculture & Natural Resources
ESF 4 Firefighting	ESF 12 Energy
ESF 5 Emergency Management	ESF 13 Public Safety & Security
ESF 6 Mass Care, Emergency Assistance, Housing, & Human Services	ESF 14 Long-Term Community Recovery
ESF 7 Logistics Management & Resource Support	ESF 15 External Affairs
ESF 8 Public Health & Medical Services	Other ESFs may defined by the Jurisdiction

Table 5: ESF Annex Examples (Chadwick)

- **Support Annexes:** "The support annexes describe common essential processes and considerations for most incidents."[116] Support annexes will generally describe the framework whereby a jurisdiction and partner agencies will execute strategies for Emergency Management and identify a coordinating agency and assisting or cooperating organizations. Typical examples of support annexes would include, but not be limited to Continuity of Government (COG)/Continuity of Operations (COOP), Financial Management, Mutual Aid, Population Protection, and Warning.

- **Hazard-Specific Annexes:** The description of the Hazard Specific Annexes for the Traditional EOP Format is identical to that of the ESF EOP Format (refer to page 117).

---

[115] (FEMA, Comprehensive Preparedness Guide (CPG) 101: Developing and Maintaining Emergency Operation Plans, November 2010)
[116] (FEMA, National Response Framework, n.d.)

3. **Agency-/Department-Focused EOP Format:** The Agency/Department EOP Format is appropriate for smaller communities and will describe individual agency or department tasks in separate sections within the plan. As with other formats, the Agency/Department EOP Format includes a basic plan section to provide "an overview of a jurisdiction's ability to prevent, protect against, respond to, and recover from emergencies."[117] Additionally, the Agency/Department EOP Format will include sections for the lead agencies for each discipline, supporting agencies, and hazard specific procedures. The level of detail provided for each jurisdictional agency or department may vary within the EOP. Lead agencies can review the sections dedicated to their agency or department and can refer to sections for other departments for greater situational awareness. Those agencies and departments, which maintain detailed stand-alone Standard Operating Procedures (SOPs) or Standard Operating Guidelines (SOGs), may require minimal information to be contained within the Agency/Department EOP. For the jurisdictions where it is appropriate to utilize the Agency/Department EOP Format, the EOP may be contained in a single plan. Examples of agencies and departments which may be included are illustrated below:

Emergency Management	Law Enforcement
Emergency Medical	Public Health
Fire	Public Works
Hospital	Others as needed

Table 6: Lead Agency/Department Examples (Chadwick)

CPG-101 provides Emergency Mangers with a Six Step Planning Process, which can be beneficial in writing EOPs. The process is concise and easy to follow: (1) Form a collaborative planning team engaging partners in the "whole community;" (2) Under the situation by identifying the threats and hazards and conducting a risk assessment; (3) Determine the goals and objectives of the plan; (4)

---

[117] (FEMA, Comprehensive Preparedness Guide (CPG) 101: Developing and Maintaining Emergency Operation Plans, November 2010)

Plan development analyzing expected action, resources, and information and intelligence; (5) Plan preparation, review, and approval; and (6) Plan implementation and maintenance. Even though the process is fairly simple; it can be very time consuming and "time is our enemy!" Therefore, many planners utilize templates, and some States provide templates to local jurisdictions to write EOPs. There is debate among Emergency Managers as to how "fill-in-the-blank" templates may detract from the planning process because such templates will inevitably limit engaging with partners and stakeholders during the development of EOPs. However, many Emergency Managers agree that a high-quality template will insure standardization and inclusion of State and Federal required information. With limited staffing and limited funding, many offices of Emergency Management opt to utilize templates as a means to sustain an approved program to meet the needs of the jurisdiction.

Comprehensive Preparedness Guide (CPG) 201: Threat and Hazard Identification and Risk Assessment (THIRA) and Stakeholder Preparedness Review (SPR) Guide

The *CPG-201: Threat and Hazard Identification and Risk Assessment (THIRA) and Stakeholder Preparedness Review (SPR) Guide* was originally released in April of 2012, updated in August of 2013, and most recently the third edition was released in May of 2018. While the THIRA and SPR are often referenced together, it is important to understand that they are two separate and closely related processes. The primary purpose of the THIRA is to "identify community-specific risks and determine the capability needed to address those risks."[118] Moreover, the THIRA provides a basis for all of the various planning functions and "sets a strategic

---

[118] (FEMA, THIRA/SPR Overview and Updated Methodology, July 9, 2018)

foundation for putting the National Preparedness System into action."[119] From 2012 to 2019, the THIRA was required to be completed annually, however, in 2019 the Federal government moved to a three-year cycle for the THIRA, while the SPR remains as an annual requirement. The primary purpose of the SPR is to estimate a community's capability, identify gaps in capabilities, and to address identified capability gaps. Working together, the THIRA and SPR assist communities to make decisions to aid in preventing, protecting against, mitigating, responding to, and recovering from the threats, which pose the greatest community risk. Development of a comprehensive and accurate THIRA and SPR will necessitate a "whole community" approach by incorporating subject matter experts (SMEs) from the community in the processes. From this point, we will examine the THIRA and SPR processes individually and how Emergency Management programs can be enhanced through a coordinated implementation of the processes:

1. **The THIRA Three-Step Process:** The THIRA is comprised of a three-step process, which is completed on a three-year cycle. The THIRA is a risk assessment, which aids in determining which threats are inherent to a community, the impacts of those threats, and what capabilities the community can maintain to address the threats. In relation to the THIRA, risk is defined as *"the potential for an unwanted outcome resulting from an incident or occurrence, as determined by its likelihood and the associated consequences."*[120] The three-step THIRA process is:

   - **Identify Potential Threats and Hazards:** It all begins by generating a concise list of the potential threats and hazards for a specific community. Emergency Mangers will rely upon experience, forecasts, historical information, input from SMEs, and available resources to generate the list. Threats and hazards are categorized as natural, technological accidents resulting from system and structure failures, or

---

[119] (FEMA, Threat and Hazard Identification and Risk Assessment (THIRA) and Stakeholder Preparedness Review (SPR) Guide, Comprehensive Preparedness Guide (CPG) 201, Third Edition, May 2018)

[120] (FEMA, Threat and Hazard Identification and Risk Assessment (THIRA) and Stakeholder Preparedness Review (SPR) Guide, Comprehensive Preparedness Guide (CPG) 201, Third Edition, May 2018)

human-caused intentional acts. Partner agencies such as the National Weather Service (NWS), United States Geological Survey (USGS), Federal and State Forest Services, and FEMA flood plain maps to conduct the threat assessment are invaluable resources to aid in the THIRA process. Additional Local, State, and Federal agencies may also provide insight to potential threats for regional specific threats and hazards.

- **Contextualize the Threats and Hazards:** *"Context Descriptions are the details about a threat or hazard needed to identify the impacts it will have on a community and includes critical details such as location, magnitude, and time of an incident."*[121] Contextualization is accomplished by estimating what impact a threat or hazard may have in a designated area of the community. This allows Emergency Managers to conceptualize "worst-case" scenarios, which would stress the community response and recovery capability.

- **Establish Target Capabilities:** This step refers back to the National Preparedness Goal Mission Areas and Core Capabilities and ties the THIRA into the National Preparedness System. The THIRA Target Capabilities for a jurisdiction are the Core Capabilities from the National Preparedness Goal applied to the local community planning. This is merely taking the core capabilities and inserting community-specific information and statistics to develop target capabilities. To aid in the process, FEMA has developed standardized target language for each capability providing the groundwork upon which to build the community target capabilities. An example of the standardized target language is: "Within (#) hours of an incident, provide emergency sheltering for (#) people; and maintain sheltering operations for (#)

---

[121] (FEMA, Threat and Hazard Identification and Risk Assessment (THIRA) and Stakeholder Preparedness Review (SPR) Guide, Comprehensive Preparedness Guide (CPG) 201, Third Edition, May 2018)

days."[122] Emergency Managers will fill in the appropriate numbers to develop the target capabilities.

2. **The SPR Process:** The SPR is also comprised of a three-step process, which is completed on an annual cycle. The SPR is a community self-assessment looking at how capabilities have changed during the last annual cycle, identified gaps between what is intended to be achieved as opposed to actual current capability, what is needed to close the capability gap, and possible funding sources. The three-step SPR process is:

   • **Assess Current Capabilities:** This is the point where Emergency Managers and the SPR stakeholders will dissect the THIRA Target Capabilities by considering how the community may have changed, how the community capabilities have changed, and the calculated current capability. Under the previous THIRA/SPR editions, this was accomplished with a 1 to 5 rating; however, FEMA modified that in the newest edition to allow communities to develop free-text descriptions to accurately rate capabilities.

   • **Identify and Address Community Capability Gaps:** Based upon the assessment of the current capability, a community can then begin to define the gaps and plan to address the gaps. Capability gaps are determined utilizing the Planning, Organization, Equipment, Training, and Exercise (POETE) model. Gaps can be categorized using POETE; for example, if responders and stakeholders lack adequate training to perform a capability, then the gap is a training gap. Once the gap is identified, POETE then provides a means to address the gap. If training is the gap, then the manner to correct the gap is to provide the appropriate training. The method identified to address the gap will need to include a timeframe for the corrective action to ensure it is completed and specify which stakeholder is accountable for the completion.

---

[122] (FEMA, Threat and Hazard Identification and Risk Assessment (THIRA) and Stakeholder Preparedness Review (SPR) Guide, Comprehensive Preparedness Guide (CPG) 201, Third Edition, May 2018)

- **Describe Impacts of Potential Funding Sources:** Emergency Mangers must determine if the capability improvements will be funded utilizing agency budgetary funding? Alternatively, does the community plan to use Federal, State, or private foundation grants to fund capability improvements? There is an associated cost, in either time or money, for every improvement. Remember, there is no guarantee that a jurisdiction will be approved for Federal or State grant funding for projects. Over the past fifteen years, there has been a gradual decrease in available governmental funding. Some Emergency Managers have attempted to seek private foundation grants for projects, however, like the governmental grants these are few and far between and increasingly difficult to obtain. The impact of disasters upon the budgets for local government has been drastic, such as seen with the COVID-19 pandemic during which many jurisdictions have been forced to downsize or cut budgets due to loss of tax revenue. Emergency Managers may be forced to strategically plan improvement incrementally over a multi-year period based upon agency budget constraints.

3. **THIRA/SPR Emergency Management Program Improvements:** As the processes of the THIRA and SPR are implemented, Emergency Management programs can be improved overall due to focused analyzation of threats and efforts to mitigate the threats. EOPs, Mitigation Plans, organizational SOGs, and so forth can incorporate the information gleaned from the THIRA and SPR processes.

Comprehensive Preparedness Guide (CPG) 502: Considerations for Fusion Center and Emergency Operations Center (EOC) Coordination

When developing a comprehensive Emergency Management planning process, Fusion Centers and Emergency Operations Centers (EOCs) will play important roles. To highlight the incorporation of the fusion process in relation to EOC operations, *CPG-502: Considerations for Fusion Center and Emergency Operations Center (EOC) Coordination* was released in May of 2010. Building towards greater understanding, let us start by defining "fusion" in relation to the fusion process. FEMA defines fusion as *"the overarching process of managing the flow of information and intelligence across all levels and sectors of government and the private sector."*[123] Expanding upon that definition, the fusion process increases the effectiveness of preventing threats due to terrorism and crime in the Local, State, Tribal, and Federal government levels. Throughout this chapter, the mission areas of the National Preparedness Goal have been a focal point and at this point, we see that the fusion process increases "Prevention," one of the five mission areas. Beyond the influence of the fusion process, we will learn that EOCs are actively engaged in all the mission areas. Continuing our forward progress of building understanding, we will review the role of Fusion Centers and EOCs along with the interactive coordination between these centers.

1. **The Fusion Center Role in the Information Sharing Environment (ISE):** "Fusion Centers are state-owned and operated centers that serve as focal points in states and major urban areas for the receipt, analysis, gathering and sharing of threat-related information between State, Local, Tribal and Territorial (SLTT), federal and private sector partners."[124] Fusion Centers are linked through the National Network of Fusion Centers (National

---

[123] (FEMA, Consideration for Fusion Center and Emergency Operations Center (EOC) Coordination; Comprehensive Preparedness Guide (CPG) 502, May 2010)
[124] ((DHS), Fusion Centers, n.d.)

Network) providing a nexus for two-way sharing of intelligence and information between all levels of government and private partners. The basic role of a fusion center is to conduct the intelligence process of "planning and direction, information gathering, processing and collation, analysis and production, and dissemination and reevaluation."[125] It all begins by analyzing "information" which is *raw unconfirmed data received through various reports*, including Suspicious Activity Reporting (SAR), and converting the information into "intelligence" which is *analyzed and confirmed data.* Intelligence is actionable because it is verified and provides knowledge, which can be acted upon by public safety and the private sector. Some of the most significant private sector partners in this process are the CI/KR owners. Similar to Fusion Centers, CI/KR owners and operators have developed Information Sharing and Analysis Centers (ISACs) under the National Council of ISACs to improve protection of their customers, facilities, and personnel. "ISACs collect, analyze and disseminate actionable threat information to their members and provide members with tools to mitigate risks and enhance resiliency."[126] Fusion Centers, ISACs, and EOCs collaborate to share information and intelligence to better protect our communities.

2. **Role of Emergency Operations Centers (EOCs):** Before we get too far along, we need to clarify what constitutes an EOC and the essential functions performed within these facilities. Many would simply describe an EOC as a temporary or permanent physical location; however, EOCs may also be mobile or virtual capabilities where jurisdictions provide "coordination of information and resources to support incident management activities, including incident or natural disaster responses and short-term recovery efforts."[127] EOCs may be staffed with dedicated full-time staff, representatives from supporting agencies and

---

[125] (FEMA, Consideration for Fusion Center and Emergency Operations Center (EOC) Coordination; Comprehensive Preparedness Guide (CPG) 502, May 2010)
[126] (About ISACs, n.d.)
[127] ((DHS), Fusion Centers vs. Emergency Operations Centers, n.d.)

organizations, and trained public safety disciplines. "Chief elected and appointed officials, as well as personnel supporting core functions, may be located at the EOC depending upon the responsibilities of their positions."[128] The configuration, design, and size of an EOC will differ from jurisdiction to jurisdiction and will be determined based upon the anticipated scope of potential operations.

3. **Collaboration between the EOC and Fusion Center:** Fusion Centers can produce intelligence products to provide EOCs with situational awareness for threats and advanced notice for potential activations. Depending upon the situation, Fusion Center personnel may be assigned as liaisons during incidents to provide EOCs with intelligence to aid in decision-making for operations. EOC personnel may, in turn, provide situational awareness and information to Fusion Centers regarding on-going operations. Fusion Centers and EOCs both provide valuable capabilities and resources to the jurisdictions they serve. Effective collaboration will require coordinated partnership development, joint training and exercising, and mutual understanding of roles and responsibilities.

Prior to reading the material in Chapter 4, would you have ever imagined that the discussion of the National Preparedness Goal would have been large as what has been covered in this chapter? And when you consider that this represents a condensation of a number of Federal documents all revolving around the seemingly simple topic of plans. Hopefully it has been an eye-opener to grasp your attention and to illustrate that when it comes to EOPs, nothing is easy and there is no such animal as a single document EOP for a jurisdiction. There are volumes of plans, whether EOPs or THIRAs or organizational EOC plans. And those various plans come in a wide variety of formats. And, yet all of the plans are developed to address the five mission areas and thirty-two core capabilities.

---

[128] (FEMA, Consideration for Fusion Center and Emergency Operations Center (EOC) Coordination; Comprehensive Preparedness Guide (CPG) 502, May 2010)

Chapter 4 Summary

Key Terms (Alphabetical Order)

Agency-/Department-Focused EOP Format
Annexes
Basic Plan
Comprehensive
Concept of Operations (CONOPS)
Context Descriptions
Continuity of Government (COOG)
Continuity of Operations (COOP)
Core Capabilities
Deliberate Plans
Emergency Support Function (ESF) EOP Format
Fusion
Fusion Center
Fusion Process
Information
Information Sharing and Analysis Centers (ISACs)
Information Sharing Environment (ISE)
Intelligence
Mission Areas
National Council of ISACs
National Network of Fusion Centers (National Network)
National Weather Service (NWS)
Protection
Stakeholder Preparedness Review (SPR)
Standard Operating Procedures (SOPs)
Standard Operating Guidelines (SOGs)
State, Local, Tribal and Territorial (SLTT)
Subject Matter Expert (SME)
Support Annexes
Suspicious Activity Reporting (SAR)

Threat and Hazard Identification and Risk Assessment (THIRA)
Traditional Functional EOP Format
United States Geological Service (USGS)

National Preparedness Goal Evolution

Chapter 4 covered how the National Preparedness Goal to achieve a secure and resilient Nation was a direct outcome of Presidential Policy Directive (PPD) 8: National Preparedness. The goal is comprised of the Five Mission Areas, 32 Core Capabilities, and the National Preparedness System, all working together to achieve the National Preparedness Goal. The National Preparedness System entails a six-part process of identifying and assessing risk, estimating capabilities, building and sustaining abilities, planning to deliver capabilities, validating capabilities, and continually reviewing and updating preparedness.

Comprehensive Emergency Management Planning

The Federal government has provided a series of Comprehensive Preparedness Guides (CPGs) which aid in the process of developing comprehensive Emergency Management plans. CPG-101 is the foundation for writing Emergency Operations Plans to use either the Traditional, Emergency Support Function (ESF), or Agency-/Department-Focused formats. CPG-201 is the guideline for conducting a Threat and Hazard Identification and Risk Assessment (THIRA). In addition, CPG-502 lays out the coordination between Fusion Centers and Emergency Operations Centers (EOCs).

In the next chapter, you will learn about Emergency Management field operations coordination.

Chapter 5: Emergency Management Field Operations

In Chapter 4, we examined the National Preparedness Goal and planning guidance for EOPs, the THIRA, and collaboration between Fusion Centers and EOCs. Shifting our study from planning to operations, Chapter 5 targets the expanse of field operations. For over a decade, methodologies in Emergency Management have widely varied, as is evidenced in the growing number of specialties within the field. You can find Emergency Managers who specialize as Community Preparedness Coordinators, EOC Managers, Grant Managers, Higher Education Emergency Managers, Hospital Emergency Managers, Planners, Private Sector Emergency Managers, Trainers, Volunteer Coordinators, and more categories are being added each year. Then there are those I refer to as "Responder Emergency Managers." In 2016, I wrote and delivered a workshop at two professional conferences on the topic of Responder Emergency Managers to address the misperception that Emergency Management was primarily limited to functions performed in an office setting. Understandably, some of the specialties in the field are dedicated to working in an office environment. However, that is not an accurate axiom across the spectrum of Emergency Management. Jurisdictions throughout the Nation rely upon professional Emergency Managers who are highly experienced in supporting field operations. The question immediately comes to mind – What are field operations? An exhaustive search does will not yield an official definition because of an apparent assumption that field operations are self-explanatory. Not willing to assume that new and prospective Emergency Managers will intuitively make the leap, I developed the following definition in 2016: *"Field operations include the performance of tasks in a natural setting by public safety, Emergency Managers, and assisting agencies to aid in response and recovery.*"[129]

Emergency Management Coordination of Field Operations

The one undeniable truth is that it is impossible to pre-determine when and where disasters will strike. Experience has shown, however, that disasters tend to occur during the most inopportune times. I have lost count over the years of the number of times that a disaster struck between midnight and the early morning, on a weekend, or on a holiday weekend. This is the main reason why Emergency Managers need to be prepared to respond 24 hours a day and 7 days a week. Part of that personal preparedness is maintaining a "Go Kit" with all of your necessary items you might need to work in a remote area with only what you can carry. In 2013, I compiled a "Go Kit" list, which includes an air card or hot spot, batteries, cell phone, laptop, multiple charging cables, small printer, surge suppressor, thumb drives, and writing tablets. Additionally, you need to be prepared to be able to work even when there is no cell service or electricity because after catastrophic disasters those services more than likely will not be functional. This is why I harp about being able to do the job of Emergency Management "old school." What I mean by that statement is that you have to be able to manage incidents using no more than pen and paper. Therefore, every effective Emergency Management "Go Kit" should also include "copies of the agency forms, FEMA IAP forms, and a few general office supplies."[130] Beyond those items, most Emergency Managers will personalize their "Go Kit" with a variety of hygiene items, flashlights, non-perishable food, and bottled water. Once a kit is completed, it should be kept in your primary vehicle and periodically maintained by replacing the food and water.

---

[129] (Chadwick, The Responder Emergency Manager, 2016)
[130] (Chadwick, Emergency Manager "Go Kit" List, 2013)

Field Operations Initial Emergency Management Response

Responding to a disaster in the field requires an understanding of the steps involved in effectively collaborating with and working alongside of Incident Commanders. Some of the important issues every Emergency Manager responding in the field must understand include knowing where and where not to park your vehicle to not interfere with life-saving operations, never running over a fire hose for any reason, engaging emergency lighting on your vehicle, and radio protocols just to name a few. Furthermore, I have broken the elements of response down to the following steps:

1. **An Incident Occurs:** At any time of any day and normally when least expected.
2. **Notification of the incident from dispatch:** From jurisdiction to jurisdiction, notification to Emergency Managers may be accomplished in several ways, by phone, public safety radio, or specialized applications.
3. **Initial response personnel deployed depending on the type of incident:** For offices with multiple Emergency Managers, one or more may be dedicated to support specific response operations.
4. **On-scene arrival:** Making entry to the scene at the appropriate location and not impeding operations.
5. **Scene size up:** This is the point where you "get eyes on" the situation and begin to determine if the incident is expanding or contracting and anticipating potential resources. Partnering with the Incident Commander, the "Responder Emergency Manager can watch for cascading issues within an incident."[131]
6. **Coordinate with the on-scene Incident Commander:** This is where the Emergency Manager contacts the Incident Commander and becomes another set of eyes to consider political implications, special circumstances, and to aid in avoiding tunnel vision.

---

[131] (Chadwick, The Responder Emergency Manager, 2016)

7. **Coordinate response of additional resources:** When it comes to resources, Emergency Managers need to "think outside of the box." You will face incidents where you do not have the perfect resource and you will have to come up with creative alternatives.

8. **Notification to response partners if necessary:** Emergency Managers will need to have a listing of mutual aid and volunteer agencies, which can provide post-disaster assistance.

9. **Deploy and Mobile Emergency Operations Center (MEOC) or support equipment:** Some Emergency Managers will have agency response assets such as a mobile emergency operations center (MEOC)/mobile incident command post trailers, communication trailers, or other support apparatus.

10. **Deploy a Volunteer Operations Center (VOC) or establish a Volunteer Process:** In large or catastrophic disasters, Emergency Mangers will need to have a process in place to coordinate volunteers. That process may include recruiting, background checking, just-in-time training, and tracking the hours worked. Even established volunteer agencies will have to be managed by Emergency Managers.

11. **Simultaneous activation of the EOC:** Some incidents will require field operations and activation of the physical EOC.

12. **Office staff man the EOC:** When you activate the EOC during field operations, someone will have to be dedicated to manning the EOC.

13. **Possible deployment of an Incident Management Team (IMT):** The ICS organization chart was presented back in Chapter 3. An IMT is comprised of the ICS personnel who are trained and qualified to hold the Command, Command Staff, General Staff, and related positions. Each State manages IMTs a little differently; therefore, I encourage you to reach out to the agency in your State, which is responsible for IMTs.

14. **Coordinate on-scene response operations:** This is the area where Emergency Managers can shine alongside the Incident Commander. Providing those extra eyes and ears is invaluable and experienced

Emergency Managers can draw upon what they have learned coordinating past responses.

15. **Coordinate recovery operations:** Firefighters, law enforcement, emergency medical personnel, public health, and public works employees roll up their operations when response ends. That is why I tell people that response is the easy part. When everyone else packs up and goes home, Emergency Managers go to work on recovery, which may last days, weeks, months, or even years. Within the National Disaster Recovery Framework, FEMA has identified six Recovery Support Functions (RSFs) which "comprise the coordinating structure for key functional areas"[132] and support the Local government encouraging partnership between Federal and State agencies, non-governmental agencies, and community stakeholders. The six RSFs are Economic, Community Planning and Capacity Building, Housing Recovery, Health and Social Services, Infrastructure Systems, and Natural and Cultural Resources. The RSFs are the objectives and work, which will monopolize the bulk of the time in recovery for Emergency Managers.

Establishment of Facilities in Support of Field Operations

The Emergency Management facilities introduced in Chapter 3 included the Incident Command Post (ICP), Staging Area, Base, Camp, Heli-Base, and Heli-spot. Aside from the ICP, the main facility, which is required on most large incidents, is the Staging Area where equipment and personnel are prepared and poised to rapidly be mobilized as needed. The resources in "a staging area should be grouped by functional use (engine strike teams and single engines are in one area, crew transportation in a separate area, and other equipment in another area)."[133] There

---

[132] (FEMA, Recovery Support Functions, n.d.)
[133] (Service, Staging Area Manager, 2014)

are a variety of other facilities, which may need to be established, depending upon the incident including, but not limited to, the following:

1. **Family Assistance Center (FAC):** In the event of a mass fatality incident or commercial aircraft accident, "the primary purpose of an FAC is to provide information to families, receive victim information from the families, and provide support services."[134] *The FAC is a location to provide care and support for the family members and friends whose loved ones have died during disasters.* Emergency Management personnel would be involved in coordinating with jurisdiction departments, social services, and volunteer agencies, which will assist in providing for the care of the family, friends, and loved ones.

2. **Family Reunification:** When disasters occur, it is not uncommon for Emergency Managers to end up with minors who need to be reunified with parents or legal guardians. *"Family Reunification is the process or location from which to manage reunifying minors with custodial parents after the occurrence of a disaster."* This can present a number of problems because the situation may involve estranged parents who have no legal status to take custody of a child. Emergency Managers can easily get into serious legal trouble if a child is released to a non-custodial parent or some other person. Family reunification will require verification of custody and may take considerable time.

3. **Shelters:** Temporary shelters are often required after a disaster. When opening a shelter, Emergency Managers need to be aware of the Americans with Disabilities Act (ADA) and Functional Needs Support Services (FNSS) requirements. A great tool to assist with ensuring your shelters are ADA/FNSS Compatible is the *"Guidance on Planning for Integration of Functional Needs Support Services in General Population Shelters"* put out by FEMA in November of 2010. "This document provides guidance to assist Emergency Managers and shelter planners in understanding the requirements related to sheltering children and adults

---

[134] (Chadwick, Family Assistance Center and Victim Information Center, 2015)

with functional support needs in general population shelters."[135] More will be covered on shelter operations in the next section of this chapter.

4. **Victim Information Center (VIC):** The VIC, like the FAC, is a facility, which is brought online in support of mass fatality incidents. "The purpose of a Victim Information Center (VIC) is to have a central location where victim ante-mortem information can be coordinated."[136] Medical examiners (MEs) or coroners and their staff will establish the *VIC* as the site *where family members can be interviewed to obtain information on a victim such as birthmarks, dental work history, surgeries or scars, and tattoos to be used for identification purposes.* Emergency Managers may be called upon to assist MEs in locating a facility to be used as a VIC and to coordinate transportation for family members, friends, and loved ones to be interviewed.

Classifications of Emergency Management Field Operations

Disasters are generally categorized as either natural, human-caused, or technological and we will start this portion of our study by briefly defining each category. *"Natural disasters include all types of severe weather, which have the potential to pose a significant threat to human health and safety, property, critical infrastructure, and homeland security."*[137] Whereas *"human-caused disasters are those resulting from human errors, intentional acts, and neglect."* In addition, our last major category; *technological disasters include commercial explosions or fires, computer infrastructure failures, dam failures, hazards materials spills, radiation exposures, and transportation accidents.* Each is its own broad category, which contains a multitude of sub-classifications and associated field operations for

---

[135] (FEMA, Guidance on Planning for Integration of Functional Needs Support Services in General Population Shelters, November 2010)
[136] (Chadwick, Family Assistance Center and Victim Information Center, 2015)
[137] ((DHS), Natural Disasters, n.d.)

Emergency Managers. Some of the classifications of Emergency Management fieldwork include:

1. **Damage Assessments:** After storms devastate a community, damage assessments must be conducted to determine the extent of the damage to residential homes and public (government) facilities, resources needed for response and recovery, and the needs of the community. Damage assessments will be covered in more detail in further in Chapter 7.

2. **Debris Removal:** Debris on roadways will impede emergency response vehicles and can threaten the safety and lives of the public and responders. Debris removal operations must begin rapidly following disasters to be able to provide emergency vehicle ingress and egress for responders and the public. An important note for Emergency Managers is that when it comes to residential debris removal, FEMA guidelines stipulate that the homeowner is responsible for moving the debris to the curb and "debris should not block the roadway."[138] Debris cannot be piled together in a single mixed pile. Debris must be separated into the six categories of electronics, large appliances, hazardous wastes, vegetative debris, construction debris, and household garbage. Additionally, most Local government regulations prohibit jurisdictional departments and emergency responders from assisting in the removal of debris from private property. The reason for the prohibition is that the jurisdiction would then have to accept financial responsibility for employees injured while working on private property, which is not normally covered by workman's compensation insurance. Moreover, the jurisdiction could be open to liability for any accidental damages to the residence or business such as broken water lines, electric lines, and incidental damages to structures.

3. **Evacuation & Accountability:** There is much more to evacuations than telling people to leave. Evacuations must be coordinated and managed correctly. Residents being evacuated from their homes must be provided

---

[138] (FEMA, Debris Removal)

with the opportunity for shelter and Emergency Managers will need to collect contact information, number and ages of family members, medical concerns, and plan for animal evacuations and shelter. Once evacuated, Emergency Managers have to maintain accountability of the evacuees are they staying with family, going to a hotel, or registering at a shelter. The last thing any jurisdiction will tolerate is having an evacuee interviewed on prime-time television and for the evacuee to claim they were kicked out of their home and left with no support.

4. **Mass Fatality Incidents:** The U.S. Department of Health & Human Services (HHS) defines mass fatalities *"as those in which there are more bodies than can be handled using local resources."*[139] Emergency Managers refer to mass fatalities as incidents where the number of deceased exceeds the jurisdictions' ability to adequately manage the incident and requires mutual aid or assistance. The primary functions conducted in mass fatality incidents are human remains recovery, decontamination when necessary, and examination for identification and death certification. The statutes for fatality management may differ from State to State; therefore, Emergency Managers will need to be familiar with the laws in their respective State laws and jurisdictional policies.

5. **Points of Dispensing (POD):** For public health emergencies, medical countermeasures (MCMs) such as antibiotics, antitoxins, antivirals, and chemical antidotes will be employed to prevent or mitigate the impact on communities as a component of the Strategic National Stockpile (SNS). Points of dispensing (PODs) are "facilities operated by local public health departments to distribute MCMs to the public."[140] Emergency Manager will work alongside of their public health counterparts in coordinating POD operations and exercising plans to establish PODs.

6. **Commodity Points of Distribution (C-PODs):** In a post-disaster environment, survivors in the community may face a situation where

---

[139] ((HHS) Services, n.d.)
[140] (Prevention, n.d.)

---

there are no utilities and retail establishments to provide food and basic supplies are not operational. *"A C-POD establishes an initial point(s) where the public can obtain life-sustaining emergency relief supplies."*[141] Typical commodities distributed will include non-perishable food, water, ice, tarps; clean up kits, and hygiene products. Emergency Manager will coordinate with a wide array of Volunteer Organizations Active in Disasters (VOADs) which provide many of these disaster relief supplies.

7. **Resource Management:** As covered in Chapter 3, resource management is a vital and complex task in coordinating disaster response. Emergency Managers will need to understand the concepts of "type" and "kind" to ensure that the appropriate resources are ordered for the tasks to be accomplished. To assist in this process, FEMA offers the free to download Incident Resource Inventory System (IRIS) software tool. "IRIS is available for use by all agencies, jurisdictions, and communities to serve as a consistent tool to inventory resources into their own database and to search/identify their specific resources for incident operations and mutual aid purposes."[142]

8. *Shelter Operations:* Aside from the previously covered information, short-term shelters are temporary locations "converted to provide safe, accessible, and secure short-term housing for disaster survivors."[143] The Authority Having Jurisdiction (AHJ) will provide a wide range of life-sustaining resources and services to provide for the safety and security of the residents being sheltered. Resources provide will include basic medical care, food, sanitation, and water. Services will include access and functional needs, health and mental health care, childcare, animal sheltering, service animal support, family reunification, laundry, transportation, and access to social services. Some jurisdictions may opt to utilize the American Red Cross to manage shelters; however, many jurisdictions chose other mechanisms and organizations to manage

---

[141] (FEMA, Distribution Management Plan Guide, August 2019)
[142] (FEMA, NIMS Resources, n.d.)
[143] (FEMA, Short-Term Shelter, n.d.)

shelters. In either case, the jurisdiction is ultimately responsible for the management of shelters and Emergency Managers will need to be engaged in this process. Shelter operations can be *congregate shelters or group settings utilizing community facilities holding hundreds of evacuees* (schools, churches, community centers, etc…), *mega-shelters or extremely large facilities such as warehouses where thousands of evacuees can be housed*, and *non-congregate shelters for single individuals or families such as hotels.*

9. **Search & Rescue (SAR) Operations:** When people are lost, in imminent danger, or trapped, SAR operations will be conducted to locate, extricate, and provide life-saving services. SAR operations are identified by the type of terrain where the search is conducted, including Cave SAR, Ground SAR, Maritime SAR, Mountain SAR, Technical SAR, and Urban SAR. Emergency Managers may be called upon to coordinate and manage the various SAR organizations working the operation and to assist in developing the Incident Action Plans (IAPs).

The Difficulties of Unique Field Operations

At the end of the day, it is not the normal types of operations (fires, floods, hurricanes, tornadoes, etc…) that will present the most difficult challenges. The unique or non-common incidents are the ones that present extreme challenges and will demand one-hundred percent focus and diligence from Emergency Managers. Gordon Graham, world renowned speaker and risk manager, summed up the facts revolving around unique incidents which he refers to as High Risk/Low Frequency incidents during a presentation on July 27, 2012. The presentation "High Risk/Low Frequency Events in the Fire Service"[144] is available for viewing on YouTube and I highly recommend every Emergency Manager to take fifteen minutes and review this humorous and educational video. When responding to unique incidents,

---

[144] (Graham, 2012)

Emergency Managers and responders will have to perform unfamiliar tasks and that is where we are placed in the highest level of danger. To emphasize how challenging unique field operations can be, I have selected four incidents I worked over the past six years to illustrate the unique challenges Emergency Mangers may face associated with field operations and these incidents may serve as case studies.

1. **United Site Services Fire:** "Bexar County OEM Case #2014-1."[145] In my position with the Bexar County Office of Emergency Management (BCOEM), I work patrolling the County on New Year's Eve and the 4th of July to rapidly respond to fires and associated emergencies. On January 1, 2014, just minutes after midnight, I was dispatched to a call for a porta-potty on fire. Initially, that may sound hilarious to you; however, I assure that the incident was anything but funny. When I was close to a mile from the location of the call, I could see flames shooting hundreds of feet into the air and that was the first clue that I would be dealing with a potentially catastrophic incident. When I arrived on-scene, I found that the property was owned by a company, which leases porta-potties all over the State of Texas, and there were thousands of porta-potties spread over the acres of the property. The porta-potties were lined up with approximately one foot between them on either side. A wooden privacy fence on the east side of the property was all that separated the porta-potty storage acreage from a residential subdivision with hundreds of homes. Some of the residents had apparently been shooting off aerial fireworks and an errant firework had landed in the middle of the porta-potties where it caught dried grass on fire and, subsequently, the porta-potties. What you have to understand is that porta-potties are manufactured from plastic, which is a petroleum product. When a porta-potty catches on fire it burns extremely hot and releases a toxic smoke. The resulting fire was in the very middle of the field of porta-potties. Firefighters could not get close to the area of the fire because of how close the porta-potties were next to each other and the vast expanse of the acreage. We brought in aerial platform fire engines

---

[145] (Chadwick, United Site Services Fire, January 1, 2014)

and water cannons to launch water streams into the fire from the perimeter. You might ask why we did not use airdrops of water from helicopters or aircraft. The answer is – helicopters and aircraft do not do nighttime water drops because it is far too dangerous. A couple of hours into fighting the fire, the winds shifted and began blowing east right towards the subdivision and the fire was whipped into a frenzy. As the fire grew so did the toxic smoke billowing from the fire and drifting over the subdivision. About an hour before bringing the fire under control, we were notified that an oil fracking company had trailers on the south end of the property containing fracking explosives. We fought that fire for almost 10 hours before bringing it under control. We were successful in stopping the fire before it engulfed any of the homes, but a section of the wooden privacy fence was heavily singed within 20 feet of the backside of several homes. The final estimate, based upon the size of the burn area, was that 1,192 porta-potties were burned to cinders during this incident. To recap the challenges; we had a massive petroleum product fire we could not readily reach in close proximity to hundreds of private residents, toxic smoke, a wind shift fanning the flames and sending the toxic smoke directly over a subdivision, deadly explosives, and the life-threatening dangers attributed to heat and burns. Definitely not a funny incident!

2. **Live Hand in Uvalde County, Texas:** "Unified Bexar-Uvalde County Situation Report."[146] I was finishing up assisting with a fire in Bexar County on April 16, 2014, when I received a call from the Emergency Management Coordinator in Uvalde County, TX (100 miles west of Bexar County). The Emergency Manager asked me if we could assist him with a hand grenade issue and if we could request the Bureau of Alcohol, Tobacco, and Firearms and Explosives (ATF) to approve deployment of a bomb squad. I told him I would start the process and notify him once we had approval. The Uvalde County Emergency Manager was out of his county on personal business at the time of the incident, which meant we

---

[146] (Chadwick, Hand Grenade - Uvalde County, April 16, 2014)

would be going into another jurisdiction to manage an incident on their behalf, which is acceptable with the appropriate permissions. This is when I received the full story of how a family had a grandfather who passed away and when they went to inventory the grandfather's home, they found a hand grenade on the mantle over the fireplace. Presumably, the grandfather had served in World War II and brought the hand grenade home as a souvenir. Not being familiar with explosives, the family called a friend who had been a volunteer firefighter for over 30 years in Uvalde. Upon inspection of the hand grenade, the firefighter took possession of it and transported it across the county and along a quarter-mile rough gravel road on his property in a cardboard box in his back floorboard of his truck. When he got the hand grenade to his house, he decided to store the hand grenade inside of his new metal barn. The firefighter later claimed he had second thoughts about the dangers of having the hand grenade and he called the ATF asking them to remove it. However, after hearing his story, the ATF found the situation to be highly questionable because the firefighter refused to call the County Sheriff because of a personal conflict with the Sheriff. This is when the firefighter called the Uvalde Emergency Manager and ultimately resulted in my involvement. We agreed to respond and provide assistance to Uvalde County, and we notified the Uvalde Sheriff of the situation and obtained permission to manage the incident. When we arrived with the bomb squad, we located the World War II era "pineapple" hand grenade in a cardboard box on top of a table in the new barn. Visually we were able to determine that the hand grenade was at least 69 years old, based upon shape, and possibly up to 75 years old. The bomb squad x-rayed the hand grenade and found that it was, in fact, completely intact with explosives and they deemed it to be highly unstable. At this point, the bomb squad notified the firefighter that protocols called for the unstable explosives such as the hand grenade to be exploded in place due to the dangers to the bomb squad if they attempted to move it. If you recall, the firefighter had placed the hand grenade inside his "new" metal barn. The firefighter immediately begged the bomb squad not to blow the explosive in place and damage his barn. The bomb squad agreed to allow the firefighter to carry the explosive by hand into the middle of a field far enough from his home and barn to safely detonate the explosive. Yes, I backed far off with the bomb squad while we watched the firefighter carry it across a plowed field over 1,500 feet from his home. Finally, the bomb squad dug a hole, packed the hand grenade and an explosive charge in the hole; we backed off, took shelter behind vehicles, and detonated the grenade. I was able to get the impressive explosion on video. The inherent dangers and unique challenges for this operation included managing an incident 100 miles outside of our jurisdiction, coordination with a Federal agency to deploy a bomb squad, and an unstable military-grade high explosive, which was at least 69 years old. The dangers to life and property in this incident were higher than most people realize because military hand grenades are designed to send shrapnel, fragments of the pineapple shaped metal casing, shooting at high velocity in 360 degrees. At any point, the hand grenade could have exploded causing serious bodily injury or death.

3. **Trench Body Retrieval:** "Bexar County Office of Emergency Management Situation Report."[147] On January 23, 2017, I was dispatched to a call for a construction worker accidentally killed in a deep trench. When I arrived, on-scene the Incident Commander explained that what had happened is that a female construction worker was doing some handwork in the bottom of a 35-foot-deep trench when a heavy equipment operator utilizing a long-arm excavator accidentally dropped the excavating bucket on her head and crushing her body. To make matters worse, the Incident Commander pointed out to me that the contractor had dug the trench without any safety shoring on the trench walls and the dirt was loose and in danger of easily collapsing in on firefighters injuring or killing them in an attempted retrieval operation. Consulting with the contractor revealed that it would take several days to install the required safety shoring and

---

[147] (Chadwick, Trench Body Retrieval, January 23, 2017)

we could not leave the body in the trench for that period of time. The only option left to us was to ask for firefighters to volunteer to enter the hazardous trench over 35 feet below the ground level to retrieve the body. To attempt to mitigate some of the hazards, we hooked safety harnesses and rescue ropes to the three firefighters who entered the trench for potential rapid extraction. The firefighters had to walk down into the trench, which was on a steep downslope over 150 feet long to get to where the body was located. The trench was only the width of the excavating bucket, which meant they had to walk in single file. When they got to the bottom of the trench, a backboard and straps were lowered in to strap the body to the backboard for extrication. After securing the body, the firefighters then had to carry the body out single file with one firefighter at the head and one at the foot. The process was slow going with the steep incline and the weight being supported in an awkward manner. The firefighters were physically and emotionally exhausted by the time they were at a level where we could safely lift them out. Under the conditions we were faced with, lives were seriously on the line and options were extremely limited. The long-arm excavator was confiscated by law enforcement as evidence of a crime, which meant it could not be utilized for the retrieval operations. Even the rescue ropes attached to the firefighters were rubbing against the edges of the trench causing the loose soil to constantly drop into the trench, which meant we could not risk raising the body on a backboard by rope. Time was working against us because it was late in the afternoon, and we were at risk of losing lighting. Adding to the complexity, the family members of the deceased female construction worker were onsite and closely examining our every move. The unique challenges we faced that day were working in an extremely dangerous situation, restrictive confines at a deadly depth underground, the unknown of whether the trench walls would suddenly collapse, daylight quickly running away from us, and doing everything we could under the circumstances to be respectful and provide for the dignity of the deceased under the scrutiny of highly emotional family members.

4. **Snakes in a Car:** "Bexar County Office of Emergency Management Situation Report."[148] This is one of the most unique and potentially deadly incidents I have ever managed during my career. On June 30, 2017, I received a call on my cellphone from dispatch that I initially thought they were pulling a prank on me. The dispatcher advised that we had a single vehicle rollover on I-35 South, and they were requesting my assistance. I replied to the dispatcher that a single vehicle rollover is not something responders normally need Emergency Management assistance. This is where it got weird as the dispatcher told me the vehicle was carrying 32 snakes, 16 of which were deadly venomous, a tortoise, and an alligator. I paused waiting for the punch line to the joke, but the joke was on me because it was true. Dispatch advised that the vehicle landed upside down, the snakes were all over the inside of the vehicle, the 75-year-old male driver and his 7-year-old grandson were entrapped in the vehicle, and firefighters on-scene could not make extrication because the snakes were everywhere, and the firefighters had no protective gear for snake bite. I immediately turned my vehicle around, engaged emergency lights, headed south, and called the Emergency Manager for one of our major hospitals. I asked the Emergency Manager if they had a supply of anti-venom and he explained that they did have some, however, they would need to know what type of snake I was dealing with since anti-venom is specific to the given snake. The Emergency Manager asked me what type of snake I was dealing with and I hurriedly told him I had 32 with 16 venomous, a vehicle entrapment with two injured, one 75-year-old male, one 7-year-old male, and firefighters unable to make vehicle extrication. This is the point when things really got interesting because the Emergency Manager told me they would begin an inventory of all anti-venom, call other hospitals for their inventory, and they placed the hospital Emergency Room (ER) on *"Divert," which is where an ER immediately shuts down receiving patients.* The Emergency Manager did that to clear

---

[148] (Chadwick, Venomous Snakes Vehicle Extrication, June 30, 2017)

the ER to potentially receive multiple venomous snakebite victims. What is important to note is that this hospital is a Level 1 Trauma Center, which is the highest level of medical care. This hospital is one of the two Level 1 Trauma Centers for Bexar County, a County with nearly 2 million in population. That cut our highest level of medical care for our citizens in half. My next call was back to Dispatch to request to have an air ambulance (helicopter) placed on stand-by to fly immediately. So, within minutes, I had a Level 1 Trauma Center on divert and AirLife gearing up to launch and I had not even gotten halfway to the scene. I began calling my contacts and searching for someone with snake handling gear and was finally successful with one of our small neighboring municipalities to the south. I arrived on-scene at the same time as the person who brought the snake tongs. Firefighters stopped a paint truck passing by on the highway and took every empty 5-gallon bucket on his truck and then broke the glass on the overturned vehicle and began extracting the snakes and dropping them in the buckets. Once the driver and his grandson were extricated, they were triaged and transported. At this point, the firefighters were able to use a response vehicle and tow strap to pull the overturned vehicle back onto its wheels and use the jaws-of-life to chop the top off the vehicle. This was my first chance to see how the snakes were being transported; they had been carried in acrylic cubes, which had shattered when the vehicle rolled. There were cards taped to the outside identifying the type of snakes. I began gathering the cards while firefighters continued to capture the snakes. The vehicle interior had to be completely torn apart on-scene because the snakes had crawled into every tiny hole they could find and they were inside the door panels, overhead panel, console, and seats. We had a pop-up canopy tent delivered to provide shade for the buckets of snakes. Since it was the end of June, we were dealing with 100 plus degree temperatures. We were extremely fortunate that no one was bitten during our operations, and I was able to stand-down the hospital and air ambulance. The firefighters captured 30 of the 32 snakes and we had no way of determining which two were missing or where they were hidden. You might think that my challenges were drawing to an end, but that is not the case. What do you do with 30 snakes, a tortoise, and an alligator on the side of a major interstate highway? None of the response agencies on-scene could take possession of the snakes. I called Animal Control, Texas Parks & Wildlife Game Wardens, and various Local and State agencies, none of which would take possession of the snakes. The Game Wardens did verify that the driver had permits to transport venomous reptiles, which was what he did for a living. In desperation, I called a private snake farm 30 miles north of our County and was able to talk them into agreeing to pick up the snakes temporarily until the owner could retrieve them. I spent another 3 hours on the side of the highway waiting for the snakes to be picked up and allowing me to go home. All in all, I was engaged in this single vehicle rollover incident for more than 8 hours. The unique challenges for this incident included extreme heat, venomous snakes, Level 1 Trauma Center diversion, air ambulance activation, snake tongs, vehicle entrapments, extrication, mutual aid, Local and State agency collaboration, and private sector partnership.

I could write a complete book on the unique operations I have been involved in over the past 35 years. However, my intention here in Chapter 5 was to demonstrate a cross-section of some of the unique challenges that can occur for Emergency Managers. These challenges will push Emergency Managers to think outside of the box because they involve issues, which are unique and potentially deadly. There is no training for unique challenges and Emergency Managers will be forced to go back to the basics and work diligently while keeping the unique challenges in the forefront of thought. The truth is that all field operations have dangerous elements, however, when responders and Emergency Managers are called upon to do things, they are not familiar with doing and in circumstances for which there is limited or no training, which is a recipe for potential disaster and deadly results.

Communications for Emergency Management Field Operations

Ask any first responder or Emergency Manager what they find to be the biggest problem area for field operations, and they will inevitably agree that communications are the most problematic. In some cases, the problem is that responding agencies have radio systems on different frequencies and are unable to communicate directly. The region where the incident occurs may have limited or spotty radio coverage. Or, in some cases, one or more of the people involved in managing the incident may be an *information hoarder; "someone who holds back information from others."* Communications are vital and can spell the difference between success and failure or life and death during field operations. Another important consideration is that communications are generally categorized as either internal or external communications. *Internal communications pertain to those communications specific to the internal audience of elected and senior officials, jurisdictional departments, and public safety response agencies.* Whereas *external communications refer to communications with the public, private sector, and volunteer agencies.* In this latter half of Chapter 5, we will investigate both internal and external communications.

Internal Communications in Support of Field Operations

Communication internally is accomplished primarily by cellphone to elected and senior officials and non-response jurisdictional departments and by public safety radios on-scene. Larger jurisdictions may have the luxury of having a dedicated professional Public Information Officer (PIO) who can manage notifications to elected and senior officials and internal departments. A PIO is worth their weight in gold during field operations because they can relieve Emergency Managers and Incident Commanders of the bulk of the burden of chasing between radio and cellphone communications. However, in some jurisdictions, the Emergency Manager may also be tasked with performing the PIO function during field operations.

Public safety radios operate on frequencies, which are restricted to public safety (Emergency Management, firefighting, law enforcement, emergency medical, and other governmental response departments) and not open to the general public, private sector, or volunteer agencies. What the average person may not realize is that there are varieties of frequency bands utilized by public safety agencies. Three of the most common frequency bands include Very High Frequency (VHF), 700 megahertz (MHz), and 800 mhz. Before the year 2000, the vast majority of the public safety radios in the United States were constructed using analog frequency modulation (FM) which is an older technology. In 1989, the Association of Public Safety Communications Officials (APCO) adopted Project 25 (P-25) to modernize public safety communications to digital technology and this effort has become known as P-25 Compliance. The Telecommunications Industry Association (TIA) announced, "the deployment of P25-compliant systems will allow a high degree of equipment interoperability, compatibility and economy of scale."[149] Basically, the change was to go from analog radios to digital radios in the hopes that public safety agencies would be better able to communicate in the field. The concept sounds good and solid on the surface. P-25 addresses the issue of *"interoperability,"* which is *"the ability of equipment or groups to operate in conjunction with one another."*[150] However, it is a much more complicated issue to be addressed than to switch from analog to digital. At the beginning of this paragraph, I explained that public safety agencies commonly operate on VHF, 700 MHz, and 800 MHz bands among others. Without getting too technical, those are completely separate frequency bands. Therefore, agencies on VHF cannot talk to agencies on 700 or 800 MHz and vice versa. Therefore, when agencies transitioned from analog to digital technology, the ability to communicate across the various bands did not change. It does not matter if you are using analog or digital when you are operating on different frequency

---

[149] ((TIA) Association, n.d.)
[150] ((DHS) Security, 2017)

bands. Therefore, the issue still exists today for agencies operating on different systems. Fortunately, there is technology to patch (route) various frequency bands through equipment, which will allow responders on divergent frequencies to communicate. Some dispatch centers and some responder vehicles will have equipment to patch frequencies. There is also a non-technical manner to work around this issue, which has been used in field operations for decades – assign one person from each agency to work shoulder to shoulder and relay vital information to personnel on their respective frequencies. The lesson to learn here is that technology is not always the answer.

Public safety agencies also utilize a variety of technology applications to facilitate communications. It is impossible to reference all of the types or brands of technologies utilized. I will refer to a couple of the technologies utilized by my jurisdiction. The first I want to highlight is *Active911* which is a mobile technology application "that coordinates with dispatchers to send notifications to emergency first responders"[151] by sending a text styled message through the application to all authorized personnel for every 911 call entered into our Computer Aided Dispatch (CAD). The messages on Active911 include the category of the incident (fire, medical, etc…), address, date and time of call, the description of what is occurring, a map link to quickly start GPS directions, link to personnel and departments assigned to the call, a chat function, and the ability for responders to tap and advise if they are responding. The Bexar County Office of Emergency Management (BCOEM) uses Active911 and we have found it to be extremely helpful. There are other similar products, however, I am not experienced with those systems to be able to offer any informed opinion. A second technology utilized by BCOEM is *Motorola's WAVE Push-to-Talk (PTT)* mobile application, which turns a cellphone into a public safety radio and "instantly connects your team across different devices, networks, and locations."[152] Bexar County and the surrounding 12 counties entered into agreement to program our primary radio frequencies into WAVE in effect patching all main frequencies (VHF, 700 MHz, and 800 MHz) when using a

---

[151] (Active911, n.d.)
[152] (WAVE Push-to-Talk, n.d.)

cellphone with the application. Again, there are numerous technologies to pick from and each jurisdiction will have to determine which, if any, technology solutions best interface with existing systems.

External Communications in Support of Field Operations

The other side of communications Emergency Managers must be conversant with is external communication, which can be employed for non-emergency information sharing and emergency notifications. As with internal communications, for those agencies with dedicated PIOs, this may be managed by the personnel assigned those duties. Non-emergency communications may include addressing partnership opportunities, asking and answering questions, and planning for events. Such communications can be managed using phones, email, or text messaging. It is vital for Emergency Managers to continually be engaged in communicating with external partners.

External communications also include emergency notifications, which are the main component for the Public Information & Warning core capability (see Table 3, page 110). Emergency notifications can be managed over numerous technology platforms, media outlets, and the multitude of social media systems available. First, let us review the four main national emergency notifications systems available:

1. **The Emergency Alert System (EAS):** The EAS "is a national public warning system that requires radio and TV broadcasters, cable TV, wireless cable systems, satellite and wireline operators to provide the President with capability to address the American people within 10 minutes during a national emergency."[153] The key here is that EAS sends messages utilizing the television as the mechanism to get the message to the public. The weakness of EAS is that only those who are viewing television at the time of the message being delivered will see it and for

---

[153] (FEMA, The Emergency Alert System (EAS), n.d.)

those who rely upon streaming services, the message may be completely missed.

2. **NOAA Weather Radio All Hazards (NWR):** The NWR "is a nationwide network of radio stations broadcasting continuous weather information from the nearest National Weather Service office."[154] NWR is also used to transmit warnings and information for all hazards along with *AMBER Alerts, which are emergency messages from law enforcement for child abductions*. The weakness with NWR is that fewer and fewer people maintain weather radios at home or work. NWR does send email alerts to those who are registered to receive the alerts; however, this may only reach a limited segment of society.

3. **The Wireless Emergency Alerts (WEA) System:** "WEA is a public safety system that allows customers who own compatible mobile devices to receive geographically targeted, text-like messages alerting them of imminent threats to safety in their area."[155] WEA provides a platform to send emergency notifications directly to all cellphones in a defined area, which means the message even goes to those who are traveling through an area. The weakness of WEA is that the cellphone owner can disable weather and AMBER alerts. Presidential alerts, though, cannot be disabled by the cellphone owner.

4. **The Integrated Public Alert & Warning System (IPAWS):** IPAWS "is FEMA's national system for local alerting that provides authenticated emergency and life-saving information to the public through mobile phones using Wireless Emergency Alerts, to radio and television via the Emergency Alert System, and on the National Oceanic and Atmospheric Administration's Weather Radio."[156] The value of IPAWS should be self-evident because it is a single platform to launch emergency notifications across EAS, NWR, and WEA reaching a greater cross-section of society. There are numerous steps, which must be completed for a jurisdiction to

---

[154] (NOAA, n.d.)
[155] ((FCC) Commission, n.d.)
[156] (FEMA, The Integrated Public Alert & Warning System (IPAWS), n.d.)

have authorization to send emergency messages over IPAWS and WEA. The agency must execute a Memorandum of Agreement with FEMA, each person seeking to be authorized to send messages must complete required training, mandatory monthly proficiency testing, and each State will have their own requirements for jurisdictions to be authorized to use IPAWS.

Emergency communications are also facilitated utilizing vendor purchased *"Opt-In" systems, which means citizens in the community must elect to be registered to receive communications through these systems.* These systems are funded by the local jurisdiction and offered free to the public. Historically, it has been found that few in the public want to voluntarily receive emergency notifications because they find them annoying or do not value the information. However, a select group of the population will register to receive information and alerts. There are many options to choose from when it comes to vendor provided systems. Jurisdictions will have to determine which, if any, systems they will purchase and utilize based upon budgetary constraints, interface with jurisdictional systems, and preference.

Overall, Emergency Managers will find strengths and weaknesses for each of the various systems to deliver emergency notifications. More importantly, the concept of employing multiple systems to reach a larger portion of the population is the most important lesson to learn. To accomplish the task of effectively advising the public of emergencies will require Emergency Managers to develop a broad knowledge base of the national emergency notifications systems, vendor purchased systems, and social media to design an overlapping emergency notification process.

For large scale disasters, the PIOs may activate the *Joint Information System (JIS), which "provides the mechanism to organize, integrate, and coordinate information to ensure timely, accurate, accessible, and consistent messaging across multiple jurisdictions and/or disciplines, including the private sector and NGOs"*[157] (non-governmental organizations). The JIS is a system for PIOs to manage

---

[157] (FEMA, Basic Guidance for Public Information Officers (PIOs), November 2007)

communications and is not a location or facility. The JIS is how multiple PIOs can coordinate and collaborate on producing a unified emergency communication message and will be comprised of policies, procedures, and mechanisms to produce emergency messages. Having an effective JIS can eliminate issues where conflicting messages are released by PIOs from a variety of agencies. When emergency messaging is inconsistent, it can easily cause confusion in the eyes of the public and may potentially lead to dangerous situations. Where the JIS is not a location, the *Joint Information Center (JIC) "is a central location that facilitates operation of the JIS."*[158] A JIC is an additional ICS facility, which Emergency Mangers may be called upon to assist with establishing a JIC to support incidents by providing a location from which PIOs can work in a collaborative effort.

The Emergency Management field operations, presented in Chapter 5, span diverse and complex issues. Beginning with our pre-disaster personal preparedness of maintaining a "go kit" and moving through the sundry of facilities and classifications of field operations. The complexities of damage assessments, debris management, evacuations and accountability, mass fatalities, points of dispensing, points of distribution, resource management, shelter operations, and search and rescue are some of the more common types of Emergency Management field operations. But, as we learned, it is not the common tasks which create our greatest challenges. The difficulties inherent in unique Emergency Management field operations are the most dangerous and present the most colossal demands. And we can either simplify or complicate those challenges through the manner in which we effectively communicate the hazards internally and externally. Truly an impressive measure of information to digest and apply as an Emergency Manager.

---

[158] (FEMA, Basic Guidance for Public Information Officers (PIOs), November 2007)

Chapter 5 Summary

Key Terms (Alphabetical Order)

Active911
AMBER Alert
Americans with Disabilities Act (ADA)
Association of Public Safety Communications Officials (APCO)
Bureau of Alcohol, Tobacco, Firearms and Explosives (ATF)
Commodity Point of Distribution (C-POD)
Computer Aided Dispatch (CAD)
Congregate Shelter
Divert
Emergency Alert System (EAS)
Emergency Room (ER)
External Communications
Family Assistance Center (FAC)
Family Reunification
Field Operations
Frequency Modulation (FM)
Functional Needs Support Services (FNSS)
Human-Caused Disasters
Incident Management Team (IMT)
Information Hoarder
Integrated Public Alert & Warning System (IPAWS)
Internal Communications
Interoperability
Joint Information Center (JIC)
Joint Information System (JIS)
Just-in-Time Training (JIT)
Mass Fatality Incident
Medical Countermeasure (MCM)
Medical Examiner (ME)
Megahertz (MHz)

Mega-Shelter
Mobile Emergency Operations Center (MEOC)
Natural Disasters
NOAA Weather Radio All Hazards (NWR)
Non-Congregate Shelter
Opt-In System
Point of Dispensing (POD)
Push-to-Talk (PTT)
Recovery Support Function (RSF)
Search and Rescue (SAR)
Strategic National Stockpile (SNS)
Technological Disasters
Telecommunications Industry Association (TIA)
Very High Frequency (VHF)
Victim Information Center (VIC)
Volunteer Operations Center (VOC)
WAVE
Wireless Emergency Alerts (WEA)

Emergency Management Coordination of Field Operations

In Chapter 5, we learned that to effectively coordinate field operations will require Emergency Managers to fully understand the initial response process and how to be a beneficial member to the response operations. It all begins with preparation in advance by building a customized "Go Kit" and then knowing how and where to enter an incident scene and coordinate closely with the Incident Commander. Part of the coordination will necessitate establishing facilities need to efficiently support field operations and familiarization with the various classifications of field operations and how each will encompass vastly different elements. Rounding out field operations, Emergency Managers have to expect the unexpected. The unique challenges faced will be a source of some of the greatest difficulties Emergency Managers will have to manage.

Emergency Communications in Support of Field Operations

Communications for field operations are generally categorized as either internal or external communications. Internal communications are specifically communications with and between our internal audience of elected and senior officials, jurisdictional departments, and public safety agencies. External communications, on the other hand, are shared with the public, private sector, and volunteer agencies. When it comes to external communications, the most important will be emergency notifications to provide the public with information and instructions related to disasters impacting the community. Emergency Managers have numerous systems with which to facilitate external emergency communications. In both internal and external communications, an invaluable member of the team is the dedicated professional Public Information Officer (PIO). However, not all jurisdictions will have the luxury of having a PIO and in those cases, the Emergency Manager may be responsible for some, or all the duties entailed in emergency communications.

In the next chapter, you will learn about emergency operations center (EOC) management and operations.

Chapter 6: Emergency Operations Center (EOC) Management and Operations

Moving from field operations in Chapter 5 to EOC Management and Operations is the next logical step in our study of Emergency Management. As a reminder, in Chapter 4 we learned that an EOC can be permanent, temporary, mobile, or virtual and they serve to coordinate information and resources in support of incident management. Many of the operations conducted in the field may also be coordinated from an EOC. In some jurisdictions an EOC may be referred to as the Emergency Coordination Center (ECC), however, for the sake of simplicity within this chapter, the term EOC will be utilized to reference both an EOC and ECC. As an integral component of managing disasters, "EOCs are a critical link for supporting Emergency Management functions before, during, and after an incident."[159] It is important to keep in mind that EOCs will come in various capabilities, shapes, and sizes; all based upon the need of the jurisdiction or agency. Many factors will have to be considered when establishing an EOC, available personnel and levels of training, the type and severity of common regional disasters, and utilizing an existing facility or new construction. From one jurisdiction or agency to another, EOCs may have extremely different or unique aspects to meet the needs of the community. There is no "cookie cutter" approach to building and designing EOCs and there is no "right" or "wrong" in how an EOC is managed or operated. There are some basics to design and operation, which are applicable to most EOCs, and those basics will embody the majority of what will be covered in Chapter 6 along with some common variations.

---

[159] (FEMA, EOC Management and Operations (G-775), December 2012)

Authorities and Benefits Associated with an Operational EOC

There is a plethora of legal guidance at the Federal, State, Tribal, Regional, and Local level pertaining to the management and operation of an EOC. These legal documents form the authorities that designate who is responsible for management, types of activation triggers, and procedures for internal and external notifications. Because the hazards, which are prone to areas, can vary, the legal authorities from one EOC to another can differ as well. Jurisdictions, which are subject to frequent flooding, will have policies and procedures addressing flooding concerns, whereas coastal jurisdictions EOC policies will likely concentrate on hurricanes and windstorms. Since the legal authorities can greatly differ, potential Emergency Managers will need to become conversant with the hazards and the policies and procedures governing EOC operations.

Aside from the differences, there are many benefits, which are derived from maintaining an operational EOC. Foremost among the benefits, the ability to swiftly activate to coordinate resources and personnel for disaster response and recovery is vital to a community. By shortening the time between the occurrence of a disaster and the initial response, Emergency Managers are better able to provide for the safety of personnel, protection of the community, stability of incidents, and basic human needs. In this section of Chapter 6, we will take a close look at the many legal authorities and benefits to gain a better understanding of managing EOCs.

Legal Statutes, Policies, and Procedures Governing EOC Management

The old saying "Variety is the spice of Life" holds true for the vast differences in the legal guidance pertaining to the management of EOCs throughout the levels of government. Federal agencies adhere to the Federal regulations; however, there are still variances between how the many Federal EOCs function based upon their mission and scope. When you look across the U.S., you find 50 States with individual constitutions and legal statutes, which serve to guide how their States operate and no two State constitutions, are alike. Breaking our governmental levels down even further, we have sovereign Tribal Nations, County, Parish, City, and Township governments, which have their own laws directing how they operate. Each of the separate levels of legislation will impact the operation of EOCs within their jurisdictions. Lumped on top of the statutes, each agency will have separate Emergency Operation Plans (EOPs), Standard Operating Procedures (SOPs), and Standard Operating Guidelines (SOGs) which translates to EOCs being similar and yet different dependent on their respective governing guidelines.

Statutes typically will be utilized to designate who has the legal authority and responsibility to carry out Emergency Management within a specific jurisdiction. In most States, the statutes establishing the Emergency Management programs will provide the guidance for how to declare local disasters, evacuation orders, rendering mutual aid, and plans for continuity of government (COOG) along with other issues. From State to State, the person or position, which is the legal authority, may be different. It is impractical to attempt to cover the statutes for all 50 States; consequently, I will briefly discuss the State of Texas statute and highly recommend that prospective Emergency Managers should refer to their appropriate State statutes. Within the State of Texas, the **Texas Government Chapter 418 Emergency Management** is the governing document for Emergency Management. The senior elected official at the county level, which is the County Judge, is designated as the Emergency Management Director for counties in the State of Texas. The County Judge has the ultimate Emergency Management authority in the State of Texas at the county level. Subordinate to counties, municipal Mayors are designated as the Emergency Management Director for a city and serve in the same capacity. Emergency Management Directors in Texas are authorized under Texas Government Code Section 418.1015 to "designate a person to serve as Emergency Management coordinator"[160] (EMC). The EMC is then authorized through a

---

[160] (Texas)

delegation of authority from the County Judge or municipal Mayor to operate the Emergency Management program for their respective jurisdiction. The EMC or an EOC Director will be responsible for the development of plans, policies, procedures, and guidelines for the management of EOCs.

Among other issues, the statutes, policies, and procedures will outline delegations of authority, evacuation and accountability, mutual aid, staffing, phases of EOC activation and activation triggers. *Triggers are events or incidents, which automatically trigger the activation of the EOC.* There are countless examples of triggers, such as: (1) weather warnings of imminent floods, ice, or snow, (2) any disaster occurring which results in a declaration of a local disaster, and (3) hurricane projected landfall within a specific number of hours to name a few. Typically, triggers are determined from jurisdiction to jurisdiction based upon the occurrence of specific disasters, which are more prevalent and have historically led to activating the EOC. So, just what does it mean when we say that we are activating the EOC? In simple terms, it is bringing in required personnel, taking actions to bring equipment and systems online, and making the EOC operational. However, in truth, it is far more complicated. Statutes, policies, and procedures will indicate levels of activation for the EOC. Most jurisdictions utilize either a four or three level activation scale. A Four Level Activation scale includes the following levels:

1. Level IV: Not Activated; daily operations as usual.
2. Level III: Actively Monitoring; limited emergency conditions where a minor emergency has or may occur requiring as few as one or two people to monitor the situation.
3. Level II: Partial Activation; an incident has or may occur requiring a small number of people to manage the incident.
4. Level I: Full Activation; A disaster/event/situation has occurred requiring full activation of all or most personnel and systems.

The only difference between a four-level and three-level activation scale is that the three-level activation does not include a category for Level IV Not Activated. However, the issue of activation is further complicated by whether the specific EOC is a hot, warm, or cold site. A hot site EOC has all equipment, systems, and utilities required to activate the EOC on a moment's notice. A warm site EOC is a facility that may have some equipment and systems, but would require bringing in laptops, phones, or other necessary equipment and will require a short period of time to be made fully operational. In addition, finally, a cold site EOC is one, which basically has four walls and a ceiling and may require bringing in all equipment and systems over a few hours to make it fully operational.

Jurisdictional legal guidelines and policies will also identify who is authorized within the jurisdiction to activate the EOC. The number of personnel authorized to activate an EOC is normally a limited number of senior elected officials, the EMC, or EOC Director. The person activating the EOC will initiate the process to recall personnel to man the EOC for the specific incident. The person responsible for activating the EOC will notify leadership, request assisting or supporting agencies to provide liaisons to work in the EOC, advise the PIO for media releases and public notifications related to the activation, or advise EOC staff to make the appropriate notifications.

EOC Benefits during Day-to-Day and Emergency Operations

There is a huge difference between having a facility designated as an EOC and having an EOC, which is beneficial to a jurisdiction. "Effective EOCs will allow communities to become more resilient over a period of time."[161] Effective jurisdictional EOCs provide numerous benefits to the communities they serve. The benefits of an effective EOC include, but are not limited to the following:

1. Assisting communities to prepare in advance to endure foreseeable incidents.
2. Providing Incident Commanders and jurisdictions with a mechanism to focus response and recovery efforts.

---

[161] (FEMA, Intermediate Emergency Operations Center Functions (G-2300), May 2019)

3. Promoting the resolution of challenges and problems faced during incidents.
4. Establishing *situational awareness (SA) which is the perception and comprehension of the details involved in an on-going incident.*
5. Conducting long-term planning for incident response and recovery operations.
6. Coordination and policy direction.
7. Resource management.
8. Prioritizing and allocating or re-allocating critical resources.
9. Providing financial and legal support.
10. Serving as a location for assisting and supporting agency liaisons to collaborate during incidents.
11. Potentially coordinating multiple response operations at a given time.
12. Collecting and analyzing incident information.
13. Information sharing and tactical support.

A myriad of types of organizations and agencies find EOCs to be a beneficial facility to their operations. Governmental agencies at the Federal, Tribal, State, and Local levels maintain EOCs to manage emergency operations. Throughout the past couple of decades, private sector businesses and non-governmental organizations have embraced incorporating EOCs into their operations as well. Major corporations, financial institutes, hospitals, universities, and utilities companies routinely build and operate EOCs to support day-to-day operations as well as emergency operations. By incorporating EOCs into daily operations, institutions are better able to maintain a high level of operational support and do not have to spend valuable time at the onset of a disaster to activate. Even many volunteer organizations have implemented the use of EOCs to provide a location from which to conduct coordination activities to better support volunteers.

Jurisdictional EOC Design and Organizational Structure Requirements

EOCs come in all configurations, shapes, and sizes to meet the specific needs of the agencies or jurisdictions, which they serve. There is no fast rule of thumb for construction, layout, location, or organizational management of an EOC. Jurisdictional population, level of government, type of agency, and budgetary constraints are but a few of the factors, which will regulate how an EOC is designed and organized. Among other factors, management models may be based upon available staffing, legal requirements, and training levels. Plunging headlong as we continue our studies to fathom the inter-workings of EOCs, we will first look to the physical designs and then to the administrative structuring of these facilities. As with most things related to Emergency Management, there is a wide variety of options when it comes to the layout of the facility. Due to the cost of building an EOC, it is common for jurisdictions to utilize existing facilities in a multi-purpose fashion where during normal day-to-day operations the rooms are used for meetings or training rooms and only during disasters will they be quickly staffed and equipped to serve as an EOC. Similarly, there are several ways to formulate the organizational management of an EOC. Flexibility is a key characteristic throughout Emergency Management and it is important to have this ability to meet the needs of the jurisdiction and for the given disasters, which may occur at any time.

Strategic and Tactical EOC Design Considerations

EOC design begins with determining the concept of how the EOC will be operated. Some jurisdictions will opt for developing a *Strategic EOC*, which *"determines and coordinates what is to be done during an incident(s)."*[162] The

---

[162] (FEMA, EOC Management and Operations (G-775), December 2012)

---

strategic EOC will focus on supporting and coordinating the needs of responding agencies. Another option is to operate as a *Tactical EOC* which "*conducts on-scene operations itself or in conjunction with first responders.*"[163] However, the function of EOCs is more complex than merely having two cut and dried methods of operation. Jurisdictions may determine to establish variations, which are hybrids along a varying spectrum between strategic and tactical EOCs. Availability of resources, the nature of a specific catastrophic disaster, political pressure, and other factors may call for the management of an incident either strategically, tactically, or in a combined manner.

1. **Example of a Strategic EOC:** COVID-19 operations are a perfect example of how a Strategic EOC coordinates with response partners for an incident. Bexar County was one of the four locations selected to receive evacuees from Wuhan China to assist with the Federal mission in February of 2020. This was over a month before Bexar County experienced the first case of community spread of COVID-19. Initially evacuees were housed on Lackland Air Force Base. The Bexar County Office of Emergency Management (BCOEM) along with numerous County offices and departments, City of San Antonio offices and departments, San Antonio Metropolitan Health District (SAMHD), Texas Health & Human Services Commission (HHSC), Texas Department of State Health Services, and Texas Division of Emergency Management (TDEM) collaborated to manage the Federal mission from the Bexar County/San Antonio EOC. BCOEM and local partners coordinated with the Office of the Assistant Secretary for Preparedness and Response (ASPR) and the Centers for Disease Control and Prevention (CDC) to provide for the needs of the evacuees. Additional Federal evacuees were flown to Bexar County from the Diamond Princess cruise ship in Japan and the Grand Princess cruise ship in California. Evacuee patient movement was managed locally with the response partners from the EOC and alternate quarantine options had to be conducted when evacuees were moved from Lackland for various

---

[163] (FEMA, EOC Management and Operations (G-775), December 2012)

reasons and were not allowed to re-enter the Air Force Base. BCOEM and local partners coordinated with the Texas Center for Infectious Disease (TCID) to house COVID-19 positive Federal evacuees. The entire operation for the Federal mission was conducted utilizing a Strategic EOC to coordinate with a myriad of partners from the Local, State, and Federal levels.

2. **Example of a Tactical EOC:** For many years, BCOEM has managed national level sports championships such as the National Basketball Association (NBA) Play-Offs and Championship games and the Professional Golfers Association of America (PGA) Valero Texas Open. Unlike the Strategic EOC where we coordinate operations, these national level championships require BCOEM to direct responders and control on-scene operations. In these championships we will have responders from the Bexar County Sheriff's Office (BCSO), Bexar County Public Works, Bexar County HazMat Team, Emergency Service District (ESD) Fire Departments, City Public Service (CPS) electrical utilities, AT&T Center management and security, Acadian Emergency Medical Service (EMS), NBA security, TDEM, Texas National Guard 6th Civil Support Team (CST), Federal Bureau of Investigations (FBI), US Department of Energy Radiological Assistance Program (RAP) Team. For these national championships, BCOEM deploys the Mobile Emergency Operations Center (MEOC) and directs the movement of all responders throughout the entire event.

Along with conceptual design, EOCs may be categorized as primary, temporary, mobile, or virtual facilities. A primary EOC will be a fixed permanent facility or location from which to manage disaster operations. Circumstance may prohibit utilizing the primary EOC for numerous reasons, alternatives must be planned for, and personnel must be trained to facilitate these predictabilities. Disasters may occur adjacent to or inside of the primary EOC, routes to the primary EOC may be impassible, utilities may be inoperable at the primary EOC, and so forth. For those purposes, temporary or alternate EOC locations need to be designated within a jurisdiction. It is wise to have multiple alternate EOCs pre-identified to plan for redundancy. Alternate EOCs may be hot, warm, or cold facilities, as previously mentioned within this chapter. Beyond fixed locations, the mobile EOC concept is a possibility for managing disaster operations. Mobile EOCs can be either configured as bus or truck platforms with a built-on box or as a trailer, which can be pulled by prime mover vehicles. The mobile EOC can provide computers, office space, radio and satellite communications, and other capabilities for managing a disaster. The final categorization for EOCs is that of the virtual EOC which has been a fairly new and growing concept over the past couple of decades. A virtual EOC may simply be the coordination of efforts remotely utilizing computers, phones, and radios. However, several applications have been developed by companies, which are designed to manage documentation of operations, resource requests, and situational awareness.

When contemplating the establishment of a fixed, primary or secondary EOC, the location is the first concern in the process. "A comprehensive hazard vulnerability analysis will help by identifying poor locations for the EOC, such as in earthquake prone areas, along fault lines, or within floodplains."[164] It does little good to place an EOC in a location, which is prone to hazards. Site selection should consider avoiding close proximity to chemical storage facilities, hazardous materials transportation routes by rail or highway, and highly congested traffic areas, which could negatively impact personnel arriving to the EOC in a timely manner for an activation. Preferably, an EOC should allow for secured access by the appropriate personnel while maintaining a high level of physical security to prevent access by unauthorized personnel. Three additional vital factors to consider are redundancy, survivability, and sustainability. *Redundancy* includes *backup communications, electricity, and water supply. Survivability* pertains to *the type of construction materials and design, such as, being built above projected flood levels and to withstand hurricane or tornado force winds.* Finally, *sustainability* relates to *mechanisms in place in the EOC, which ensure the capability to maintain extended*

---

[164] (FEMA, Intermediate Emergency Operations Center Functions (G-2300), May 2019)

operations. Contracts to provide for meals, security, and necessary supplies are typical mechanisms of sustainability.

The next task is to determine an effective and efficient layout to maximize the interior space of the EOC. The configuration of the EOC layout will be dependent upon the number of people expected to work within the facility and potentially the types and sizes of operations, which would be considered typical for the jurisdiction. When it comes to working space, FEMA recommends that you "multiply a minimum of 50 square feet per person."[165] Interior space should allow for personnel to move about easily and to be able to speak to each other with limited interference. EOCs situated in earthquake, fire, flood, and hurricane regions may have to base the layout upon the projection for the number of people expected to be working during catastrophic disasters. Conducting a hazard assessment plays a role in determining both the location and layout of a jurisdictional EOC.

Design of the EOC will depend on many factors; however, the most important factor is for the facility to be designed to be flexible to meet the needs of a myriad of incidents. Those agencies which may be required to work alongside of each other more often should be seated close by within the EOC to enhance cooperation. A multi-purpose design, which allows for quickly modifying the interior space to meet operational needs is extremely valuable in saving time and potentially lives. EOCs should also be designed with the understanding that at some point technology can and will fail and, in that case, supplies should be readily at hand to revert to "old school" pencil and paper, easels with large paper pads, or markers and dry erase boards. Along those lines, many EOCs have begun using wall sized dry erase areas which when clean provide a visually appealing setting and can be immediately utilized during disasters to begin capturing and displaying vital information. Additionally, breakout rooms for separate meetings and workspace should be included in the EOC design to allow for command, staff briefing, and media briefing areas.

---

[165] (FEMA, Intermediate Emergency Operations Center Functions (G-2300), May 2019)

Planning for flexibility also pertains to staff support options, which should be considered in EOC design. For example, some jurisdictions have chosen to have staff sleeping areas while others have chosen to have furniture in office spaces which can let down into a small bed for extended operations. Far more EOCs, however, are designed with the adage in mind "You don't have to go home, but you can't stay here." Typically, plans for staff sleeping areas or office sleeping will result in little rest because rest cycles are often interrupted and comfort is problematic under the best of conditions, which leads to issues of fatigue for long-term operations. EOC design is more than form and function; for incidents, requiring activation over an extended period of time comfort becomes more of a necessity than a nicety.

Selection of an Appropriate EOC Organizational Structure

Beyond the physical design, the organizational design of an EOC may vary and should be well thought out to provide for the needs of the community. Just as there are numerous external design and layout considerations, the management of an EOC can be conducted in several manners. Each jurisdiction will determine the organizational management structure for their EOC. Some of the more common forms of EOC organizational management include the following:

1. **Incident Command System (ICS) Structure:** The ICS or ICS-Like structure mirrors ICS in the field. The EOC will have an assigned Incident Commander (IC), Command Staff, and General Staff, which coordinates directly with the ICS in the field or, in some cases, may operate as a Tactical EOC where the EOC staff are directing the field operations. The ICS model is a more "response-centric organizational structure."[166]

2. **Emergency Support Function (ESF) Structure:** The ESF structure is more common in State and Federal EOCs; however, some local jurisdictions have opted to utilize this structure as well. The ESF model aligns with the

---

[166] (FEMA, EOC Management and Operations (G-775), December 2012)

15 ESFs enumerated in Chapter 4 for planning. In an EOC utilizing the ESF structure, personnel will be assigned to oversee each of the 15 ESF areas. The ESF structure may require more personnel to fill the positions and, therefore, be less adaptable to jurisdictions where trained personnel are limited.

3. **Functional or Departmental Structure:** The Functional or Departmental structure will be organized by disciplines, such as Firefighting, Law Enforcement, Medical, Public Works, Public Health, and so forth. Typically, the assigned leadership for each discipline will manage their personnel in coordination with other functional or departmental leaders under this system.

4. **Hybrid ICS-ESF Structure:** More and more agencies are adopting a Hybrid ICS-ESF structure where some elements of the EOC organizational management are more ICS and others are more ESF in nature. One benefit of the hybrid management structure is that some components will mirror the field operations and others will mirror the State and Federal operations. However, it should be pointed out that a Hybrid structure will require personnel trained to be able to effectively interact with their counterparts and to be able to function collaboratively within the EOC.

5. **Incident Support Model (ISM) Structure:** The ISM structure will be organized with an EOC Director, Public Information Officer, Situational Awareness Section, Planning Support Section, Resources Support Section, and a Center Support Section. "EOC staff in jurisdictions or organizations that use an ISM structure typically focus exclusively on support functions rather than operations or managing actual response/recovery efforts."[167] Normally the ISM EOC Director does not set EOC objectives, but rather will establish tasks to support the incident response.

---

[167] (FEMA, Intermediate Emergency Operations Center Functions (G-2300), May 2019)

Primary Functions and Personnel Qualifications of Successful EOCs

EOC personnel are far more important than the EOC facility itself. You are only as strong as the people who comprise your team. It is important to point out that Emergency Managers new to the career field should never underestimate Emergency Management personnel from smaller jurisdictions. It has been my experience that quite often the personnel from rural jurisdictions can very well have an expansive trove of experience and are capable of thinking outside of the box more effectively than many of their larger jurisdiction peers. The reason has become evident, as I have built lasting professional relationships with Emergency Managers from a variety of jurisdictions. Emergency Managers from smaller jurisdictions are called upon constantly to perform at a high level with very few resources at hand and they have become ingenious in doing so. Several years ago, I was privileged to attend a logistics staging exercise in Uvalde, Texas where Charlie Waller serves as the Emergency Management Coordinator. Charlie is someone for whom I have great respect and I have learned more from than I can articulate in a single sitting. Had I been called upon to conduct this particular staging exercise; I would have had a Power Point presentation and handouts and we would have looked at aerial views with diagrams of entry and exit routes and potential clusters of resources. Oh, it would have looked impressive, but it would have lacked much compared to Charlie's presentation. Charlie accomplished more than I could have with all of the vast technology I could bring to bear and he did it with a handful of supplies. Charlie held the exercise at the facility that was being planned for use and he set up a "sand box" styled presentation with a piece of plywood stretched over a table, an aerial map printed by his jurisdiction, clear plastic sheeting lain over the map, dry erase markers, and little toy vehicles he purchased at a local discount store. I calculated that Charlie might have spent approximately $30 on all of the resources we used. In the end, the result was that we were able to see exactly how the vehicles would travel into the staging area and exit upon deployment, we heard about and saw the areas to be used, moved the toy vehicles between the various areas on the map, drew arrows on the plastic sheeting along with traffic control measures, and then conducted a walk-through of the facility. The map was the only resource you could identify as technological, but everyone left knowing exactly what would be required without question. My advice to you as upcoming Emergency Managers is to find yourself a "Charlie Waller" and become a sponge soaking up all that you can learn from them.

Common EOC Management Functions and Responsibilities

Everything that is done within an EOC revolves around the central theme of coordination. Flowing from that concept, the four most common EOC functions are recognized as "Information Management, Resource Management, Planning, and Policy and Coordination."[168] However, a more comprehensive list is found in the *Emergency Operations Center Skillset User Guide*, which was released in September 2018 as a component of the National Qualification System (NQS). The EOC Skillsets are divided into two categories: (1) Level of Responsibility and (2) Function. The Level of Responsibility category is subdivided between Coordination and Individual Contribution, Leadership, and Policy and Direction, which relates to the various personnel working in an EOC. The Function category is far more expansive in listing the tasks accomplished by individuals working in an EOC with the following 17 functions:

1. Action Tracking
2. Center Management
3. Document and Records Management
4. EOC Facility Management
5. Finance
6. Legal Counseling
7. Organizational Representation
8. Performance Improvement

---

[168] (FEMA, Intermediate Emergency Operations Center Functions (G-2300), May 2019)

9. Planning
10. Public Affairs Coordination
11. Recovery Coordination
12. Resource Ordering and Acquiring
13. Resource Sourcing
14. Resource Tracking
15. Safety Advising
16. Situational Awareness
17. Understanding the Resource Requirement

"EOC Skillsets establish minimum criteria for EOC qualifications — they do not cover the full range of activities that EOC personnel perform."[169] The functions listed above are elements of the countless types of operations, which are managed from an EOC. Nearly every day EOC staff across the nation are faced with managing an infinite number of incidents, which could never have been imagined in impacted jurisdictions. In those instances, Emergency Managers have to fall back upon accomplishing tasks, which are common across large-scale disasters. Therefore, we will review some of the common tasks, which are conducted for many of the feasible operations EOC staff coordinate.

1. **Calculating the Burn Rate:** This is the calculated hourly cost of equipment, personnel, and supplies. There is no single jurisdiction in the nation, which can afford to sign a blank check for the cost of a disaster. Calculating the cost is important so that jurisdictions do not deplete their operating budget. The hourly burn rate is utilized in determining whether less costly tactics to address the disaster must be implemented.

2. **Documentation:** There is a saying in Emergency Management – "If it isn't written down, it didn't happen." That is true for a great many things we are required to do as Emergency Managers. When developing plans, strategic and tactical emergency plans must be written to provide proof that a jurisdiction had a plan. When measures are taken to aid in the

---

[169] (FEMA, National Incident Management System: Emergency Operations Center Skillsets User Guide, September 2018)

response or recovery from a disaster, the tasks completed must be written down as evidence that due diligence has been maintained. There is always a legal liability to what Emergency Managers do and the only way to mitigate that liability is to write down everything. The compiled documentation will be catalogued and filed in case actions ever come into question and to support expense costs. Catastrophic disasters will generate mountains of documentation and all the documentation must be maintained as per the jurisdictional retention policy, in most cases 8 to 10 years.

3. **Donations Management:** Emergency Managers refer to donations' management as the "disaster after the disaster" because you face such an uphill obstacle. Well-intentioned people will run to their cupboards and pull out their unwanted and outdated canned and boxed goods and raid their closets of the clothes not worn in years. When those things get dumped on jurisdictional doorsteps, quite literally sometimes, Emergency Managers inherit the task of sorting through it and separating what is usable from what is garbage. The problem is – "What do you do with the donated garbage?" If the media catch you or someone posts that you have thrown away donated goods, regardless of the condition of the goods, you will be crucified in the eye of the public. Some of the examples of the types of donated items I have seen include expired canned goods that are bulging, opened box foods which were half eaten, moldy bread, waxed beans, a leopard print leotard, prom dresses, used underwear, socks with holes in them, and a single athletic shoe just to name a few.

4. **Evacuation and Re-Entry:** The work of evacuation may be conducted in the field by first responders; however, it must be supported from the EOC. Emergency Managers may have to coordinate the opening and staffing of shelters, food and water, medical support, social services, and more during a disaster. Once electrical power, gas, water, and wastewater are back online the task of re-entry will need to be planned out by Emergency Managers. Re-Entry is not as simple as just opening the doors and telling people to come on back home. Emergency Managers often face

circumstances, which warrant Phased Re-Entry, which is where complicating issues prohibit allowing residents to completely move back into their homes. This typically occurs when utilities have not been fully restored, emergency services are limited, roadways are impassible in areas, and safety is at great risk. Dependent on the disaster, there may be several phases to fully reoccupy an area. The three common phases are (1) Look and Leave, (2) Partial Re-Entry, and (3) Full Re-Entry.

- **Look and Leave:** The look and leave phase is utilized when an area is extensively damaged and it is unsafe to allow residents to move back to their homes. This phase allows the residents to come in and observe their home to see the extent of damage. It is important to understand that the longer people are prohibited from seeing their home will only add to their level of anxiety. When establishing a Look and Leave Phase, normally there is a single-entry point where residents are advised to show their identification or some documentation, which establishes that they are truly residents in the impact area. This phase is only during daylight hours and residents are only allowed to drive to and view their home without exiting the vehicle and then they must depart.

- **Partial Re-Entry:** It is not uncommon for houses within an impacted area to have greatly varying levels of damage. The Partial Re-Entry Phase allows for some residents to be allowed to reoccupy their home while others may be allowed to begin cleanup, collection of personal property, and repairs.

- **Full Re-Entry:** When all emergency services, infrastructures, roads and bridges, and utilities are online and homes can be safely reoccupied then full re-entry can proceed.

5. **Recovery:** Of all the tasks, which Emergency Managers will be called upon to accomplish, recovery is the most extensive. Picking up the pieces of society after a disaster and weaving them back together is a painstaking process. Factors spanning from the extent of damage, financial tax base

stability, and level of resilience make it impossible to predetermine how long it will take for a community to recover.

6. **Volunteer Management:** As discussed in Chapter 5, Emergency Managers must have a plan to manage volunteers, especially unaffiliated or spontaneous volunteers. Established volunteer agencies will manage their volunteers under the guidelines set forth in jurisdictional plans. However, those who wish to volunteer after a disaster are more problematic. Emergency Managers can attempt to direct these individuals to standing volunteer organizations, but even doing so may create touchy situations. The perception of governmental officials seen as encouraging people to volunteer with faith-based agencies can be construed as promoting religion. On the other side of that coin, discouraging volunteers from volunteering with a faith-based agency can be perceived as being adversarial towards religious organizations. It is also possible that there will be those who volunteer after a disaster with unscrupulous motives. Some criminals may hope that during the confusion that they can find opportunities to take advantage of the situation for their own benefit. For these reasons, Emergency Managers may be required to set up volunteer operations to conduct background checks on potential volunteers, provide training, and scheduling.

EOCs provide the platform from which to monitor a disaster to formulate situational awareness and to develop a *common operating picture (COP)* or *integrated situational awareness process to collect, share, and display information.* Emergency Managers will utilize a variety of systems to paint the picture of what is occurring and the potential for the situation to improve or worsen. Weather conditions can be monitored from any number of systems including the National Weather Service (NWS), National Hurricane Center (NHC), and United States Geological Survey (USGS). Riverine and streambed monitors can provide real time data on flooding. State and U.S. Forest Service agencies can produce *Keetch-Byram Drought Index (KBDI)* modeling which *"is an index used to determine forest fire potential.*"[170] Unfortunately, there is no crystal ball to view the future and inevitable outcomes. However, Emergency Managers can piece together a COP to aid response and recovery operations and to support responders and response partners.

Identification and Qualification of EOC Personnel

As we move into the realm of identifying and qualifying personnel to hire and work within an EOC it is important to state at the very beginning "it is more important to find the right person for the specific EOC position than to simply "fill the seat" for the purposes of being perceived as having a fully-operational EOC."[171] While there are entry-level positions in Emergency Management, developing the skillsets to work effectively in an EOC takes time. EOC staff should have considerable knowledge of the critical tasks to be performed. Working in an EOC during a disaster can be a pressure cooker. Therefore, those who hold EOC staff positions should be people who are highly skilled, capable of multi-tasking under extreme pressure situations, able to efficiently work with limited oversight, and reliable to produce work products accurately and timely. That does not mean that there are not any opportunities to train personnel. However, the truth is that an EOC cannot function effectively if key or numerous positions are filled with trainees.

So, where do we begin to find staffing for our jurisdictional EOCs? Start with permanent (full-time) Emergency Management staff. Never lose sight of the fact that most jurisdictions across the nation have a one- or two-person Emergency Management department or office. That means that Emergency Managers will have to supplement the full-time Emergency Management staff with other personnel. Reaching into the first responder agencies is an easy decision because those personnel will have knowledge of response and recovery operations. However, you cannot just limit that to law enforcement, fire fighters, and emergency medical

---

[170] (Service, Keetch-Byram Drought Index (KBDI), n.d.)
[171] (FEMA, Intermediate Emergency Operations Center Functions (G-2300), May 2019)

technicians. Additional highly qualified personnel can be found in codes, environmental, public works, and public health departments. We can also incorporate personnel from volunteer organizations to serve as liaisons for their specific agencies. Lastly, retired professionals with an interest in serving in an EOC can aid in rounding out staffing.

Several other concerns arise when identifying EOC staff, which must be addressed. Aside from the initial staff, alternate staff will need to be identified to cover multiple operational periods and support staff to sustain day and night operations. Ultimately, stress and exhaustion will pay a toll upon extended EOC operations. No matter the level of experience, stress can negatively impact staff and should be planned for long before activation. EOC staff should be trained to recognize the signs of stress and exhaustion in co-workers and how to manage stress in a healthy manner before, during, and after EOC activations. To aid in stress management, many jurisdictions have partnered with peer-to-peer support and critical incident stress management (CISM) trained teams to provide group and one-on-one support. A prime example of long-term operations stress is *"COVID Fatigue which is a form of disaster fatigue brought on by the prolonged impact on life by the COVID virus where those affected are tired of being careful, cooped up, scared, and living in an abnormal reality."* After working many months of extended hours and no days off, I can assure you that COVID Fatigue is real and it is not something that has just impacted the response community. Americans have basically been trapped in their homes for the better part of a year and we have begun to see how that has deeply changed people's actions and personalities. Only time will tell what the long-term impact COVID Fatigue will be for all of us.

Training and cross training must be prevalent in EOC operations to qualify EOC staff, cover for staff illnesses, and provide coverage for staff turnover. The NIMS Training Program provides the beginning level list of courses required for personnel working in an EOC. At a minimum, all personnel who work in an EOC must have the IS-100 Introduction to the Incident Command System and IS-700, An Introduction to the National Incident Management System online FEMA courses. Incident personnel with leadership responsibilities must also have the IS-800

National Response Framework, An Introduction, the IS-2200 Basic Emergency Operations Center Functions, and the G-191 Emergency Operations Center/Incident Command System Interface courses. The IS-800 and IS-2200 are both FEMA online courses; however, the G-191 is an in-person 8-hour course. Finally, incident personnel designated as leaders or supervisors must have all of the preceding and complete the E/L/G-2300 Intermediate Emergency Operations Center Functions 23-hour in-person class. "As recipients and sub recipients of Federal preparedness grants, jurisdictions and organizations must achieve, or be actively working to achieve, all of the NIMS Implementation Objectives."[172]

Chapter 6 illustrates that there truly is a mountain of information to learn for Emergency Managers when it comes to EOC management and operations. Each jurisdiction or agency must first begin by analyzing their respective authorities, statutes, policies, and procedures for how their EOC must be managed. Then consideration must be given to designing the facility to meet the needs of the community served and the organizational structure which will be employed. Will the EOC be strategic by serving as a facility to coordinate efforts or will it be tactical in actually directing response operations? Will your agency utilize an ICS, ESF, Departmental, Hybrid, or Incident Support Model structure? Which all leads to ensuring that personnel are trained and qualified to perform the necessary functions within the chosen organizational structure.

---

[172] (FEMA, National Incident Management System Training Program, 2020)

Chapter 6 Summary

Key Terms (Alphabetical Order)

Assistant Secretary for Preparedness and Response (ASPR)
Bexar County Sheriff's Office (BCSO)
Burn Rate
Centers for Disease Control and Prevention (CDC)
City Public Service (CPS)
Civil Support Team (CST)
Cold Site
Common Operating Picture (COP)
COVID Fatigue
Critical Incident Stress Management (CISM)
Emergency Coordination Center (ECC)
Emergency Operations Center Skillsets
Emergency Management Coordinator (EMC)
Emergency Service District (ESD)
Federal Bureau of Investigations (FBI)
Full Re-Entry
Hot Site
Keetch-Byram Drought Index (KBDI)
Look and Leave
National Basketball Association (NBA)
National Hurricane Center (NHC)
National Qualification System (NQS)
Partial Re-Entry
Professional Golfers Association of America (PGA)
Radiological Assistance Program (RAP)
Redundancy
San Antonio Metropolitan Health District (SAMHD)
Situational Awareness (SA)
Strategic EOC
Survivability

Sustainability
Tactical EOC
Texas Center for Infectious Disease (TCID)
Texas Health & Human Services Commission (HHSC)
Trigger
Warm Site

Operational EOC Authorities and Benefits

In Chapter 6, we learned that Emergency Operations Centers (EOCs) provide vital services for their respective jurisdictions to support response and recovery operations. Local, State, and Federal regulations dictate requirements for EOC operations. Legal statutes, policies, and procedures work hand in hand with emergency operations plans (EOPs), standard operating procedures (SOPs), and standard operating guidelines (SOGs) to form the authorities, which guide EOC operations. The legal authorities include instructions on activation, delegations of authority, evacuations, and triggers. Emergency Managers must have a strong working knowledge of the authorities and how to manage an EOC in compliance with regulatory guidance to better serve their communities. Effectively managed EOCs are a base for community preparedness where the benefits of tactical support to responders, resolution of challenges, establishment of situational awareness, long term planning, resource management, and information sharing come to fruition.

Jurisdictional EOC Design and Organizational Structure

The truth is that there is no single design for an EOC, which allows jurisdictions to customize EOCs based upon local needs and capabilities. EOCs may be structured as either strategic coordination centers or tactical centers, which work alongside of responder's on-scene to support operations. Jurisdictions planning on establishing EOCs can choose between primary, temporary (alternate), mobile, or virtual EOC facilities. Hazard assessments should be conducted for potential EOC locations to ensure that the facility will not be impeded by hazards. Three primary issues are to assure the EOC is constructed with redundancy, survivability, and sustainability in mind. While emerging technology should be incorporated into each EOC, Emergency Managers must recognize that technology can and will fail. This will necessitate Emergency Managers to be prepared to do the work in an "old school" fashion with pen and paper when all else fails. Beyond the physical attributes of an EOC, the organizational structure of EOCs may also be varied to meet the needs of a community. EOCs may be managed with an ICS, ESF, Functional/Departmental, Hybrid ICS-EOC, or Incident Support Model (ISM) structure.

EOC Functions and Personnel Qualifications

The basic functions performed in an EOC are information management, resource management, planning, and policy and coordination. Those functions were expanded under the National Qualification System (NQS) EOC Skillsets to incorporate 17 skillsets, which encompass the detailed work performed in, and EOC. Other common tasks Emergency Managers will perform in an EOC are the calculation of the hourly burn rate, documentation, donations management, evacuation and re-entry planning, and recovery operations. The right personnel must be selected and qualified to do the required work within an EOC. Appropriate training, cross- training, and exercising of the selected personnel will aid in the qualification process. Emergency Managers cannot afford to lose sight of the training requirements mandated by the NIMS Training Program because compliance is mandatory to be eligible as a recipient or sub-recipient for Federal grant programs.

In the next chapter, you will learn about Federal Assistance for Presidential Declared Disasters.

Chapter 7: Federal Assistance for Presidential Declared Disasters

Following on the study of EOC Management and Operations, we come to the examination of Federal assistance provided under Presidentially Declared Disasters. There is an ocean of misunderstanding when it comes to Federal assistance in declared disasters. Therefore, the goal for providing the information in this chapter is to correct misinformation and to put accurate information into the hands of Emergency Managers and those seeking to enter into this career field. Navigating through the gauntlet of the process to receive Federal assistance will necessitate beginning with the request for assistance process and continue through the Public Assistance (PA) and Individual Assistance (IA) programs. Admittedly, there are many more subtleties to Federal assistance than will be covered in this text. The intention of this chapter is to cover the basic components to set a foundational level of knowledge for Emergency Managers in regard to Federal assistance.

The Local, State, and Federal Disaster Declaration Process

When considering the disaster declaration process, the first step is to ensure that the three levels of the process to ultimately reach a Presidential Disaster Declaration are understood for Emergency Managers. Failure to fully comprehend the declaration process can easily spell ruin for a jurisdiction. Equally important is for Emergency Managers to possess the ability to quickly determine whether or not an incident may even qualify for a Presidential declaration because those incidents, which do not qualify, will be the responsibility of the local jurisdiction for the financial burden.

Every year States request Presidential declarations and for various reasons those requests for declarations are denied leaving the States and Local jurisdictions to cover the costs. In some cases, Local governments are left with taking out emergency loans or utilizing large portions of their *"rainy day funds"* which are *accounts set aside as emergency contingency funds*. Knowledgeable Emergency Managers can predict whether a Presidential declaration is likely and guide their jurisdictions to be better poised to make decisions, which will lessen the economic impact of disasters. In some cases, a single disaster may bankrupt jurisdictions because they did not understand the declaration process and they assumed that Federal funding would be forthcoming. Cities, towns, and other local jurisdictions can face long-term economic downfall after disasters, which will result in decreased services to the community, loss of jobs, loss of taxable revenue to support the Local government, loss of businesses, collapse of the housing market, and further trickle-down impact upon the residents. Emergency Managers must be cognizant of how mismanaging a single disaster can cause catastrophic impact on their communities and residents.

Local Disaster Declaration and Request for State Assistance

The axiom "All disasters are Local disasters" reminds us that every disaster occurs in a Local community. Not only does each disaster occur locally, but all disasters are a local disaster at the beginning, in the middle, and at the end of the incident. The residents at the local level will feel the brunt of any disaster and they will be the ones who will suffer the most through the response and long-term recovery. As Emergency Managers, we must prepare for the consequences of disasters negatively impacting our communities. Some of those preparations begin at the planning stage by conducting accurate hazard and threat assessments, establishing mitigation projects to lessen the impact of potential disasters, training responders and leadership, and developing mutual aid agreements with our regional response partners. *"Mutual aid agreements establish the terms under which assistance is provided between two or more jurisdictions within a state and between states, and can be with and between private sector entities, NGOs, and other whole community partners."*[173]

The first step towards a Local Declaration of Disaster is for the Local government to exceed its capability to adequately respond to an incident. That includes utilizing the resources and personnel from the Local government and exceeding the capabilities of our mutual aid partners to be able to manage the incident without assistance from the State. For some disasters, it will be immediately identifiable that the incident will in fact exceed the Local capability to manage the incident. Massive floods, hurricanes, tornadoes, wildfires, and such will necessitate an immediate need for State assistance. Different States may have different processes; therefore, it is vital that Emergency Managers become aware of their specific requirements in their respective States. In this chapter, I will refer to the process in the State of Texas, which should be similar to most States. Emergency operations plans (EOPs) may contain triggers for catastrophic disasters, which direct the jurisdiction to issue a Declaration of Disaster before the impact of the incident or after such time as available resources and personnel have been exhausted. The declaration process is a fairly quick and easy task because most States have a fill in the blank Declaration of Disaster template. A copy of the wording for a Texas Local Declaration of Disaster, which is completed and signed by a County Judge or City Mayor, is provided below:

DECLARATION OF DISASTER

WHEREAS the [County of _____ / City of _____] on the ____ day of _____ ,20__, has suffered widespread or severe damage, injury, or loss of life or property (or there is imminent threat of same) resulting from

        [Briefly describe the disaster situation.], and

---

[173] (FEMA, National Incident Management System Guideline for Mutual Aid, November 2017)

WHEREAS, the [County Judge/Mayor] of _____ has determined that extraordinary measures must be taken to alleviate the suffering of people and to protect or rehabilitate property,

NOW, THEREFORE, BE IT PROCLAIMED BY THE [COUNTY JUDGE/MAYOR] OF _____:

1.   That a local state of disaster is hereby declared for _____ pursuant to §418.108(a) of the Texas Government Code.

2.   Pursuant to §418.018(b) of the Government Code, the state of disaster shall continue for a period of not more than seven days from the date of this declaration unless continued or renewed by the [City Council/Commissioners Court] of _____.

3.   Pursuant to §418.018(c) of the Government Code, this declaration of a local state of disaster shall be given prompt and general publicity and shall be filed promptly with the [City Secretary/County Clerk].

4.   Pursuant to §418.018(d) of the Government Code, this declaration of a local state of disaster activates the [county/city] Emergency Management plan.

5.   That this proclamation shall take effect immediately from and after its issuance.

ORDERED this the _____day of _____ , 20__ .

_____signature_____

[County Judge/Mayor][174]

Once the Declaration of Disaster is signed by the County Judge or City Mayor it is transmitted to the State Operations Center (SOC) where it will be reviewed by the Governor who will authorize State resources and personnel to be deployed to the impacted community to assist the Local jurisdiction for the incident. Normally, phone calls will have proceeded and followed the transmittal of the Declaration of Disaster to the SOC and its arrival will be anticipated at the State level. The time period to produce, transmit, and receive authorization from the Governor is literally

---

[174] (Texas Local Declaration of Disaster)

completed in minutes, so there is relatively little delay. One common misconception to overcome is that the State does not come in and take over the management of the incident, but rather comes to assist because the main responsibility is that of the Local government. When the Governor authorizes State assistance that opens the doors to access resources and personnel from across the State, which will be managed by the State.

The State of Texas is divided into regions and districts under the Texas Division of Emergency Management (TDEM) and each district has a TDEM District Coordinator whose job is to coordinate with Local governments on a day-to-day basis and during disasters. "In their response role, they deploy to incident sites to assess damages, identify urgent needs, advise local officials regarding state assistance, and coordinate deployment of state emergency resources to assist local emergency responders."[175] Most States have a system to make some resources and personnel immediately available even before the Local Declaration of Disaster is being processed. In Texas, the applicable District Coordinator will receive all requests for resources through *WebEOC*, which is *a web-based platform for monitoring incidents, ordering and tracking resources, and coordinating efforts between all response partners.* Within WebEOC State of Texas Assistance Request (STAR) is created and the TDEM District Coordinator will determine whether the resources can be provided through the Region or to be forwarded to the SOC or other State agency or forwarded to FEMA under a Presidential Declaration. The STAR is the equivalent of the FEMA ICS-213 Resource Request (ICS-213RR) which is required to request resources during a disaster.

---

[175] ((TDEM), Regions, n.d.)

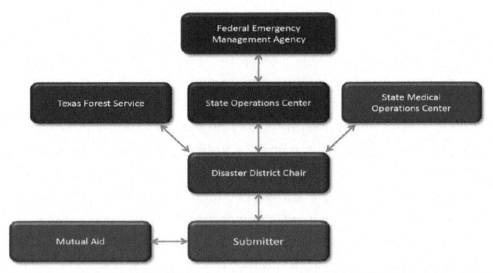

Figure 3: State of Texas Assistance Request (STAR) Process (TDEM)

Governors' State Disaster Declaration and Request for Federal Assistance

Similar to the process at the Local government level, when a State has exceeded its capability to respond to a catastrophic disaster the State may issue a Declaration of Disaster and request Federal assistance. *The Robert T. Stafford Disaster Relief and Emergency Assistance Act, 42 U.S.C. §§ 5121-5207* (the Stafford Act) §401 states": "All requests for a declaration by the President that a major disaster exists shall be made by the governor of the affected state."[176] The Governors' declaration and request for Federal assistance is forwarded to the appropriate FEMA Region where it is reviewed and forwarded to the President. The declaration of disaster is filed immediately and the Request for Public Assistance must be filed within 30 days after an area is designated as eligible. Local, State, and Federal officials will conduct a preliminary damage assessment (PDA) to determine the

---

[176] (FEMA, Diaster Declaration Process Fact Sheet, May 2011)

extent of damage to the affected community. Several simultaneous elements are occurring during the Governors' request; the State Emergency Operation Plan (EOP) is activated, information is provided on the nature and extent of Local and State resources committed to the disaster, an estimate is provided on the damage severity to the private and public sectors (governmental facilities), an estimate on the amount and type of Federal assistance to be provided, and the Governor will have to certify that all Local and State expenditures comply with the applicable cost-sharing rules. "Based on the Governor's request, the President may declare that a major disaster or emergency exists, thus activating an array of Federal programs to assist in the response and recovery effort."[177] Governors may issue a State Declaration of Disaster before the impact of certain incidents, which are considered triggers for issuing a declaration such as hurricanes, tornadoes, tsunamis, and other catastrophic level disasters. A pre-emptive declaration is issued in these cases to make State resources immediately available and request Federal resources to assist Local communities impacted by the disaster. In the case of disaster occurring on Native American properties the Declaration of Disaster will be issued by the Indian Tribal Chief Executive and for U.S. Territories the Territorial Governor has the authority to issue a Declaration of Disaster.

Presidential Disaster Declaration and Federal Assistance

Once FEMA receives a Declaration of Disaster from a State Governor with a request for Federal assistance, the request will be reviewed to determine if the incident meets the criteria for Federal assistance and it is then forwarded to the Office of the President of the United States. For various reasons a State Declaration of Disaster and request for assistance may be denied by the President. It is important for Emergency Managers to be aware of this truth because in those instances the State and Local jurisdictions will bear the brunt of the impact with little or no

---

[177] (FEMA, A Guide to the Disaster Declaration Process and Federal Disaster Assistance)

Federal assistance. When Federal assistance is authorized, the President has a choice between two types of Federal disaster declarations. The first type of Federal declaration is an *Emergency Declaration* to *"supplement State and local efforts in providing emergency services, such as the protection of lives, property, public health, and safety, or to lessen or avert the threat of a catastrophe in any part of the United States."*[178] The total amount of financial assistance from the Federal government under an Emergency Declaration is limited to not more than $5 million for a single incident and if that financial limit is exceeded the President is required to make a report to Congress to justify the cost. The second type of Federal declaration is a *Major Declaration "for any natural event, including any hurricane, tornado, storm, high water, wind-driven water, tidal wave, tsunami, earthquake, volcanic eruption, landslide, mudslide, snowstorm, or drought, or, regardless of cause, fire, flood, or explosion, that the President believes has caused damage of such severity that it is beyond the combined capabilities of state and local governments to respond."*[179] A Major Declaration of Disaster opens up a wide array of Federal assistance programs to be made available to State and Local jurisdictions. Not every Federal program is activated for every major declaration. The determination for which Federal assistance programs will be authorized for a single disaster is based upon a review of the Governor's request and the specific needs identified during the preliminary damage assessment (PDA) and any additional damage assessments. The three general categories of Federal assistance to be provided under a Major Declaration are:

1. **Public Assistance** – Assistance "for repair of infrastructure, public facilities, and debris removal, and may include repair or replacement of non-Federal road, public buildings, and bridges and implementation of mitigation measures."[180]

2. **Individual Assistance** – Assistance to repair residences and businesses or personal property loses, temporary housing, and other individual needs.

---

[178] (FEMA, Diaster Declaration Process Fact Sheet, May 2011)
[179] (FEMA, Diaster Declaration Process Fact Sheet, May 2011)
[180] (FEMA, Fundamentals of Emergency Management, IS-230d, December 16, 2013)

3. **Hazard Mitigation Assistance** – funding for measures designed to reduce future loses to public and private property.

Below is a diagram of the request for assistance process from the Local jurisdiction, State, and Federal government.

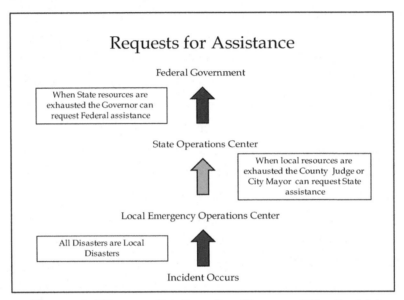

Figure 4: Disaster Declaration Process (Chadwick)

FEMA's Public Assistance (PA) Grant Program

After a disaster, State and Local leaders along with community residents, are hoping to receive grants (free money) from the Federal government, however, you will learn that Public Assistance (PA) grants are much more elusive to qualify for and receive than is perceived by the general public. "FEMA's Public Assistance Program provides supplemental grants to state, tribal, territorial, and local governments (STTLs), and certain types of private non-profits so that communities can quickly respond to and recover from major disasters or emergencies."[181] Emergency Managers need to understand that public assistance applies primarily to government owned buildings, bridges, parks, and roads damaged in a disaster. In this section of Chapter 7, the focus will be on eligible recipients and work, Federal cost share, and State and County thresholds for receiving PA grants.

While there are certain conditions where private non-profit organizations (PNP) facilities may apply, the focus for this study is on the government owned or public facilities. The topic of PNPs is outside of the scope of this text, therefore, to gain more information on PNP eligibility, please refer to the Stafford Act.

Eligibility for Public Assistance (PA)

There are numerous steps in the process of qualifying for PA grants and it begins with understanding who are considered to be eligible recipients or applicants. Per FEMA, "State and Territorial governments, including the District of Columbia, American Samoa, the Commonwealth of the Northern Mariana Islands, Guam, Puerto Rico, and the U.S. Virgin Islands, are eligible Applicants" and "Federally recognized Indian Tribal Governments, including Alaska Native villages and organizations (hereinafter referred to as "Tribal Governments"), are eligible Applicants."[182] From State to State, there are many variants of what constitutes a Local government; the following provides a list of potentially eligible Local governments.

1. Counties and Parishes
2. Cities, Boroughs, Municipalities, Towns, and Townships
3. School Districts in some cases
4. Intrastate Districts
5. Councils of Governments

---

[181] (FEMA, Public Assistance Program Overview, n.d.)
[182] (FEMA, Public Assistance Program and Policy Guide, April 2018)

6. Regional and Interstate Government agencies
7. State-Recognized Tribes
8. Special Districts which are established by State law
9. Applications for rural communities, public entities not listed, unincorporated towns and villages may be submitted by the State or other political subdivision of the State.

The next step is to determine eligibility of a prospective *facility*, which is "*a building, works, system, or equipment, built or manufactured, or an improved and maintained natural feature.*"[183] For a natural feature to be considered eligible it must designed and constructed as an improvement such as a slope which has been terraced or a channel which has been realigned, an enhancement to the unimproved natural feature, and be maintained by the applicant on a regular basis. Eligible public facilities include airports, flood control, irrigation, navigation, power, reclamation, water, wastewater, or watershed systems; non-Federal highways, roads, or streets; and buildings, structures, or systems for cultural, educational, or recreational purposes.

Once eligible facilities have been determined, eligible work projects can be identified for the facilities. Eligible work is divided between *Emergency Work to implement emergency protective measures and conduct debris removal* and *Permanent Work for the restoration of damaged facilities and hazard mitigation projects to protect facilities from future damages*. Examples of permanent work include restoring or repairing roads and bridges, water facilities, buildings, equipment, utilities, parks, recreational, and other public facilities.

The final element for eligibility is determining whether the costs claimed by an applicant are eligible. Not all costs incurred due to an incident qualify as being eligible for reimbursement under the Public Assistance (PA) Grant Program. To be considered eligible, costs must be:

1. "Directly tied to the performance of eligible work;
2. Adequately documented;

---

[183] (FEMA, Public Assistance Program and Policy Guide, April 2018)

3. Reduced by all applicable credits, such as insurance proceeds and salvage values;

4. Authorized and not prohibited under Federal, State, Territorial, Tribal, or local government laws or regulations;

5. Consistent with the Applicant's internal policies, regulations, and procedures that apply uniformly to both Federal awards and other activities of the Applicant;

6. Necessary and reasonable to accomplish the work properly and efficiently."[184]

FEMA defines *reasonable cost as cost, which does not exceed the cost a prudent person would pay under the prevailing circumstances at the time an applicant, determines to incur the cost.* FEMA evaluates reasonableness based on whether the cost is ordinary and necessary for the facility or work type and if it is comparable to the current market cost for similar work. What that translates to is that inflated costs for price gouging after a disaster would not qualify. The general rule of thumb is that the cost must be equivalent to that which would be charged for the work the day before a disaster occurs. FEMA may disallow all or part of the costs reported by an applicant if it is determined not to be a reasonable cost.

Calculating State and County Public Assistance (PA) Thresholds

There is a vast amount of confusion when it comes to what is commonly referred to as "reimbursement" for local jurisdictions to attempt to recoup funds expended on response and recovery for catastrophic disasters rising to the level of being a Presidentially Declared Disaster. There are several assumptions that people can make which are far from the truth when it comes to the potential for reimbursement. One assumption is that every major disaster will qualify for Federal

---

[184] (FEMA, Public Assistance Program and Policy Guide, April 2018)

assistance; however, the honest answer is that few disasters qualify. Another assumption is that reimbursement is something which happens quickly, or that a Local government can immediately be reimbursed for the costs associated with a disaster. For catastrophic disasters, which qualify for reimbursement, it may very easily take one or multiple years to receive the funds that are authorized. Everything is predicated upon *thresholds, which* are *minimum levels of monetary costs related to disasters, which must be exceeded to qualify for Federal grant money for Public Assistance (PA)*. The thresholds are determined by a mathematical formula, which is based upon *"per capita," or the "per unit of population: by or for each person."*[185] There are two thresholds, which must be met to qualify for Federal reimbursement under PA; the County threshold and the State threshold. Every year FEMA revises the *"per capita indicator"* or *the multiplier (number) which is applied to the population number for the County or State to determine the specific threshold*. The FEMA "Per Capita Impact Indicator and Project Thresholds"[186] report lists the 2021 per capita indicator at the County level is $3.89 and at the State level, it is $1.55. To determine a County threshold, multiply $3.89 times the official population. For example, if a County population is 2,000,000 (two million) the equation would be $3.89 x 2,000,000 making the threshold $7,780,000. This specific County would have to incur over $7,780,000 in damages to public facilities (bridges, buildings, parks, and roads) for a single disaster to qualify for Public Assistance (PA) from the Federal government. However, on top of that the State must meet its threshold for the same incident. Take the State of Texas as an example, which has a population of approximately 29.8 million and multiply that by $1.55 to obtain the State threshold of $46,190,000. For jurisdictions to qualify for PA they must meet the County threshold and the State must meet the State threshold. As Counties and States grow in population, the corresponding per capita threshold increases. Every year the per capita indicator increases along with the population. Additionally, in December 2020 FEMA proposed, "to substantively revise the Estimated cost of assistance disaster declaration factor that FEMA uses to review a Governor's request for a major disaster under the Public Assistance Program." All that is known at this

---

[185] (Per Capita, n.d.)
[186] (FEMA, Per Capita Impact Indicator and Project Thresholds, 2020)

---

time is that FEMA is asking to "substantially" raise the per capita indicator. Speculation has swirled around figures as high as $8.00 per capita which would raise the threshold astronomically. The argument from FEMA is that States and Local jurisdictions are responsible for their disasters and should bear the majority of the financial burden for maintaining their communities.

Federal Cost Share Eligibility

Under a Presidential Declared Disaster, the grant amount FEMA provides through the Public Assistance (PA) program is subject to a cost share between the Federal government and the Local jurisdiction. "*Cost Share*, also known as non-Federal share, or match, is *the portion of the costs of a federally assisted project or program not borne by the Federal Government.*"[187] What that means is that when a Local community experiences a catastrophic disaster and they qualify for PA, the community may apply for reimbursement of expenses and, if costs are eligible, the Federal government will reimburse a portion of the costs. Typically, the Federal portion of the cost share is 75% of the eligible costs and the Local jurisdiction is responsible for the remaining 25% of the total costs plus covering all ineligible costs. On rare occasions the Federal government may increase the Federal cost share to 90% in limited circumstances.

Local jurisdictions are authorized to offset the 25% cost share through cash contributions, in-kind services, and donated materials or equipment. This allows communities to reduce their amount of financial exposure to some extent. The types of offsets, which are allowed, include volunteer labor, donated equipment, donated supplies and materials, and logistical support. "The offset for volunteer labor is based on the same straight-time hourly labor rate, and fringe benefits, as a similarly qualified person in the Applicant's organization who normally performs similar

---

[187] (FEMA, Cost Sharing, n.d.)

work."[188] "Reasonable logistical support for volunteers doing eligible work, such as donations warehousing and management related to eligible Emergency Work, may be eligible either for funding (if the Applicant provides the logistical support) or as a donations credit (if a third party provides the logistical support), subject to approval by FEMA."[189]Additionally, FEMA maintains an approved equipment rate list to determine the amount of equipment costs which may be applied towards the 25% cost share. Eligible costs for donated supplies and materials are based upon the current commercial rate.

COVID-19 is the exception to the rule when it comes to cost sharing. On February 2, 2021, President Joe Biden issued a memorandum on COVID-19 stating, "FEMA shall provide a 100 percent Federal cost share for all work eligible for assistance under Public Assistance Category B, pursuant to sections 403 (42 U.S.C. 5170b), 502 (42 U.S.C. 5192), and 503 (42 U.S.C. 5193) of the Stafford Act."[190] Pause to consider the totality of the cost of COVID-19 on every community in the United States and keep in mind that covering 100 percent of the cumulative costs across the entire nation will be an extreme impact on the Federal budget for decades. That is always the part that is often forgotten; there is no such thing as free money. That cost will be rolled into the Federal debt for many years to come and the same is true for every other disaster in which PA is authorized.

FEMA's Individual Assistance (IA) Grant Program

Where public assistance is Federal grant funding provided to levels of government, individual assistance (IA) is Federal grant funding provided to individuals and households in the aftermath of a Presidentially Declared Disaster. IA grants and services offered to disaster survivors comprise the Individuals and

---

[188] (FEMA, Public Assistance Program and Policy Guide FP 104-009-2 , April 2017)
[189] (FEMA, Public Assistance Program and Policy Guide FP 104-009-2 , April 2017)
[190] (Memorandum on Maximizing Assistance from the Federal Emergency Management Agency, February 2, 2021)

Households Program (IHP). As will be articulated within this section, with a few exceptions, homeowners are generally the main recipients of IA grants. Emergency Managers must bear in mind that IA grants are only eligible under a Presidential Disaster Declaration. Small, medium, and in some cases large disaster which do not rise to the level of a Presidential Disaster Declaration will not qualify for IA grants for individual homeowners. Therefore, most disasters do not qualify and, in those cases, local communities and individuals will be responsible for covering the costs of response and recovery without Federal financial assistance.

Overview of the Individual Assistance (IA) Programs

Public assistance (PA) and individual assistance (IA) are two sides of the same coin. One side serves to provide Federal grant funding to aid in the restoration of Local governmental functions and infrastructure and on the other side "Individual Assistance is provided by the Federal Emergency Management Agency (FEMA) directly to eligible individuals and families who have sustained losses due to disasters."[191] *Individual assistance (IA) is an umbrella designation encompassing assistance, services, volunteer agency collaboration, and the Individuals and Households Program (IHP).* This section will provide an overview to address mass care, case management, crisis counseling, legal services, unemployment, and volunteer agency assistance. The larger component of the IHP will be covered in the following section.

The *Mass Care and Emergency Assistance (MC/EA) component of IA "is the provision of life-sustaining services to disaster survivors as defined in the National Response Framework."*[192] To accomplish the monumental tasks of MC/EA requires collaboration of government at all levels, private sector partners, and volunteer agencies working together to provide for the emergency care of communities and

---

[191] (Individual Assistance, 2018)
[192] (FEMA, Individual Assistance Program and Policy Guide (IAPPG), January 2019)

individuals impacted by catastrophic disasters. There are seven activities within MC/EA supporting the whole community:

1. Sheltering:
2. Feeding
3. Distribution of emergency supplies
4. Support for individuals with functional needs support concerns
5. Family reunification
6. Support for pets and service animals
7. Mass evacuee support

The **Disaster Case Management (DCM) component of IA is a "partnership between a case manager and a disaster survivor to develop and carry out the survivor's long-term recovery plan."**[193] The DCM program provides individuals with a single point of contact to aid in assessing unmet needs and creating a plan for emotional, financial, physical, and spiritual stability. The goal of DCM is to return households to a state of independence. While DCM is not a form of financial assistance, it may lead to monetary assistance coming from governmental or private sector partners and faith-based disaster relief programs.

The Crisis Counseling Assistance and Training Program (CCP) component of IA provides financial assistance to States, territories, tribal, and Local governments to fund crisis counseling or contracted counseling services through local mental health providers within an impacted community. **"Crisis Counseling means the application of individual and group treatment procedures which are designed to help alleviate the mental and emotional crises and their subsequent psychological and behavioral conditions resulting from a major disaster or its aftermath."**[194] The CCP does not replace current mental health services, but rather the award augments services offered locally to survivors of disasters. CCP provides free counseling services to offer disaster survivors short and long-term psychological support.

---

[193] (Federal Disaster Case Management Program)
[194] (FEMA, Individual Assistance Program and Policy Guide (IAPPG), January 2019)

The **_Disaster Legal Services (DLS)_** component of IA **_"provides free legal help to low-income disaster survivors."_**[195] The disaster legal services are provided through an agreement between FEMA and the Young Lawyers Division of the American Bar Association (ABA). The attorneys only provide legal advice for cases, which do not generate fees. Typical types of legal assistance provided by DLS include:

1. Insurance claims for loss of life, loss of property, and medical bills
2. Preparing powers of attorney, wills, and replacing legal documents lost in disasters
3. Reviewing contracts for home repairs
4. Assisting with landlord issues
5. Documentation for proof of ownership of homes
6. Assisting with FEMA appeals

The **_Disaster Unemployment Assistance (DUA)_** component of IA **_"provides temporary benefits to people who, as a result of a major disaster, lost or had their employment or self-employment interrupted."_**[196] To qualify for disaster unemployment assistance, an individual's job must have been lost or interrupted due to a Presidentially Declared Disaster and must not be eligible for normal unemployment insurance benefits. Additionally, qualification factors for individuals in disaster impact communities meeting any of the following conditions may qualify:

1. Due to the disaster, the individual no longer has a job or a place of work
2. The individual is unable to reach the job location
3. Damage to the job site has interrupted work
4. The individual was in the process of starting a new job that no longer exists
5. Disaster related injuries prevent the individual from working

---

[195] (Disaster Legal Services (DLS), 2020)
[196] (Disaster Unemployment Assistance, 2021)

6. The head of household died as a result of the disaster leaving the individual in a position of having to assume being the major household support

Everyone knows that established volunteer organizations in local communities are among the first to respond to assist with disaster operations and are among the last to close up shop. However, engaging volunteer organizations during disaster response and recovery requires effective coordination. The volunteer coordination component of IA is managed by FEMA's Volunteer Agency Liaison staff in collaboration with State and Local governments. The FEMA Voluntary Agency Coordination Section provides technical assistance; coordination and subject matter expertise to partners who are addressing gaps in resources, providing financial support and additional support to survivors after government assistance is exhausted."[197]

The Individuals and Households Program (IHP)

The Individuals and Households Program (IHP) component of IA is designed to provide direct financial assistance and services to qualifying individuals who have incurred uninsured or underinsured damages and expenses. It is important to note up front that the IHP is not a substitution for insurance and it does not compensate individuals for the total losses sustained by a disaster. FEMA financial assistance is provided after verifying that the individual or household is not insured and once approved, the total amount of assistance will be far less than the cost of repairs or replacement.

IHP assistance is divided into the two categories of Housing Assistance and Other Needs Assistance (ONA). Housing Assistance is further sub-divided between Financial Housing Assistance and Direct Housing Assistance. Financial Housing

---

[197] (FEMA, Individual Assistance Program and Policy Guide (IAPPG), January 2019)

Assistance "refers to funds provided to eligible applicants for temporary lodging expenses, rental of temporary housing, or repair or replacement of a damaged primary residence."[198] FEMA defines a *primary residence* as "*The home where the applicant lives during the major portion of the calendar year, or The home that is required because of proximity to employment, including agricultural activities that provide 50% of the household's income.*"[199] Additionally, Lodging Expense Reimbursement (LER) may be provided by FEMA to assist disaster survivors with out-of-pocket expenses for temporary lodging or rental assistance may be provided when homeowners or renters are displaced from their primary residence. Housing assistance may also be provided in the form of home repair assistance or replacement assistance when a primary residence is destroyed as the result of a Presidentially declared disaster, which is referred to as Direct Housing Assistance. In order to be eligible for IHP, the person must be a U.S. citizen, non-citizen national, or qualified alien, and:

- Sustained losses in a Presidentially declared disaster area
- The damages occurred to the primary residence
- The primary residence is uninhabitable or inaccessible
- The needs caused by the disaster are not able to be met through any other form of disaster assistance or insurance
- The homeowner has insufficient or no insurance

The Other Needs Assistance (ONA) "program provides money, if you qualify, for necessary expenses and serious needs caused by the disaster."[200] A *necessary expense* is defined by FEMA as *a cost attributed to purchasing an item, procuring a service, or payment for other activities that meet a serious need.* And, the definition of a *serious need* is "*the requirement for an item or service that is essential to an applicant's ability to prevent, mitigate, or overcome a disaster-caused hardship, injury, or adverse condition.*"[201] ONA is divided between

---

[198] (FEMA, Individual Assistance Program and Policy Guide (IAPPG), January 2019)
[199] (FEMA, Individual Assistance Program and Policy Guide (IAPPG), January 2019)
[200] (FEMA Individuals and Households Program (IHP) - Other Needs Assistance , 2019)
[201] (FEMA, Individual Assistance Program and Policy Guide (IAPPG), January 2019)

assistance provided by FEMA that does not require the applicant to apply for a Small Business Administration (SBA) loan or "non-SBA Dependent" and the assistance that does require the applicant to apply for an SBA loan or "SBA Dependent." The non-SBA Dependent ONA applies to assistance with funeral expenses, medical or dental expenses as a verified direct result of injuries sustained during the disaster, childcare, miscellaneous expenses, critical needs for lifesaving or life-sustaining items, and clean and removal assistance for homes inundated by floodwaters. The SBA-Dependent ONA, requiring application for SBA loans, includes financial assistance for personal property, transportation, moving and storage, and group flood insurance assistance. The types of personal property eligible for SBA loans under ONA are appliances, clothing, furnishings, and *essential tools* that are *required as a condition of employment.*

Damage Assessments and Maximum Individual Assistance (IA)

Making sense of Individual Assistance (IA) can be extremely complicated. However, it begins to make more sense once you begin to look at it from the vantage of conducting damage assessments. When discussing IA, damage assessments only apply to homes and not businesses because businesses are required to have insurance to cover damages. Likewise, most homes that are less than 25 years old will be covered by insurance because mortgage companies require homes to be insured for the duration of the mortgage. With that understanding, to qualify for IA, the home must be uninsured or underinsured, however the latter is deceptive, and FEMA will determine if a home qualifies as underinsured. Additionally, the home must be the primary residence, not a vacation home or rental home and the damage must be classified as either Major or Destroyed to qualify. Even when homes do qualify, in this section you will learn that the amount of financial assistance provided by IA is far less than the value of the home and the assistance is not intended to cover the total costs associated with completely repairing or replacing a home.

There are three types of damage assessments which are conducted to determine the extent of disaster related damages: the Rapid Assessment, Windshield Assessment, and Site Assessment.

1. Rapid Assessment
   - Conducted immediately following the disaster
   - Focuses on life safety issues of search and rescue, evacuation, and treatment of the injured
   - Determines the immediate human needs of food, water, and shelter
   - Evaluates re-establishment of transportation and utilities
   - Takes into account operation of critical facilities for medical and emergencies
   - Establishes the boundaries of the damage area
2. Windshield Assessment
   - Conducted concurrent with or immediately after the Rapid Assessment
   - Teams drive through the damage area counting and categorizing the extent of damage
   - Quickly conducted if the area is accessible
   - Excellent method for moderate to large scale disasters
3. Site Assessment
   - Primary method for damage assessments for government-owned infrastructure or for an SBA assessment
   - Slow and very resource dependent

Damage classifications are divided into two categories; those damages caused by means other than water fall into the first category. There are four classifications of damage: Affected, Minor, Major, and Destroyed. A home is classified as Affected if the structure has received cosmetic or minimal damage (minimal missing shingles and siding, broken windows, damaged porch or carport, damaged outbuilding, etc...) and is immediately habitable. Generally speaking, damages to carports, garages, outbuildings, and porches are not eligible for IA. Homes are classified as Minor for nonstructural damage when they may be habitable in a short period of time (numerous missing shingles, damage to chimney, small holes to roofing or siding, etc...). Homes are classified as Major for significant damage requiring extensive repairs (failure or partial failure to structural components such as roof rafters or joists over essential living areas, walls, or partial failure of the foundation with shifting of the residence or more than 6 inches). Finally, homes classified as Destroyed when they are a total loss (only the foundation is remaining, complete failure of two or more of the main structural elements, or it is confirmed as an imminent danger due to land or mud slides or sinkholes). Only the homes which are classified as Major or Destroyed will qualify for IA and then based upon the per capita indicator the local jurisdiction will have to meet or exceed the required number of qualifying homes. For Bexar County, TX; the threshold to qualify for IA grants for 2021 is estimated by the Texas Division of Emergency Management (TDEM) as a total of 600 to 1,000 uninsured homes classified as Major or Destroyed for a single Presidentially Declared Disaster. When jurisdictions do not meet the threshold to qualify for IA, homeowners may qualify for low interest SBA loans if more than 25 uninsured homes or businesses classified as 40% or more damage.

Damages due to flooding or water are the second category and are calculated based upon the level of water on the structure which is determined by viewing the water line. Due to the difference in construction; the classifications for mobile homes are different from those for single or multi-family homes.

1. Single/Multi-Family Homes
   - Affected: Water level in a crawlspace or unfinished basement; no submerged mechanical components.
   - Minor: Water level is between 1 and 3 inches in an essential living area, but below 18 inches.
   - Major: Water level is above 18 inches or above electrical outlets or basement is full.
   - Destroyed: Water level at or above the roofline or higher; or a complete failure of two or more main structural elements.
2. Mobile Homes
   - Affected: Cosmetic damages, skirting missing, damages to porch, or carport, or damages to outbuildings.

- Minor: Water level is at the floor line but has not entered the living space, damage to bottom board, insulation, or ductwork; no structural damages.
- Major: Water covered the floor system entering the living space but is below the roof, or the mobile home has been shifted off of its foundation.
- Destroyed: Water level at or above the roofline or higher; or the frame is twisted or compromised.

The bottom-line question for Individual Assistance (IA) is, what can a homeowner whose home has been classified as Major or Destroyed potentially receive in terms of financial assistance? There is a definitive maximum amount of funding for IA to individuals and households. On October 16, 2019, FEMA published a "notice that the maximum amount of IHP financial assistance provided to an individual or household under section 408 of the Stafford Act with respect to any single emergency or disaster is $35,500 for housing assistance."[202] However, the average FEMA IA grant for a disaster claim "is about $5,000 on average per household"[203] or less. Emergency Managers must be leading the narrative, to set expectations, after a disaster to educate the public on the truth that Federal assistance will not come close to covering the costs of damages and loss.

Hazard Mitigation Assistance Grants

FEMA defines *hazard mitig*ation as *"any sustainable action that reduces or eliminates long-term risk to people and property from future disasters."*[204] The goal of hazard mitigation is disrupt the cycle of damage caused by a disaster, efforts to

---

[202] (FEMA, Notice of Maximum Amount of Assistance Under the Individuals and Households Program, October 16, 2019)

[203] (FEMA, Overcoming Objections, n.d.)

[204] (FEMA, Hazard Mitigation Assistance Grants, n.d.)

rebuild, and repeated disaster damage. Hazard mitigation can be accomplished through various methods or construction projects designed to reduce future disaster impacts. FEMA manages the Hazard Mitigation Grant Program (HMGP) for eligible projects to reduce a community's vulnerability, promote safe and resilient communities to withstand disaster disruptions, to lessen the requirements for response and recovery resources, and to encourage communities to be more self-reliant. This section will provide an overview of the eligible recipients and projects under the Hazard Mitigation Grant Program. Chapter 9 pertaining to various Emergency Management grant programs will delve more into the types of Hazard Mitigation grants.

Eligible Hazard Mitigation Grant Recipients

State, Local, Tribal, and Territorial (SLTT) governments can apply for hazard mitigation grants in the wake of a presidentially declared disaster that has impacted their communities. Homeowners and business are not eligible to apply directly for hazard mitigation grants but may benefit through sub-applicant assistance for their local community under certain circumstances. The impacted State, Tribal, or Territorial government will designate one agency as the Applicant for HMGP funding and Local governments such as counties and cities will be considered sub-applicants. Similar to Public Assistance (PA) grants, HMGP funding recipients are responsible for conducting a preliminary damage assessment prior to applying for HMGP funding and those assessments will assist in identifying potential mitigation projects.

There are three steps involved in applying for Hazard Mitigation funding: (1) Project scoping or proposing specific projects to reduce or eliminate the risks of hazards, (2) Project Development or refining of project concepts based upon feasibility, cost-effectiveness of the projects, and examination of regulatory requirements, and (3) Project Submission after evaluating inherent issues and consideration of alternatives. The application, along with the identified sub-applicants must be submitted to FEMA within twelve months of the presidentially declared disaster. FEMA will then review the application to determine eligibility of the projects submitted and if approved "awards funds to the recipient, which disburses the funds to its sub-recipient – generally a local government entity"[205] to disburse and oversee funding to the sub-applicant Local governments. Projects must be completed within thirty-six months of the close of the application period.

Eligible Hazard Mitigation Grant Projects

There is a wide array of hazard mitigation projects that may be eligible to aid communities to rebuild better, safer, and stronger to become resilient when faced with future disasters. To receive approval from FEMA, the projects must be cost-effective, reduce or eliminate the risk of future natural disaster damages, meet International Building Codes, align with the community hazard mitigation plan, and meet the requirements of Environmental and Historic Preservation (EHP) standards or statutes. Eligible hazard mitigation projects can include:

- Acquisition or "buy outs" of residential and business properties to enable relocation of the owners to safe areas.
- Protection of residential and business properties with installation of permanent barriers that prevent inundation of floodwaters, such as flood-proofing, floodwalls, or levees.
- Elevation of structures above flood levels.
- Reconstruction of damaged structures on elevated foundations.
- Retrofitting of structures making them more resistant to earthquakes, floods, wildfires, winds, or other natural disasters.
- Retrofitting utilities and infrastructure to make them more resilient to natural disasters.
- Constructing safe rooms for communities or residents in areas prone to hurricanes or tornadoes.

---

[205] (FEMA, After You Apply: Things to Know and Do After Applying for Hazard Mitigation Grant Program Funding, 2021)

- Stabilizing slopes to prevent or reduce damages to structures.
- Improving drainage or constructing flood reduction projects.
- Post-disaster enforcement of building codes.
- "Developing and adopting hazard mitigation plans, which are <u>required for state, local, tribal and territorial governments</u> to receive funding for their hazard mitigation projects."[206]

Taken in its totality, in Chapter 7, the disaster declaration process combined with all that is involved in public assistance (PA), individual assistance (IA), and hazard mitigation contains a lot to wrap your mind around when it comes to Federal assistance. There are hurdles along the path, including county and State thresholds, cost-sharing, damage assessments, and far fewer Federal dollars than the public may assume. Put it all together and you can see why hazard mitigation is so important. It is much better to avoid the negative results involved in a natural, man-made, or technological disaster altogether.

---

[206] (FEMA, Hazard Mitigation Grant Program (HMGP), 2021)

Chapter 7 Summary

Key Terms (Alphabetical Order)

American Bar Association (ABA)
Cost Share
Crisis Counseling
Crisis Counseling Assistance and Training Program (CCP)
Disaster Case Management (DCM)
Disaster Legal Services (DLS)
Disaster Unemployment Assistance (DUA)
Emergency Declaration of Disaster
Emergency Work
Environmental and Historic Preservation (EHP)
Essential Tools
Facility
Hazard Mitigation
Hazard Mitigation Grant Program (HMGP)
Individual Assistance (IA)
Individuals and Households Program (IHP)
Lodging Expense Reimbursement (LER)
Major Declaration of Disaster
Mass Care and Emergency Assistance (MC/EA)
Mutual Aid Agreement
National Flood Insurance Program (NFIP)
Necessary Expense
Other Needs Assistance (ONA)
Per Capita
Per Capita Indicator
Permanent Work
Preliminary Damage Assessment (PDA)
Primary Residence
Private Non-Profit (PNP)
Public Assistance (PA)

Rainy Day Funds
Rapid Assessment
Reasonable Cost
Serious Need
Site Assessment
State of Texas Assistance Request (STAR)
State Operations Center (SOC)
State, Tribal, Territorial, and Local (STTL)
Threshold
Volunteer Agency Liaison (VAL)
WebEOC
Windshield Assessment

Navigating the Disaster Declaration Process

Chapter 7 opened with learning that the very first step towards Federal disaster assistance is the Local government response; as the saying goes "All disasters begin and end local." When disasters strike the Local government will respond and engage regional mutual aid partners. Once the Local government has exceeded its capability to respond, the County Judge or City Mayor may issue a disaster declaration and forward the appropriate notification to the State for assistance. The Governor will then authorize State resources to assist with the response and recovery operations. When a disaster exceeds the States' capability to respond, the Governor will issue a disaster declaration and forward it to FEMA for review. FEMA will then forward eligible requests to the President who may then issue a Presidential Disaster Declaration authorizing Federal assistance.

The Public Assistance (PA) Grant Program

FEMA's Public Assistance (PA) grant program provides funding to State, Tribal, Territorial, and Local governments for disaster damages to buildings, bridges, parks, and roads. Additionally, under some circumstances PA grants may be provided to specific private non-profit organizations. For Local governments to qualify to receive PA grants, both the County and the State must meet or exceed the thresholds based upon the per capita for the population established by FEMA. Even after qualifying for PA assistance, reimbursement may take months or years dependent upon the documentation compiled and submitted to FEMA. Even for public facilities that qualify, the 75% Federal and 25% Local cost share will reduce the overall amount of PA grant assistance received.

The Individual Assistance (IA) Grant Program

The FEMA Individual Assistance (IA) grant program may provide assistance to individuals and households in the aftermath of a Presidentially Declared Disaster. Many of the IA programs do not provide direct monetary assistance. Programs such as mass care, case management, crisis counseling, legal services, and volunteer coordination are vital IA programs provide services rather than finances. While unemployment assistance, housing assistance, and qualifying other needs assistance comes in the form of direct funding to the individuals or households. However, qualifying for IA funding is conditional upon the damage classification and meeting the required number of uninsured homes classified as Major or Destroyed for the jurisdiction. When jurisdictions do not meet the required number of qualifying homes, the homeowners may qualify for low interest SBA loans.

The Hazard Mitigation Grant Program

Where the Public Assistance (PA) and Individual Assistance (IA) grant programs are established to address the aftermath of disasters, the Hazard Mitigation Grant Program (HMGP) is focused on developing plans and implementing projects to eliminate or reduce the impact of natural disasters on communities. It all revolves around this whole concept of resilience or making communities safer and stronger to be prepared to weather the effects of natural disasters. FEMA maintains an entire office dedicated to resilience that "aims to build a culture of preparedness through insurance, mitigation, continuity, preparedness programs and grants."[207] It is important to highlight that the mission of FEMA's Resilience Office includes promoting the need for communities, homeowners, and businesses to be insured against natural disasters. Many home and business owners don't even realize that home and business insurance typically does not cover flooding. Which is all the more reason for Emergency Managers to be engaged in educating the public on community preparedness, the National Flood Insurance Program (NFIP), and ways to enhance their own resilience to natural disasters.

In the next chapter, you will learn about Emergency Management Training and Exercise Programs.

---

[207] (FEMA, Resilience, 2020)

Chapter 8: Emergency Management Training and Exercise Programs

Training and exercises are a way of life for Emergency Managers. Continually we face new challenges, improved tactics from lessons learned, upgraded equipment and technology, and new personnel entering the field requiring training and exercising to improve response and recovery capabilities. It cannot be over-emphasized that Emergency Managers are lifelong students and the method for testing our training is through conducting and evaluating exercises. This sets up the cycle of planning, training to the plan, exercising the plan, evaluating the training, and updating the plan to do it all over again on a continuous cycle of preparedness. The Emergency Management training cycle covers a wide spectrum of topics covering various types of disasters, hazards, threats, and incident management.

No matter how much knowledge we may possess from years of experience, Emergency Managers will never know it all or know enough to meet all of the potential challenges in the communities we serve. Towards those ends, it is imperative to recognize that untested knowledge is a single point of weakness that may result in a catastrophic failure at the very worst time and, therefore we should embrace training and exercises. Our dedication to training and improvement, coupled with the experience we gain through real-world disaster response makes us better Emergency Manager and our communities better prepared for whatever challenges may come our way. It is through embracing learning throughout our careers that we become true professionals in this field.

Introduction to Emergency Management Training

As has been illustrated throughout this text, Emergency Management is an expansive field filled with complex operations. The enormous responsibilities make it all the more imperative that Emergency Managers must be knowledgeable of the building blocks and Federal regulations which guide all phases of Emergency Management. Comprehension of Emergency Management history and development of the Incident Command System (ICS) allows those working towards entering this field to gain from the benefit of the lessons learned and best practices adopted through centuries of disaster response. Those lessons have transformed into the preparedness goals implemented across the United States and are the impetus behind the evolution of how Emergency Management plans are structured.

Awareness of the field operations of Emergency Managers, emergency medical technicians (EMTs), fire fighters, law enforcement, public health, and public works drives effective management of disasters and emergencies at the tactical level. Transitioning our knowledge from tactics proficiency to strategic coordination within emergency operations centers (EOCs) enhances the capability and capacity for Emergency Managers to safeguard our residents and communities. Then top it all off with insight into the overarching disaster declaration process and the result is Emergency Managers possessing the knowledge and skills to be able to serve and succeed with confidence.

Needless to say, there is so much to learn for both entry-level and experienced Emergency Managers over our lifetimes. Fortunately, one of the outcomes of generations of disaster response in the nation is the establishment of the FEMA Emergency Management Institute (EMI) which "offers self-paced courses designed for people who have Emergency Management responsibilities and the general public."[208] As of June 10, 2021, FEMA offers 210 free independent study Emergency Management courses which can be accessed online through EMI.

---

[208] (FEMA, Distance Learning, n.d.)

Annually, new and updated courses are added to EMI to address changes, new technologies, and improved procedures. Every potential or life-long Emergency Manager has the ability to complete cost-free training at our own pace on a wide range of new and vital topics.

Do not underestimate the value of the courses provided online by EMI simply because they are free and self-paced. A majority of the material utilized to develop Emergency Management college courses can be learned through the courses administered by EMI. Further value added by these courses is evident in the fact that FEMA has developed an accredited partnership "where you can convert your FEMA EMI Independent Study courses into college credit from Frederick Community College."[209] Where most colleges and universities charge between $200 to $400 per credit hour or more for college credit, FEMA's partnership provides an avenue for people to attain critical Emergency Management knowledge that can easily be converted to college credit for $90 per semester hour through Frederick Community College. Those credit hours can lead to an Associate of Applied Science (AAS) degree and/or be transferred to higher-level degree programs.

The Purpose of Emergency Management Training and Qualifications

Objectives behind training and qualifying Emergency Managers and first responders are grounded within the National Incident Management System (NIMS) and the National Qualification System (NQS). All the way back in Chapter 3, the characteristics and components of NIMS were presented to begin forming a bedrock of knowledge in Emergency Management. The identified central perspective of NIMS is to provide a comprehensive approach for all levels of government and the private sector to collaboratively "prevent, protect against, mitigate, respond to, and

---

[209] (Emergency Management Study, n.d.)

recover from incidents."[210] The three major NIMS components of resource management, command and coordination, and communications and information management contribute to forming the basis upon which to build competency in Emergency Management. Along with the comprehensive approach of NIMS to promote proficiency, "the National Qualification System (NQS) provides a foundational guideline on the typing of personnel resources within the NIMS framework, plus supporting tools."[211]

What it all boils down to is that for the nation to effectively develop a comprehensive approach to managing disasters demands training of all governmental and non-governmental Emergency Managers and responders to a common standard. The result of training to a standard is that Emergency Managers and responders from any jurisdiction in any State can quickly and efficiently integrate in and assist with disaster operations in any other jurisdiction or State. Beyond training, the process of qualifying personnel to attain "an ability, characteristic, or experience that makes you suitable for a particular job or activity"[212] is vital to Emergency Managers being able to adequately perform during disaster operations. Which plays directly into how the Incident Command System (ICS) promotes utilizing the highest qualified personnel to manage incident response.

Emergency Management Course Codes and Categories

Every Emergency Management training class is assigned a course code and is categorized based upon the type of training and level of personnel qualification. Course codes indicate the level of government conducting the training, location, in-person versus distance training, virtual instructor-led, or the level to which personnel will be qualified to operate. Unlocking the course codes can aid

---

[210] (FEMA, National Incident Management System, Third Edition, October 2017)
[211] (FEMA, NIMS Components - Guidance and Tools, 2021)
[212] (Qualification, n.d.)

Emergency Managers in planning and conducting a comprehensive training program.

Three main sources comprise the bulk of the official Emergency Management course codes. First among the sources is FEMA's Emergency Management Institute (EMI); that includes online and in-resident training. Aside from the 210 online courses previously mentioned, "EMI provides resident course training to Federal, state, local, tribal, territorial (SLTT), volunteer, public, and private sector officials to strengthen Emergency Management core competencies for professional, career-long training."[213] The FEMA EMI course codes are:

E   Residential courses provided at FEMA's National Emergency Training Center (NETC) in Emmitsburg, Maryland.

G   Residential courses provided by State/Local/Tribal and/or agency trainers. "A significant portion of EMI's training is conducted by state Emergency Management agencies and identified by the EMI-developed/state-delivered G course code."[214]

IS   Courses provided as Independent Study through FEMA's EMI online portal (https://training.fema.gov/is/crslist.aspx).

K   Residential courses provided over Adobe Connect.

L   Residential courses provided at offsite facilities such as FEMA's Center for Domestic Preparedness (CDP) located in Anniston, Alabama and the FEMA Logistics Center located in Frederick, Maryland.

V   Residential courses provided by Video Teleconference (VTC).

The second official source for Emergency Management course codes is the United States Fire Administration's (USFA) National Fire Academy (NFA), which is co-located with FEMA's NETC in Emmitsburg, Maryland. "To supplement and support State and local fire service training programs, the NFA delivers educational and training courses having a national focus."[215] The NFA offers training to promote

---

[213] (FEMA, EMI Course Codes, 2021)
[214] (FEMA, EMI Course Codes, 2021)
[215] ((NWCG), The Mission, Purpose, and Course Codes of the United States Fire Administration's National Fire Academy, n.d.)

professional development for fire fighters, emergency responders, Emergency Managers, and partner organization professionals. The NFA course codes are:

C   College-level courses.

F   Field delivered courses.

I   Courses offer In-Service.

N   Courses offered regionally.

O   Off-Site courses offered through State training systems.

P   Pilot courses.

Q   Self-Study courses.

R   Residential on-campus courses.

T   Train-the-Trainer courses.

W   Weekend State delivered courses.

Y   Courses endorsed by the NFA and/or courses developed at the State level.

The third official source for Emergency Management course codes is the National Training and Education Division (NTED), which is a division under the National Preparedness Directorate (NPD). "NTED serves the Nation's first responder community, offering more than 200 courses to help build skills that responders need to function effectively in mass consequence events."[216] Where EMI and NFA course codes primarily identify the method of course delivery, NTED course codes identify the individual's level of responsibility on an incident. There are three levels of courses identified by NTED: Awareness (AWR), Performance (PER), and Management and Planning (MGT). *Awareness level courses* are *developed to provide responders with the abilities to recognize and report hazards or catastrophic incidents or to provide skills necessary to investigate hazardous materials and/or incidents involving potentially explosive devices. Performance level courses* are *developed to train those responders who will be performing tasks related to initial response and catastrophic incidents, such as insuring safety of responders and the public, search and rescue, and HazMat decontamination. Management level courses* are *developed to provide incident managers with the*

---

[216] (National Training and Education Division (NTED) Course Catalog, n.d.)

knowledge to develop incident plans and coordinate over-arching incident coordination for catastrophic incidents.

Providers of Emergency Management Training

The great news is that at the Federal, State, and Local levels there are a plethora of Emergency Management training providers. In the first few pages of this chapter alone, the Center for Domestic Preparedness (CDP), Emergency Management Institute (EMI), National Emergency Training Center (NETC), National Fire Academy (NFA), and the National Training and Education Division (NTED) have been identified as training providers. While it is not practical to be able to list every possible training provider, this text will attempt to address a broad cross-section of potential providers. One alliance of Emergency Management training providers is the National Domestic Preparedness Consortium (NDPC). The NDPC "is a partnership of several nationally recognized organizations whose membership is based on the urgent need to address counterterrorism preparedness needs of the nation's emergency first responders within the context of chemical, biological, radiological, and explosive WMD hazards."[217] The training providers comprising the NDPC include:

1. **Center for Domestic Preparedness (CDP):** CDP "provides advanced, all-hazards training to approximately 50,000 emergency responders annually from state, local, tribal, and territorial governments, as well as the federal government, foreign governments, and private entities, as available."[218]
2. **Counter Terrorism Operations Support (CTOS) Program at the U.S. Department of Energy (DOE) Nevada National Security Site (NNSS):** CTOS "located northwest of Las Vegas, Nevada provides First Responder CBRNE Training in unique, authentic, and safe WMD venues using

---

[217] (National Training and Education Division (NTED) Course Catalog, n.d.)
[218] (Center for Domestic Preparedness (CDP), n.d.)

---

realistic training scenarios."[219] The acronym CBRNE stands for Chemical-Biological-Radiological-Nuclear-Explosive hazards.

3. **Energetic Materials Research and Testing Center (EMRTC) of New Mexico Tech:** EMRTC "provides world-class training in explosives, firearms and explosive site safety in association with the U.S. Department of Homeland Security, the U.S. State Department and other Federal and State agencies."[220]

4. **National Center for Biological Research and Training (NCBRT) of Louisiana State University (LSU):** NCBRT "is a nationally recognized center for emergency preparedness and response training located at Louisiana State University's flagship campus in Baton Rouge, Louisiana."[221]

5. **National Disaster Preparedness Training Center (NDPTC) of the University of Hawaii:** "NDPTC is authorized to develop and deliver training and educational programs related to homeland security and disaster management, with a specific focus on natural hazards, coastal communities, and the special needs and opportunities of islands and territories."[222]

6. **National Emergency Response and Rescue Training Center (NERRTC) through Texas Engineering Extension Service (TEEX):** "NERRTC prepares state and local officials for the management challenge posed by WMD through hands-on, scenario-driven training and computer-based simulations."[223]

7. **Security and Emergency Response Training Center (SERTC) operated by the Transportation Technology Center, Incorporated (TTCI):** As a subsidiary of the Association of American Railroad, SERTC serves to train "not only the transportation service industry, but also the public sector

---

[219] (Center for Radiological Nuclear Training, n.d.)
[220] (Energetic Materials Research and Testing Center (EMRTC), n.d.)
[221] (National Center for Biological Research and Training (NCBRT), n.d.)
[222] (National Disaster Preparedness Training Center, n.d.)
[223] (National Training and Education Division (NTED) Course Catalog, n.d.)

emergency response community, the chemical industry, government agencies, and emergency response contractors from all over the world"[224] to safely manage HazMat rail tank car incidents.

A second Emergency Management training partnership is the Rural Domestic Preparedness Consortium (RDPC) which "was established to lead the development and delivery of homeland security all-hazards preparedness training to rural communities across the Nation."[225] The RDPC is led by Eastern Kentucky University and other higher education partners include Eastern Tennessee State University, North Carolina Central University, Northwest Arkansas Community College, The University of Findlay, and University of California – Davis.

At the graduate collegiate level, the Center for Homeland Defense and Security (CHDS) at the Naval Postgraduate School serves as the premier Homeland Security training provider for executive and graduate level education. "Since 2003, CHDS has conducted a wide range of programs focused on assisting current and emerging leaders in Homeland Defense and Security to develop the policies, strategies, programs and organizational elements needed to defeat terrorism and prepare for and respond to natural disasters and public safety threats across the United States."[226]

Additional Emergency Management training providers are available at the Federal, State, and Local government levels and through associations and private or non-governmental agencies. Discipline specific agencies such as the Federal Law Enforcement Training Center (FLETC), National Sheriff's Association (NSA), International Association of Fire Chiefs (IAFC), and International Association of Fire Fighters (IAFF) provide training for law enforcement and fire fighters. Other agencies which offer training across disciplines are the National Weather Service (NWS) and Office of Bombing Prevention (OBP). Additionally, State and Local offices of Emergency Management (OEM)/Emergency Management Agencies

---

[224] (About SERTC, n.d.)
[225] (National Training and Education Division (NTED) Course Catalog, n.d.)
[226] (Center for Homeland Defense and Security (CHDS), n.d.)

(EMA), fire and law enforcement academies, forest service agencies, and health and human service organizations also provide valuable training for Emergency Management and responder personnel. Lastly, volunteer training is available through the American Red Cross, faith-based organizations, and the Community Emergency Response Team (CERT) programs.

Foundational Emergency Management Training

The concept of what comprises foundational training can be summed up with the single term "minimum." By now, the reader should recognize that the field of Emergency Management is far-reaching. As such, there is no possibility of a person ever completing the entirety of Emergency Management training, which necessitates establishing minimum levels of training to form a foundation upon which to build through years of continued training and experience. The handful of foundational courses in the field are merely stepping-stones for entering into the training process. As stated at the beginning of this chapter, Emergency Managers are lifelong students. I describe the Emergency Management training process to interns as that of reverse engineering an onion. The foundational courses are the core of Emergency Management knowledge and each successive course adds consecutive inter-related layers of knowledge.

Unfortunately, it is not uncommon for potential or new Emergency Managers to express frustration with attempting to identify a *"glide path,"* which is *"a course of action that leads easily to an expected outcome"*[227] for training. Partially, the difficulty is rooted in the truth that there is no single set of courses required to become an Emergency Manager. Just like the field, there are too many variables involved and varieties of Emergency Managers. The hazards of a specific jurisdiction may dictate the requirements for training, agency policies and procedures may influence training, and the level of government or organization may

---

[227] (Glide Path, n.d.)

establish distinct training to achieve their mission and goals. However, there are common core courses which are the bedrock upon which to build a foundation of Emergency Management comprehension to perform the basic functions of the career.

The National Incident Management System (NIMS) Training Program

Beyond the establishment of course codes and identification of training providers, the next logical discussion is the composition of foundational Emergency Management training. The *2020 National Incident Management System Training Program* outlines "a path for developing and maintaining NIMS and provides guidance for Authorities Having Jurisdiction (AHJ) in developing their training plans."[228] The NIMS Training Program is a guiding baseline providing assistance to Authorities Having Jurisdiction (AHJ) while being flexible enough to allow AHJs to tailor training based upon their explicit needs. One stipulation is that AHJs must meet or be actively working towards meeting the requirements contained in the *NIMS Implementation Objectives for Local, State, Tribal, and Territorial Jurisdictions* to qualify as recipients or sub-recipients of Federal preparedness grants. While it is true that qualification for preparedness grants is tied to NIMS training compliance, a common misperception is that public assistance (PA) grants for communities following a disaster or emergency are tied to the NIMS Training Objectives. Embracing NIMS training compliance is highly recommended by the Federal government, but communities that have not fully integrated NIMS training are not penalized by the Federal government when they are devastated by disasters.

Understandably, the daunting task of training every Emergency Manager and responder across the nation is beyond the ability of any single organization. Therefore, "NIMS training exists as a component of the National Training and

---

[228] (FEMA, National Incident Management System Training Program, Summer 2020)

Education System (NTES)—a network of students, training providers, and higher education partners building a more secure and resilient nation."[229] The NIMS Training Program establishes an approach to training that is consistent with the NTES and categorizes foundational training based upon the four NIMS Command and Control systems:

1. ICS: Tactical on-scene operations personnel.
2. EOC: Strategic incident coordination personnel.
3. PIO: Public Information Officers managing the Joint Information Center (JIC)/Joint Information System (JIS).
4. MAC (Policy) Group: Senior policy decision-makers.

Foundational Emergency Management training is further subdivided between those personnel who are entry level or all non-supervisory, mid-level incident personnel with leadership roles, and senior incident personnel with supervisory responsibilities. The only foundational course identified for the MAC (Policy) Group is the G-402, whereas the graphic below illustrates the foundational training for ICS, EOC, and PIO personnel with a couple sensible additions of the E/L/G-300 and E/L/G-400 for EOC supervisory personnel and the G-289 that is typically provided in conjunction with the G-290 for PIO personnel.

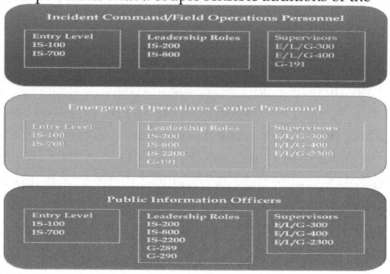

The Independent Study (IS) courses are available online through FEMA's training website

Figure 5: NIMS Foundational Training (Chadwick)

---

[229] (FEMA, National Incident Management System Training Program, Summer 2020)

(https://training.fema.gov/is/crslist.aspx) and the in-person classes are offered at the Local and State levels as well as at FEMA's NETC campus in Emmitsburg, MD. The course codes along with the course names for the NIMS Foundational Training are as follows:

> E/L/G-300 Intermediate Incident Command System for Expanding Incidents (a 3 day in-person class; prerequisites include completion of the IS-100, IS-200, IS-700, and IS-800)
>
> E/L/G-400 Advanced Incident Command System, Command and General Staff (a 2 day in-person class, prerequisite of completion of the E/L/G-300)
>
> E/L/G-2300 Intermediate Emergency Operations Center Functions (a 3 day in-person class)
>
> G-191 ICS – EOC Interface (a 1 day in-person class)
>
> G-289 Public Information Officer Awareness Training (a 1 day in-person class)
>
> G-290 Basic Public Information Officer (a 2 day in-person class)
>
> G-402 NIMS Overview for Executive/Senior Officials (a 4 hour in-person class)
>
> IS-29 Public Information Officer Awareness (online)
>
> IS-100 Introduction to the Incident Command System (online)
>
> IS-200 Basic Incident Command System for Initial Response (online)
>
> IS-700 An Introduction to the National Incident Management System (online)
>
> IS-800 National Response Framework, An Introduction (online)
>
> IS-2200 Basic Emergency Operations Center Functions (online)

Hazardous Materials (HazMat) Training

The challenges and demands upon responders and Emergency Managers combined with handling life-threatening materials in time limited circumstances makes it crucial to receive training that "is relevant to their work and tailored to their expected duties and tasks"[230] on a HazMat incident. Accidental or intentional release when handling or transporting HazMat can lead to death of responders or substantial and long-term threats to public health and environmental impact. Granted that Emergency Managers should not have "hands-on" HazMat during incidents; however it is dangerous to have people involved in coordination and planning if they have no HazMat training to comprehend the inherent hazards.

The enormous volume of HazMat training is so massive that it is impractical to cover in depth in this text and, therefore the topic will be covered as an overview limited to the levels of HazMat training. There are four levels of hazardous materials response and training which are based upon the type of work responders are trained to perform on HazMat incident scenes. Simply stated, hazardous materials are a category of response that is inclusive of Chemical, Biological, Radiological, Nuclear, and Explosive (CBRNE) substance incidents. The two terms of HazMat and CBRNE are often utilized synonymously. Descriptions of HazMat response and training levels are provided below:

1. **Awareness:** The awareness level of response and training is the basic level and focuses on training responders to recognize and identify HazMat, protect themselves and the public, secure the scene, and to call for properly trained responders to manage the incident. Awareness level responders work in what is referred to as the *Cold Zone* or *area free of contamination.*

2. **Operations:** The operations level HazMat responder is trained to assist in evacuations, establishment of exclusion areas, decontamination procedures, proper wear of personal protective equipment (PPE), and conducting the defensive operations of "absorption, damming and diking, diverting, retention, vapor dispersion and suppression."[231] Operations HazMat responders typically work within the *Warm Zone area between the Cold Zone and the area where the hazardous materials are present.* Decontamination is conducted in the Warm Zone to remove hazardous

---

[230] (Cresswell, 2021)
[231] (The Different Levels of Hazardous Materials Response, 2011)

---

substances from responders and serves as a barrier to prevent hazardous substances from contaminating the Cold Zone.

3. **Technician:** HazMat technicians or HazMat Techs are highly trained to take offensive "hands-on" actions while wearing chemical protective PPE and utilizing specialized monitors and equipment. HazMat techs are trained to work inside of the *Hot Zone area where hazardous substances have been released.*

4. **Specialist:** The highest level of training for hazardous materials is the HazMat Specialists which are personnel trained in advanced levels of biology, chemistry, and handling of hazardous substances. Typically, HazMat Specialists are trained to manage commercial highway transport vehicle or railway HazMat incidents.

All Hazards Incident Management Team (AHIMT) Training

In Chapter 2 of this text, the definition of *All Hazards* was introduced to explain the value of focusing planning and training upon the *common tasks responders perform for incidents regardless of shape, size, or complexity.* Add to that the concept of an *Incident Management Team (IMT)*, introduced in Chapter 5, or *personnel trained to hold specific Incident Command System (ICS) positions or position-specific training.* The outcome then is the *All Hazards Incident Management Team (AHIMT)* which is a title referring to *a team of personnel who have received advanced ICS position-specific training to be able to respond to and manage incidents regardless of shape, size, or complexity.* FEMA's EMI maintains the NIMS ICS All-Hazards Position Specific Training Program website with the goal of providing "advanced level training needed by personnel responsible for managing incidents of greater complexity than those typically encountered during routine operations."[232]

---

[232] (FEMA, NIMS ICS All-Hazards Position Specific Training Program Official Website, n.d.)

AHIMT training was developed to standardize minimum qualification criteria for personnel responding to incidents. AHIMTs are *typed* or *defined by level of capability to respond to and manage incidents based upon the corresponding Incident Complexity types* presented in Chapter 3. In 2011, FEMA issued the *NIMS Guideline for the Credentialing of Personnel* to guide AHJs in developing a process to qualify AHIMT personnel. FEMA replaced the 2011 version in 2017 with the *National Incident Management System Guideline for the National Qualification System* (NQS). "The National Qualification System (NQS) supplements the Resource Management component of the National Incident Management System (NIMS) by establishing guidance and tools to assist stakeholders in developing processes for qualifying, certifying, and credentialing deployable emergency personnel."[233]

The three key terms utilized in the NQS operations concept are qualification, certification, and credentialing. While the terms are definitely inter-related, they are distinct. *Qualification* is defined as *the process through which personnel are enabled to perform position-specific duties and the documentation of performance capabilities for the assigned position.* A component of the qualification phase is the completion of a position task book that "lists the competencies, behaviors and tasks required for successful performance in specific positions."[234] *Certification* is defined as *the process whereby an AHJ or third party recognize an individual for having met established standards to be qualified for holding a specific position.* The certification entails review of individual performance records and evidence for the completion of required tasks. Lastly, "*Credentialing is the process of providing documentation that identifies personnel and verifies their qualifications for certain positions.*"[235] The culmination of the NQS process is conducted by the AHJ issuing a credential or identification card to identify the individual's qualification and affiliation.

---

[233] (FEMA, National Incident Management System Guideline for the National Qualification System, November 2017)

[234] ((NWCG), NWCG Task Book for the Position of Incident Commander Type 3, June 2009)

[235] (FEMA, National Incident Management System Guideline for the National Qualification System, November 2017)

As presented in Chapter 6, in September of 2018, FEMA issued the *National Incident Management System Emergency Operations Center Skillsets User Guide* to mirror the system of qualifying, certifying, and credentialing AHIMT personnel for personnel working within an EOC. "As a part of the National Qualification System (NQS), EOC Skillsets support standardized qualifications for EOC personnel, while remaining flexible enough to accommodate EOCs of all sizes and kinds."[236] AHJs can select between the various skillsets to build EOC position task books to meet their jurisdictional requirements. Additionally, the EOC skillsets aid in developing a national vocabulary to communicate capabilities for various EOC position titles that perform similar tasks.

Exercise Program Management

Moving beyond training, Emergency Managers come to the task of exercising the agency plans and training to evaluate realistic performance expectations. This is the final step in the Planning, Organizing, Equipping, Training, and Exercising (POETE) process. Jurisdictions transition from developing plans, organizing teams, equipping personnel, training to standards, to exercising planned capabilities. Exercises are vital to the whole community because they provide an opportunity to evaluate performance in a controlled environment and identify areas for improvement. Once challenges or improvements have been identified, a corrective action plan can be developed to address those areas of concern and improve response capability.

Experienced Emergency Managers know that the worst possible time for new personnel and partners to learn local processes is during any real-world disaster or emergency response because time is critical and it is improbable to bring people up to speed in the midst of an incident. Exercises allow communities and jurisdictions to test their plans in a controlled environment outside of the chaos intertwined in

---

[236] (FEMA, National Incident Management System: Emergency Operations Center Skillsets User Guide, September 2018)

disaster response. New equipment, personnel, and policies can then be integrated into and familiarized with existing or revised plans through an effective exercise program. Different categories and types of exercises can be utilized for various audiences and purposes making it possible to walk-through a scenario in a classroom or briefing room with key leadership, testing teams or groups on a specific task a field environment with responders, or evaluating larger numbers of leadership and responders and deploying apparatus.

Categories and Types of Emergency Management Exercises

There are two categories and seven types of Emergency Management exercises. The first category of exercises is *Discussion-Based Exercises* that are used to *familiarize participants with plans, policies, and procedures in a guided or facilitated format.* Discussion-Based exercises do not involve moving personnel or equipment and the types include:

1. **Seminars:** Informal discussions or briefings to present new or revised plans, policies, or procedures.
2. **Workshops:** Similar to seminars, however workshops include the development of a work product during the workshop in the form of a draft plan or policy.
3. **Tabletop Exercises (TTX):** Scenario-based discussions involving key leadership and decision-makers working through a hypothetical incident.
4. **Games:** Competitive simulations involving two or more teams utilizing data, policies and procedures, and rules depicting a real-world incident.

The second category of exercises is *Operations-Based Exercises* that *involve the mobilization or movement of personnel and resources in response to a planned hypothetical emergency.* The types of operations-based exercises include:

1. **Drills:** Coordinated evaluation of capabilities of personnel to perform a specific function or operation, such as a fire drill.

2. **Functional Exercises (FE):** Mobilization or movement of a limited number of personnel and resources to evaluate command, control, and coordination for multi-agency/multi-discipline/multi-jurisdictional incident response.

3. **Full-Scale Exercises (FSE):** Mobilization or movement of a large number of personnel and resources to evaluate command, control, and coordination for multi-agency/multi-discipline/multi-jurisdictional incident response.

A well-coordinated exercise program will typically be progressive in nature. New information or resources will be introduced in a Seminar and followed by a Workshop to develop or improve policies. The next step is to conduct a Tabletop Exercise (TTX) to work through potential issues with leadership, plans, or policies. Then operational teams can be tested on their individual elements through Drills. And, finally, a Functional (FE) or Full-Scale Exercise (FSE) can be conducted to evaluate the collaborative response efforts. A progressive exercise program is a good pattern to follow to insure understanding from leadership working in an EOC to the individuals and teams in the field.

Designing and Facilitating Emergency Management Exercises

FEMA initially released the *Homeland Security Exercise and Evaluation Program (HSEEP)* in 2002 to provide "a set of fundamental principles for exercise programs, as well as a common approach to program management, design and development, conduct, evaluation, and improvement planning."[237] HSEEP presents another attempt to standardize the tasks associated within Emergency Management across the nation. However, it is important to dispel some misconceptions often attributed to HSEEP. Foremost, HSEEP is a guide or tool to be used for agencies in

---

[237] (FEMA, Homeland Security Exercise and Evaluation Program (HSEEP), January 2020)

their exercise programs, but it is not a mandate to utilize a specific format or template. Rather, templates are available on the HSEEP website (https://www.fema.gov/emergency-managers/national-preparedness/exercises/hseep) merely to assist agencies and jurisdictions to easily design and develop exercises. Additionally, FEMA does not recognize agencies or exercises as being HSEEP Compliant or HSEEP Certified.

"HSEEP doctrine is based on national best practices and is supported by training, technology systems, tools, and technical assistance."[238] Program management is a process identified in HSEEP for integration and oversight of exercises over an extended period of time. The approach involves senior leadership working in collaboration with stakeholders from the whole community to develop a multi-year preparedness plan to address regional hazards, risks, and threats. Part of this process is incorporating the Integrated Preparedness Cycle to plan, organize/equip,

Figure 6: Preparedness Cycle (FEMA)

train, exercise, and evaluate/improve to meet the challenges identified by the community. Periodically, an Integrated Preparedness Planning Workshop (IPPW) is conducted with representatives of the whole community to establish "the strategy and structure for an exercise program, in addition to broader preparedness efforts, while setting the foundation for the planning, conduct, and evaluation of individual exercises."[239] The product produced in this workshop is the Integrated Preparedness Plan (IPP) that documents the efforts of the preparedness cycle towards managing community disasters and generally covers a three-year timespan.

Exercise planners utilize the information from the IPP to design exercises to test emergency operations plans and procedures along with response capability and capacity. The exercises are designed to evaluate performance based upon the five mission areas and thirty-two core capabilities described in the *National*

---

[238] ((TDEM), About the State Exercise Program, n.d.)
[239] (FEMA, Homeland Security Exercise and Evaluation Program (HSEEP), January 2020)

Preparedness Goal that were covered in Chapter 4. Designing exercises includes determining a purpose, scope, setting of objectives, establishing evaluation goals, developing the scenario, and planning through the hypothetical incident from beginning to end. The exercise scenario may be presented as a scripted narrative or as a timeline sequence of events and should be a plausible or realistic incident consistent with community hazards, risks, and threats.

Exercises are planned by agencies and jurisdictions for a variety of reasons including plan testing, equipment and procedure evaluation, and to meet State and/or Federal mandates. The mandates may differ slightly from State to State, therefore Emergency Managers should consult with their respective State to ensure compliance. In Texas, Jurisdictions that receive Emergency Management Performance Grants (EMPG) are required to conduct at least one annual exercise and to "Conduct and evaluate a Full-scale Exercise at least once every three (3) years."[240] Additionally, a jurisdiction may be required to conduct an annual exercise of the Strategic National Stockpile (SNS) point of dispensing (POD) operation and a Full Scale (FTX) HazMat exercise once every three years.

Exercise Evaluation and Improvement Planning

The exercise documentation forms the framework for conducting and evaluating exercises. Depending upon the category and type of planned exercise, the documentation may range from being fairly simplistic to extremely complex. Where Seminars and Drills may be designed and facilitated with brief straightforward documentation, Tabletop (TTX) and Functional (FE) or Full-Scale (TTX) exercises will require detailed documentation. The HSEEP process provides recommendations for potential documentation to consider developing when planning Discussion- and Operations-Based exercises. Exercise planners will determine the extent of documentation for the type of exercise planned and the

---

[240] ((TDEM), FY2020 Local Emergency Management Performance Guide, November 2019)

participants. Tables depicting the types of documents associated with Discussion- and Operations-Based exercises are provided below:

Potential Documentation for Discussion-Based Exercises		
Document	Description	Distributed To
Situation Manual (SitMan)	Background and reference for participants.	All
Player Handout	Supplements or replaces the SitMan; participant quick reference.	Players
Facilitator Guide	Instructions for facilitators to guide participants.	Exercise Facilitators
Presentation	Multi-media presentation.	All
Exercise Evaluation Guides (EEGs)	Tools for collecting data to evaluate performance in a standardized manner.	Evaluators
Participant Feedback Form	Tool to collect participant information to develop and After-Action-Report (AAR) and Improvement Plan (IP).	All
Table 7: Discussion-Based Exercise Documents (FEMA – Modified Chadwick)		

Potential Documentation for Operations-Based Exercises		
Document	Description	Distributed To
Exercise Plan (ExPlan)	General information on exercise objectives and scope for participants.	Players and Observers
Player Handout	Supplements or replaces the SitMan; participant quick reference.	Players
Ground Truth	Detailed scenario elements to add to realism and guide achievement of objectives.	All
Controller/Evaluator (C/E) Handbook	Specific information for controllers and evaluators, may be contained in the ExPlan or as a standalone document.	Controllers and Evaluators
Master Scenario Events List (MSEL)	Timeline of scripted actions and events to be injected by controllers to prompt participants.	Controllers, Evaluators, and Simulator
Extent of Play Agreement	Agreement outlining a participant jurisdiction/organization level of involvement in the exercise.	Exercise Planning Team
Exercise Evaluation Guides (EEGs)	Tools for collecting data to evaluate performance in a standardized manner.	Evaluators

Control Staff Instructions (COSIN)	Detailed guideline on procedures and responsibilities for control, simulation, and support; may be a component of the C/E Handbook.	Controllers, Simulators, and Exercise Support
Evaluation Plan (EvalPlan)	Instructions for observing and evaluating an exercise.	Evaluators
Table 8: Operations-Based Exercise Documents (FEMA – Modified Chadwick)		

A diverse mixture of exercise participants will assist in the overall effectiveness and success of exercises. The more detailed operations-based exercises are typified by multi-discipline and multi-jurisdictional participants, while the lesser detailed discussion-based exercise may primarily involve a single agency or jurisdiction. Within the exercise documentation, numerous official titles are employed to describe the exercise participants and their respective roles or responsibilities. Some of the more common participant titles are:

1. **Actor:** Role player simulating officials or disaster victims.
2. **Controller:** Manages and monitors exercise pace and prompts actions to maintain exercise flow.
3. **Evaluator:** Subject-Matter Experts (SMEs) selected to observe and evaluate exercise performance.
4. **Facilitator:** Leads and guides the exercise to remain focused on planned objectives.
5. **Observer:** Individual who is not a direct participant and is observing, typically from a non-participant agency.
6. **Participant:** Any individual involved in the exercise.
7. **Player:** Individual with an active role in discussion or performance of exercise tasks.
8. **Simulator:** Delivers scenario messages or injects representing actions, conversations, or changes to the scenario to prompt participants to engage in corresponding activities or decision-making.

The ultimate goal of exercise evaluation and improvement planning is the production of an After-Action Report (AAR) and an Improvement Plan (IP). At the conclusion of an exercise, the exercise documentation and participant evaluations are compiled into an *After-Action Report (AAR) document "to capture observations of an exercise and make recommendations for post-exercise improvements."*[241] The areas for improvement are captured to form the basis of the *Improvement Plan (IP)* by *listing the issues or areas to be improved, corrective action to be taken, the agency or individual responsible for implementing the corrective action, and a date for the completion of the corrective action assigned.*

Training and exercises are two areas to which I have devoted a sizeable portion of my career in Emergency Management for two main reasons; (1) I want to be as best prepared I can be to perform the tasks associated with disaster response and (2) professional development is as much about how you aid others in preparing as it is about yourself. The field of Emergency Management is an arena like none other. Emergency Managers have to be able to immediately shift gears when the peaceful moments of tranquility are pierced with erupting chaos from the next tragic incident striking our community. That is why I am grateful for all that has come before me and the processes and programs which have been established in Emergency Management. The founding of FEMA's EMI online training program is a game changer making free training available to anyone interested to work through at your own pace and for those who are interested they can easily convert many of the courses to college credit at a fraction of the cost of traditional college or university fees. Additionally, through a nationwide network of trainers and providers, courses can be accessed for entry level and advanced level Emergency Managers on a wide range of topics. Specialized training is also available for HazMat and All Hazards courses and those requiring discipline specific training. All of which leads to participating in or planning exercises to test and improve upon our skills. That is how we prepare ourselves to Organize Chaos!

---

[241] (FEMA, FEMA Glossary, n.d.)

Chapter 8 Summary

Key Terms (Alphabetical Order)

Actor
After-Action Report
All Hazards Incident Management Team (AHIMT)
Awareness (AWR)
Chemical-Biological-Radiological-Nuclear-Explosive (CBRNE)
Center for Homeland Defense and Security (CHDS)
Certification
Cold Zone
Community Emergency Response Team (CERT)
Control Staff Instructions (COSIN)
Controller
Controller/Evaluator (C/E) Handbook
Counter Terrorism Operations Support (CTOS)
Credentialing
Department of Energy (DOE)
Discussion-Based Exercises
Drills
Emergency Management Institute (EMI)
Emergency Management Performance Grants (EMPG)
Energetic Materials Research and Testing Center (EMRTC)
Emergency Medical Technician (EMT)
Evaluation Plan (EvalPlan)
Evaluator
Exercise Evaluation Guides (EEGs)
Exercise Plan (ExPlan)
Extent of Play Agreement
Facilitator
Facilitator Guide
Federal Law Enforcement Training Center (FLETC)
Full-Scale Exercise (FSE)

Functional Exercise (FE)
Games
Glide Path
Ground Truth
Hot Zone
Homeland Security Exercise and Evaluation Program (HSEEP)
Improvement Plan (IP)
Integrated Preparedness Plan (IPP)
Integrated Preparedness Planning Workshop (IPPW)
International Association of Fire Chiefs (IAFC)
International Association of Fire Fighters (IAFF)
Louisiana State University (LSU)
Management and Planning (MGT)
Master Scenario Events List (MSEL)
National Center for Biological Research and Training (NCBRT)
National Domestic Preparedness Consortium (NDPC)
National Disaster Preparedness Training Center (NDPTC)
National Emergency Training Center (NETC)
National Preparedness Directorate (NPD)
National Qualification System (NQS)
National Sheriff's Association (NSA)
National Training and Education Division (NTED)
National Training and Education System (NTES)
Nevada National Security Site (NNSS)
Observer
Office of Bombing Prevention (OBP)
Operations
Operations-Based Exercises
Participant
Participant Feedback Form
Performance (PER)
Planning, Organizing, Equipping, Training, and Exercising (POETE)
Player
Player Handout
Qualification
Rural Domestic Preparedness Consortium (RDPC)
Security and Emergency Response Training Center (SERTC)

Seminars
Simulator
Situation Manual (SitMan)
Specialist
Tabletop Exercises (TTX)
Technician
Texas Engineering Extension Service (TEEX)
Transportation Technology Center, Incorporated (TTCI)
Typed
United States Fire Administration (USFA)
Video Teleconference (VTC)
Warm Zone
Workshops

Essentials of Emergency Management Training

In Chapter 8, we learned that Emergency Management is an extremely expansive topic and involves preparation to meet the ever-changing elements of society. Because hazards, risks, and threats are continually changing and evolving, Emergency Managers must embrace the life of being a student and continuously training. To provide a starting point to address the non-stop need for training, FEMA developed the Emergency Management Institute (EMI) online training courses. As of the writing of this text, EMI maintains 210 free, self-paced, Independent Study (IS) courses which are open to anyone. Further adding to the value of the online courses, FEMA partnered with Frederick Community College to provide an avenue for obtaining college credit for many of the courses and the opportunity to complete an accredited Associates Degree and transfer credit to higher-education universities.

The goals of Emergency Management training are grounded in the *National Qualification System (NQS)* and *National Incident Management System (NIMS)*. The NQS is a guiding outline for typing Emergency Managers and responders in a standardized fashion to ensure personnel are qualified to effectively and rapidly integrate with other Emergency Managers and responders from across the nation. The sheer magnitude of providing training for all Emergency Managers and responders in the United States (US) requires a national network of providers and trainers at the Federal, State, and Local government levels in coordination with non-governmental agencies.

Emergency Management Training Foundations

Every Emergency Manager has and does begin at the same point, having to take the first steps of completing the minimums in training. For those who are seeking a glide path, the **2020 *National Incident Management System Training Program*** contains a path to begin the journey. To that end, the ***National Training and Education System (NTES)*** is the network of students, providers, and higher education partners to build national resiliency and establishes a training approach built upon the four NIMS Command and Control Systems of personnel working in ICS, EOC, PIO, and MAC (Policy) Group positions.

As recommended in the NIMS Training Program, the basics of Emergency Management learned in FEMA's online courses and learning is enhanced through a variety of in-person courses. Due to the inherent dangers involved in hazardous materials response, Emergency Managers should also work towards developing a knowledge base of the incremental levels of training for HazMat to include the Awareness, Operations, Technician, and Specialist levels. Additionally, advanced level training for All-Hazards Incident Management Teams (AHIMT) including experiential documentation in task books, qualifying, certifying, and credentialing personnel to field highly qualified Emergency Managers and responders in the aftermath of catastrophic disasters should be a part of all comprehensive training programs. Finally, keeping with the NQS structure for All-Hazards training, the NQS EOC Skillsets were developed to qualify EOC personnel and Emergency Managers through a similar standardized process to that of the AHIMT.

Emergency Management Exercise Programs

Exercises are a tool to evaluate training, plans, policies, and procedures to ensure the capability to perform the necessary functions in real-world disasters and emergencies. Emergency Management exercises are distinguished between the two categories of Discussion-Based and Operations-Based exercises. Discussion-Based exercises include Seminars, Workshops, Tabletop Exercises (TTX), and Games. Operations-Based exercises include Drills, Functional Exercises (FE), and Full-Scale Exercises (FSE). Regardless of the category or type, the Homeland Security Exercise and Evaluation Program (HSEEP) is a guideline for the design and evaluation of exercises. The evaluation of exercises culminates in the development of an After-Action Report (AAR) and Improvement Plan (IP) to round out the preparedness cycle and to make meaningful advancements in disaster readiness.

In the next chapter, you will learn about a variety of State and Federal Emergency Management Grant Programs.

Chapter 9: State and Federal Emergency Management Grant Programs

Emergency Management grant programs generally are born in response to catastrophic disasters that are far beyond the ability of State, Tribal, Territorial, and Local (STTL) governments to handle without financial assistance. Some of the Federal grant programs are short-lived in terms of providing for assistance for a limited number of weeks, months, or years. However, other Federal grant programs that have been established during a single natural or manmade disaster have developed into continuing programs. This chapter will provide an overview of the Federal programs for preparedness and disaster-specific grants along with examples of how some of these grant programs have come into existence.

The devastating terrorist attacks carried out against the civilian population of New York and the United States on September 11, 2001, awakened a sense of awareness for public safety. While these cowardly actions resulted in catastrophic injury upon America, it also opened funding streams in the form of Federal grants to enhance Federal, State, Tribal, Territorial, and Local prevention of and preparedness for terrorist attacks. September 11th became referred to as 9/11 and these attacks "changed the face of homeland security as well, (and even introduced the term "homeland security" to the American lexicon), so that such a horrific act would never be repeated."[242] One Federal grant program with origins in 9/11 that continues today after two decades is the Homeland Security Grant Program (HSGP) that will be further elaborated in this chapter.

---

[242] (Post 9/11 Federal Grants, n.d.)

Four years later, Hurricane Katrina ravaged the Gulf coast communities in several States, particularly in New Orleans, at the end of August in 2005. As was documented in Chapter 1, one result of the identified challenges associated with Hurricane Katrina was the development of the *Post-Katrina Emergency Management Reform Act* (PKEMRA) or Public Law 109-295. Sections 661 and 662 of the PKEMRA pertain specifically to grant funding as an outpouring to address response and recovery issues identified in the Act. Emergency Management Assistance Compact (EMAC) grants totaling $4,000,000 were appropriated in 2008 "to assist State and local governments, emergency response providers, and organizations representing such providers with credentialing emergency response providers and the typing of emergency response resources"[243] and $175,000,000 in Emergency Management Performance Grants (EMPG). EMAC is an all-hazards and all-disciplines compact for mutual aid and "offers assistance during governor-declared states of emergency or disaster through a responsive, straightforward system that allows states to send personnel, equipment, and commodities to assist with response and recovery efforts in other states."[244]

Another surge of Federal grant funding came in response to Super Storm Sandy that crippled East coast communities in 2012. Through the *Sandy Recovery Improvement Act (SRIA)* of 2013 or Public Law 113-2, Congress appropriated in excess of $50 billion that was shared across all affected States. Grants were authorized for a wide range of programs, including "grants for public assistance permanent work projects on the basis of fixed estimates for the timely or cost-effective completion of work."[245] This grant funding made it possible for numerous communities to rebuild infrastructure and homes in the wake of Super Storm Sandy.

More recently, the "*Coronavirus Aid, Relief, and Economic Security (CARES) Act (2020)* and the *Coronavirus Response and Consolidated Appropriations Act (2021)* provided fast and direct economic assistance for American workers, families,

---

[243] (Congress, October 4 2006)
[244] ((EMAC), n.d.)
[245] (FEMA, Sandy Recovery Improvement Act of 2013, 2021)

small businesses, and industries."[246] The ***Coronavirus Aid, Relief and Economic Security (CARES) Act*** of 2020 provided $2.2 trillion dollars in assistance to COVID-19 and the ***Coronavirus Response and Consolidated Appropriations Act*** of 2021 provided an additional $2.3 trillion. No one can estimate how long it will take to calculate the total costs of COVID-19 across all Federal, State, Tribal, Territorial, and Local governments and the private sector. It may very well take several years to see the end of the tunnel on these costs and the financial impact will be felt within the United States for generations.

With the exception of the grant funding for COVID-19, the amount of annual preparedness grant funding has decreased every year over the past many years. Post 9/11 grant funding skyrocketed, especially in the larger urban metropolitan areas of the country. However, in the years since and as time has passed from the terrorist attack on New York and the U.S., the concern over funding to protect against terrorism has dwindled. Similarly, as presented in Chapter 7, FEMA has already signaled that a change is coming in the formula for determining the State and County thresholds and thereby reducing the amount of disaster-related grant funding available across the entire nation and that trend is most likely going to continue because it is not economically feasible for the United States to continue to provide massive grant funding year after year. The impact of COVID-19 grant funding, in conjunction with preparedness and disaster-related grant funding, is adding trillions of dollars in national debt that will have to be re-paid at some point.

Overview of Emergency Management Grant Programs

While the roots of many Emergency Management grant programs are found in some of the worst catastrophes in the history of the United States, there is so much more to grant development and structures. One important fact to understand is that grants do not stand alone. All Emergency Management grants are founded

---

[246] (Treasury, n.d.)

upon the tenets of, wait for it, Emergency Management. Yes, grants are yet another example of how all of the foundational knowledge of Emergency Management is so vital to successful professionals in the field and, as will be evident, all that has been previously covered in this text is integral to Emergency Management grants.

When it comes to procuring grant funded services or supplies, evaluating grant needs is not simply cherry picking from the latest list of flashy fashions or supposed trends in Emergency Management. Oh, but there are plenty of vendors who are gambling upon impressing or influencing Emergency Managers to purchase equipment, programs, and technology based on no more than appearance and a desire to have the newest toy. Don't be swayed by the smiles and platitudes of every salesperson who comes along. Remember that first and foremost all vendors are in business to sell us their wares. However, that doesn't mean that all vendors are disreputable or not to be trusted. Many vendors have a proven track record of dedicated support to Emergency Management operations. And the best vendors will investigate how to be a positive impact on Emergency Management programs before making their first sales pitch.

So, if we don't want to be led around by the nose chasing the newest and shiniest products and services, how does a professional Emergency Manager select appropriate grant projects? Start by crafting "a detailed plan considering all aspects of the endeavor to be funded and how performance will be evaluated."[247] Emergency Managers can develop this plan by reviewing community history, existing strategic plans, and the jurisdictional hazards. In this manner, grant project will be built upon realistic need and not perceived need. As will be discovered in this chapter, Federal and State Emergency Management grants require documentation to prove eligibility and to assure that funding is applied to project that will have a positive impact on the communities receiving funding.

---

[247] (FEMA, Fact Sheet: A Guide to Grant Writing for Resources or Recovery Assistance, 2021)

The Intersection of Emergency Management Grants and the National Preparedness Goal

As introduced in Chapter 4, the National Preparedness Goal is achieved by implementing the National Preparedness System. One component of the system entails estimating capability requirements in relation to the five mission areas of prevention, protection, mitigation, response, and recovery. The mission areas then become the basis for developing strategic plans, conducting training, writing and evaluating exercises, and formulating an effective Emergency Management grant program.

Generally speaking, there are two broad categories of Emergency Management grants; the first are the grants designated for preparedness and the second are those that are disaster related. Both categories are aligned with the five mission areas of the National Preparedness System (see Figure 7 below). Preparedness grants relate specifically to the prevention and protection mission areas; more will be addressed on preparedness grants. Then disaster related grants, some of which were presented in Chapter 7 as elements of the Presidentially declared disaster process, pertain to the mitigation, response, and recovery mission areas.

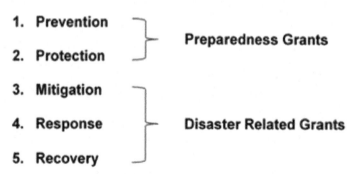

Figure 7: Mission Areas and Grants (Chadwick)

Strategic Plans Provide a Basis for Preparedness Grant Projects

While it can be argued that every emergency operations plan (EOP) is an important element for preparedness grant project management, the Threat and Hazard Identification and Risk Assessment (THIRA) and the Stakeholder Preparedness Review (SPR) are crucial components in grant management. Both the THIRA and the SPR were covered in Chapter 4 and these strategic plans focus on terrorism related threats and are the cornerstone for preparedness grants. The concept is that preparedness grant projects will work towards preventing against and protecting from the impact of potential terrorist acts in communities within our nation.

As a reminder, the THIRA Three Step Process is to identify threats and hazards, contextualize the threats, and then establish target capabilities to address the threats. The THIRA identified threats provide one mechanism for identifying equipment, services, and supplies that can positively enhance a jurisdiction's capabilities and serve as potential grant projects. Additionally, the related SPR provides a second mechanism for formulating effective grant projects. The SPR process of assessing capabilities, identifying and addressing community capability gaps, and determining impacts of potential funding sources is an exemplary example of how to identify potential grant projects to strengthen our communities.

Continuing the theme of strategic planning, in September of 2019, the Department of Homeland Security (DHS) adopted the *Strategic Framework for Countering Terrorism and Targeted Violence* (CTTV Framework) that contains the "vision for reinvesting in programs and efforts that have enhanced our security, while incorporating key strategic changes that will allow us to address the threats we currently face."[248] In conjunction with the CCTV Framework, DHS developed a

---

[248] (Security, Strategic Framework for Countering Terrorism and Targeted Violence , September 2019)

corresponding Public Action Plan and an internal Implementation Plan. The three DHS documents define actions and progressive steps to achieve the goals of the CCTV Framework. The CCTV Framework identifies four goals to address potential terrorism and *targeted violence* which is defined as *"any incident of violence that implicates homeland security and/or DHS activities in which a known or knowable attacker selects a particular target prior to the violent attack."*[249] The four goals of the CCTV Framework are:

1. **Goal 1:** Understand the Evolving Terrorism and Targeted Violence Threat Environment, and Supporting Partners in the Homeland Security Enterprise Through Specialized Knowledge.
2. **Goal 2:** Prevent Terrorists and Other Hostile Actors from Entering the United States, and Deny Them the Opportunity to Exploit the Nation's Trade, Immigration, and Domestic and International Travel Systems.
3. **Goal 3:** Prevent Terrorism and Targeted Violence.
4. **Goal 4:** Enhance U.S. Infrastructure Protections and Community Preparedness.

Regional Homeland Security Grant Management

When it comes to regional grant management, my experience is based upon how grants are managed regionally in Texas. Differences may exist from State to State, therefore new or prospective Emergency Managers should investigate how grants are managed within their specific State. In Texas, preparedness grants are initially managed through the Council of Governments (COG), sometimes referred to as the Regional Council. *"A COG is an association that consists of elected public officials who come from the major local governments within an urban or metropolitan area."*[250] Elected officials or their designated representative make up

---

[249] (Security, Strategic Framework for Countering Terrorism and Targeted Violence: Public Action Plan, September 2020)
[250] (Vlassis, 2007)

the Regional Emergency Preparedness Advisory Committee (REPAC) and one of their functions is to receive grant project proposals, rank the proposals in order of priority for the region, and then approve funding for the grant projects selected. "Projects must address capability targets and gaps identified during the Threat and Hazard Identification and Risk Assessment (THIRA) process and are assessed in the Stakeholder Preparedness Review (SPR)."[251] Often the grant projects that focus on supporting the needs of the region, as opposed to just benefitting a single jurisdiction, will be scored higher on the ranking of projects approved for grant funding.

Once preparedness grant projects are approved, first by the region and then by the State, funds are released to the local government making the funding request. From that point, the authority having jurisdiction (AHJ) will administer the grant funds and the State will audit the expenses to ensure funds are only expended on authorized purchases. Furthermore, the State may conduct annual audits of grant funded equipment for several years and any plans for sale or redistribution of grant funded equipment must be approved by the State. Think of grant funding as the "carrot and the stick." The "carrot" is the offer of "free" money in the form of Federal grants. However, the "stick" is that the State and Local governments must strictly adhere to the requirements of administering the funding in accordance with the project proposals and the equipment and supplies which are purchased under grant funding must be inventoried and remain accountable through the entire grant cycle.

State and Federal Preparedness Grant Programs

States, Tribal, and Territorial governments are the primary recipients of preparedness grants and, in turn, these funds are further allocated in varying proportions across the regions based upon established criteria. Typically, the larger

---

[251] (Homeland Security Grant Information, n.d.)

and more urban regions will receive the bulk of the preparedness grant funding because those regions contain more critical infrastructure and are considered to be more susceptible to acts of terrorism. Higher concentration population densities combined with large numbers of critical infrastructure will be two of the major criteria for determining distribution of preparedness grants. This does not prohibit rural communities from receiving preparedness grants, however fewer funds will be allocated to less populated regions with minimal critical infrastructure.

Ultimately, "FEMA has the statutory authority to deliver numerous disaster and non-disaster financial assistance programs in support of its mission, and that of the Department of Homeland Security, largely through grants and cooperative agreements."[252] The important take away here is that statutes or laws are the driving force behind Federal preparedness grants. The manner in which grant funding is budgeted by Congress, the distribution of funds across the entire nation, and the accountability and administration of Federal preparedness grants is pursuant to Federal laws and regulations. That said, current or prospective Emergency Managers must comprehend the applicable laws to be successful in obtaining and managing preparedness grants. Mismanagement of preparedness grants, whether intentional or unintentional, can easily result in legal repercussions and the loss of Federal funding for a jurisdiction. The long-term impact from loss of jurisdictional integrity can result in the administering councils or committees responsible for distributing funding to completely discount those jurisdictions from future preparedness grant project consideration.

The Preparedness Grant Process

The first thing to understand is that there are some types of equipment or services that are prohibited from being purchased utilizing preparedness grant funding. A couple of examples of prohibited purchases are telecommunications and

---

[252] (FEMA, FEMA Preparedness Grants Manual, Version 2, February 2021)

video surveillance equipment or services produced by Huawei, ZTE, Hytera, Hangzhou, and Dahua or any subsidiary or affiliate. These prohibitions are mandated in the *John S. McCain National Defense Authorization Act for Fiscal Year 2019* (FY2019 NDAA). Other restrictions may be applied at the State or Local level to how preparedness funds are utilized. It is incumbent upon all Emergency Managers to consult the Authorized Equipment List (AEL) prior to investing considerable time and effort formulating a grant proposal that is prohibited by law. "The Authorized Equipment List (AEL) is a list of approved equipment types allowed under FEMA's preparedness grant programs."[253] Purchases of equipment not included on the AEL must be pre-approved by FEMA. Recipients are also required to verify that potential vendors have not been barred from doing business by the State or Federal government and that contracted services comply with Environmental Planning and Historic Preservation (EHP).

After allowable grant projects have been selected, the jurisdiction will need to prepare and submit a grant application through the appropriate system utilized within the State prior to the established deadline and for the relevant grant program Notice of Funding Opportunity (NOFO). "FEMA will not review applications that are received after the deadline nor will it consider these late applications for funding."[254] Extensions may be granted by FEMA when good cause is justified, however it is the applicant's responsibility to justify the purpose for the extension based on issues such as technical problems, exigent circumstances, or statutory requirements. However, extensions will not be granted automatically. Applicants are required to receive a Unique Entity Identifier and register in the System for Award Management (SAM) or State system to submit a grant application. Applicants failing to comply with any of the steps required to submit an application prior to the deadline may be disqualified from grant project consideration. The steps for a grant applicant to follow are:

---

[253] (FEMA, FEMA Preparedness Grants Manual, February 2020)
[254] (FEMA, FEMA Preparedness Grants Manual, Version 2, February 2021)

1. "Apply for, update, or verify their Data Universal Numbering System (DUNS) number from Dun & Bradstreet and Employer Identification Number (EIN) from the Internal Revenue Service;
2. In the application, provide a valid DUNS number, which is currently the unique entity identifier;
3. Have an account with login.gov;
4. Register for, update, or verify their System for Award Management (SAM) account and ensure the account is active before submitting the application;
5. Create a Grants.gov account;
6. Add a profile to a Grants.gov account;
7. Establish an Authorized Organizational Representative (AOR) in Grants.gov;
8. Register in the Non-Disaster Grants Management System (ND) Grants;
9. Submit an initial application in Grants.gov;
10. Submit the final application in ND Grants, including electronically signing applicable forms; and
11. Continue to maintain an active SAM registration with current information at all times during which it has an active federal award or an application or plan under consideration by a federal awarding agency."[255]

During the post award period of a grant, applicants and grant expenditures will be monitored and audited by both the State, Tribal, and Territorial government and FEMA to ensure compliance with applicable regulations, laws, grant guidance, and the terms and conditions of the award. Awards may be terminated in part of whole by FEMA for noncompliance, with consent of the recipient, or when requested by the recipient. Finally, all financial records and documentation pertinent to the grant award must be retained for at least three years from the close out of the grant and local policies may mandate longer terms of retention.

---

[255] (FEMA, FEMA Preparedness Grants Manual, Version 2, February 2021)

Grant Funding Supporting National Campaigns and Programs

A number of national campaigns and programs are supported by Federal preparedness grant funding. Among those programs generally supported are Active Shooter Preparedness, Community Lifelines, Soft Targets and Crowded Places, Strategic Framework for Countering Terrorism and Targeted Violence, and Whole Community Preparedness. Most of these campaigns or programs have been presented at various points throughout this text, however we will briefly review them individually from a grant funding perspective.

1. **Active Shooter Preparedness**: In an effort to enhance whole community preparedness, DHS and FEMA may authorize funding for products, resources, and tools to prepare for and respond to active shooter incidents.

2. **Community Lifelines**: Preparedness grant projects related to Community Lifelines enhance continuity of government and sustaining critical services to improve economic security, human health, and safety during and after disasters.

3. **Soft Targets and Crowded Places (ST-CP)**: "ST-CPs are those locations or environments that are easily accessible to large numbers of people on a predictable or semi-predictable basis that have limited security or protective measures in place."[256] Preparedness grants can be utilized to address the unique challenges associated with protecting soft targets and crowded places.

4. **Strategic Framework for Countering Terrorism and Targeted Violence (CTTV)**: Counterterrorism is a core priority of the Department of Homeland Security (DHS) and preparedness grants support efforts to detect, prevent, protect against, and mitigate terrorism and targeted violence.

---

[256] (FEMA, FEMA Preparedness Grants Manual, February 2020)

5. **Whole Community Preparedness**: The entire concept of whole community preparedness revolves around the understanding that protecting our communities requires the teamwork of all levels of government, faith-based organizations, the private sector, and individuals and families. Preparedness grants can be utilized to improve all facets of whole community preparedness.

National Preparedness Goal Grant Alignment

When it comes to the grants that are aligned with the National Preparedness Goal, there are numerous major preparedness grants to be reviewed. As a reminder, the goal is succinctly stated, "A secure and resilient Nation with the capabilities required across the whole community to prevent, protect against, mitigate, respond to, and recover from the threats and hazards that pose the greatest risk."[257] This brief and concise statement is a foundation for all of the preparedness grants that are developed to achieve the goal. The review of the preparedness grants, in support of the Goal, will begin with the Emergency Management Performance Grant (EMPG) and move on to the Homeland Security Grant Program (HSGP), and then end off with Terrorism- and Transportation-Specific Grant Programs.

1. **Emergency Management Performance Grant (EMPG)**: "The purpose of the Emergency Management Performance Grant (EMPG) Program is to provide Federal funds to states to assist state, local, territorial, and tribal governments in preparing for all hazards."[258] Like disaster related grants, later in this chapter; the EMPG program employs a cost share match component. For 2021, EMPG utilizes a 50/50 cost share where 50% is the Federal portion and the remaining 50% is non-Federal cash or in-kind match. As with all Federal grants, there are restrictions on using EMPG funds for items such as Small Unmanned Aircraft Systems (SUAS). "All

---

[257] (FEMA, National Preparedness Goal, 2020)
[258] (TDEM, Emergency Management Performance Grant, n.d.)

requests to purchase Small Unmanned Aircraft Systems (SUAS) must comply with Information Bulletin (IB) 426 and must include the policies and procedures in place to safeguard individuals' privacy, civil rights, and civil liberties in the jurisdiction that will purchase, take title to, or otherwise use the SUAS equipment."[259]

2. **Homeland Security Grant Program (HSGP)**: "The Homeland Security Grant includes a suite of risk-based grants to assist state, local, tribal and territorial efforts in preventing, protecting against, mitigating, responding to and recovering from acts of terrorism and other threats."[260] As a component of DHS preparedness grants, HSGP funding supports the national prioritization to support specific major urban areas and State fusion centers in addition to building and sustaining core capabilities. HSGP is comprised of three individual grant programs funding preparedness to meet the five mission areas and thirty-two core capabilities.

   - **Operation Stone Garden (OPSG)**: "The OPSG Program supports enhanced cooperation and coordination among Customs and Border Protection (CBP), United States Border Patrol (USBP), and local, Tribal, territorial, state, and Federal law enforcement agencies."[261] OPSG funds efforts to secure U.S. international borders and water borders. These grant funds are awarded to State Administrative Agencies (SAAs) of Border States and then State, Local, and Tribal law enforcement organizations can apply as sub-recipients. OPSG funding targets improving law enforcement operational capabilities in States bordering Canada, Mexico, and those States with international water borders.

   - **State Homeland Security Program (SHSP)**: "The State Homeland Security Program (SHSP) is a core assistance program that provides funds to build capabilities at the State, local, tribal, and territorial

---

[259] (TDEM, Emergency Management Performance Grant, FY2021 Grant Guidance, 2021)
[260] (FEMA, Homeland Security Grant Program, 2021)
[261] (Operation Stonegarden (OPSG) Program, n.d.)

levels, to enhance our national resilience to absorb disruptions and rapidly recover from incidents both natural and manmade as well as to implement the goals and objectives included in State homeland security strategies and initiatives in their State Preparedness Report (SPR)."[262] SHSP funds are allocated only for terrorism preparedness and all proposed grant projects must focus on preventing, protecting against, mitigating, responding to, and recovering from terrorist incidents. While SHSP supports terrorism preparedness, the efforts employed by the grant funding can also support all-hazards preparedness and grant recipients are required to illustrate how project proposals serve this dual use of grant funds. SHSP funding is awarded to State Administrative Agencies (SAAs) for all States and U.S. Territories. In turn, law enforcement, public safety, and non-profit organizations may apply as sub-recipients through their respective States.

- **Urban Area Security Initiative (UASI)**: "The UASI program is intended to provide financial assistance to address the unique multi-discipline planning, organization, equipment, training, and exercise needs of high-threat, high-density Urban Areas, and to assist these areas in building and sustaining capabilities to prevent, protect against, mitigate, respond to, and recover from threats or acts of terrorism using the Whole Community approach."[263] Like SHSP grants, UASI funds must address terrorism preparedness and serve the dual purpose of meeting the concerns of all-hazards preparedness. The main difference is that UASI grants are only awarded to high-density Urban areas. Initially, UASI grants are awarded to State Administrative Agencies (SAAs) and then law enforcement, public safety, and non-profit organizations may apply as sub-recipients.

---

[262] (State Homeland Security Program (SHSP), n.d.)
[263] (Urban Area Security Initiative (UASI) Program, n.d.)

3. **Additional Terrorism-Specific Preparedness Grant Programs**: In addition to HSGP, the Nonprofit Security Grant Program (NSGP) and the Tribal Homeland Security Grant Program (THSGP) are focused on the enhancement of State, Local, Tribal, and Territorial (SLTT) along with nonprofit agencies in prevention of, protection against, response to, and recovery from potential terrorism and all-hazards incidents. Congress authorizes these preparedness grant programs to strengthen our communities in a comprehensive manner. They provide an overlapping approach with HSGP emphasizing State and Local communities, NSGP highlighting high-risk nonprofit agencies, and THSGP supporting Tribal communities.

- **Nonprofit Security Grant Program (NSGP)**: The State Administrative Agencies (SAAs) are the only agencies eligible to apply for NSGP grants to assist eligible nonprofit organizations that are identified as being at high risk of potential terrorist attacks. "Eligible nonprofit organizations are those organizations described under section 501(c)(3) of the *Internal Revenue Code of 1986, Title 26 of the U.S.C.*, and exempt from tax under section 501(a) of such Code."[264] These nonprofit agencies are required to be located within one of the UASI designated urban areas.

- **Tribal Homeland Security Grant Program (THSGP)**: Recipients of THSGP funds must be identified as directly eligible tribal governments that are federally recognized as meeting the criteria contained within Section 2001 of the *Homeland Security Act of 2002*. "Among these eligibility criteria, a tribe can qualify as a directly eligible tribe if it is located on or near an international border or a coastline bordering an ocean or international waters, along with meeting other required criteria."[265] Additionally, tribes located within 100 miles of an international border or ocean coastline may qualify.

---

[264] (FEMA, Fiscal Year 2021 Nonprofit Security Grant Program (NSGP), 2021)
[265] (FEMA, Fiscal Year 2021 Tribal Homeland Security Grant Program (THSGP), 2021)

4. **Transportation-Specific Preparedness Grant Programs**: There are four transportation infrastructure grant programs designed to promote sustainability and risk-based security efforts to protect the public while traveling against terrorist acts. The transportation-specific programs are the Intercity Bus Security Grant Program (IBSGP), Intercity Passenger Rail (IPR) Program, Port Security Grant Program (PSGP), and the Transit Security Grant Program (TSGP). Each of these programs covers a very specific layer of transportation infrastructure.

- **Intercity Bus Security Grant Program (IBSGP)**: "Eligible applicants under the FY 2021 IBSGP are private operators providing transportation by an over-the-road bus that have completed a vulnerability assessment and developed a security plan that the DHS Secretary has approved as described in Section 1531 of the ***Implementing Recommendations of the 9/11 Commission Act of 2007***."[266] To be considered eligible, private transportation buses must meet either one or both of the criteria of operating a fixed-route intercity bus service within one or more UASI areas and/or operate a charter over-the-road bus service providing at least 50 annual trips to one or more UASI areas.

- **Intercity Passenger Rail (IPR) Program**: "The National Railroad Passenger Corporation (Amtrak) is the only entity eligible to apply for funding under the IPR Program."[267] The IPR program establishes three National Priority Areas and minimum spending requirements for Amtrak. The priority areas are to enhance cybersecurity, enhance the protection of Soft Targets and Crowded Places (ST-CP) and allotting 5% of grant funding for this effort, and to address emerging threats through an additional 5% of funding.

- **Port Security Grant Program (PSGP)**: "PSGP is focused on supporting increased maritime cybersecurity, port-wide maritime security risk

---

[266] (FEMA, Fiscal Year 2021 Intercity Bus Security Grant Program (IBSGP), 2021)
[267] (FEMA, Fiscal Year 2021 Intercity Passenger Rail (IPR) Program, 2021)

management, enhancing maritime domain awareness, supporting maritime security training and exercises, and maintaining or reestablishing maritime security mitigation protocols that support port recovery and resiliency capabilities."[268] PSGP grant funding must be utilized to address port security vulnerabilities identified by the U.S. Coast Guard (USCG) and the Area Maritime Security Committee (AMSC). Facility operators, port authorities, and State and Local governments subject to a Maritime Security Plan, as defined in *46 U.S.C. § 70103(b)* are eligible applicants.

- **Transit Security Grant Program (TSGP)**: "Eligible transit agencies are determined based on daily unlinked passenger trips (ridership) and transit systems that serve historically eligible Urban Area Security Initiative (UASI)-designated urban areas."[269] While certain ferry system operators may be eligible recipients, the ferry systems that choose to participate in the TSGP program are not eligible to also receive PSGP funding.

State & Federal Disaster Related Grant Programs

Switching gears from preparedness grants that primarily pertain to the prevention and protection mission areas, disaster related grants are directly related to the mitigation, response, and recovery mission areas. Previously, in Chapter 7, we partially covered Individual Assistance (IA) grants, Public Assistance (PA) grants, and the Hazard Mitigation Grant Program (HMGP) funding under Presidentially declared disasters. In this section, we will review the IA, PA, and Hazard Mitigation Assistance (HMA) processes along with investigating the Fire Management Assistance Grant (FMAG) program and the FMAG process.

---

[268] (FEMA, Fiscal Year 2021 Port Security Grant Program (PSGP), 2021)
[269] (FEMA, Fiscal Year 2021 Transit Security Grant Program (TSGP), 2021)

As has been demonstrated in most of the Federal grant programs, disaster related grants are initially awarded to State, Tribal, and Territorial governments. Local governments, authorized State agencies, and eligible nonprofit organizations may then apply as sub-recipients to the grant under the management of the award recipient. The end result is that Federal, State, Tribal, Territorial, and Local governments work collaboratively to manage all disaster related grants in support of impacted communities across the nation.

Individual Assistance (IA) Grant Process

The FEMA Individual's and Households Program assistance process begins with the disaster survivor's application. After a Presidentially declared disaster, FEMA works with the State, Tribal, and Territorial governments to identify the Individual Assistance (IA) designated areas, establishes the initial registration period, and provides multiple methods for disaster survivors to apply for assistance. FEMA offers four options for disaster survivors to apply for assistance:

1. Disaster survivors may apply on the internet at www.disasterassistance.gov or by Smartphone after downloading FEMA's application from www.fema.gov or through the mobile application store.
2. Disaster survivors may apply by toll-free telephone at 800-621-3362, through Text Telephone (TTY) for hearing and speech disabled disaster survivors at 800-462-7585, or for those using Video Relay Service (VRS) at 800-621-3362.
3. Disaster survivors may apply in-person at a Disaster Recovery Center (DRC) in or near their disaster impacted community. "FEMA and applicable STT governments and communities work together to quickly

establish DRCs in convenient locations within an area impacted by a disaster."[270]

4. Or FEMA may send Disaster Survivor Assistance (DSA) teams into disaster impacted communities to help survivors apply for assistance in coordination with representatives from the State, Tribal, Territorial, and Local governments.

The disaster registration period is divided between the initial, extension, and late registration periods. It all begins with the date of the Presidential declaration and the date of the IA designation within the declaration. The initial registration period is 60 days from the date of the declaration and the IA designation. When requested by State, Tribal, and Territorial governments, FEMA may extend the registration period. Extensions may be granted under situations such as the need to establish deadlines for multiple contiguous disaster impact areas, high volume registrations, barriers to registration like loss of electricity, also the FEMA Regional Administrator or their designees may approve an extension for up to 60 days, and subsequent extensions are required to be approved by the FEMA IA Division Director (IADD). Lastly, FEMA will allow up to an additional 60 days as a grace period for late registrations. However, no applications will be accepted beyond the grace period and all late registrations must be accompanied by a letter and documentation from the applicant justifying claims of extenuating circumstances.

Applicants registering for IA disaster assistance are required to declare and self-certify, under penalty of perjury, that they are U.S. citizens, non-citizen nationals, qualified aliens, or parents or guardians of minors meeting those same criteria and to acknowledge the *Privacy Act* terms and make a Declaration of Eligibility. Additionally, applicants must provide their name and Social Security Number (SSN) and that of secondary or co-applicants, both current and pre-disaster addresses, names of all household occupants, contact information, household insurance information, pre-disaster annual household income, documented disaster losses, and direct deposit banking account information.

---

[270] (FEMA, Individual Assistance Program and Policy Guide (IAPPG), Version 1.1, May 2021)

The next step in the process is for FEMA to verify the applicant's loss claims. FEMA standardizes loss verification by conducting onsite inspections, geospatial inspections, and by inspecting the applicant's documentation. At the discretion of FEMA, alternate methods of verification may be employed. Onsite inspections are conducted by contract inspectors who assess damages, but contractors do not determine IA funding eligibility. Geospatial inspections are conducted utilizing various techniques and technology, including aerial and satellite imagery and remote sensing technology. Geospatial inspections provide the ability to rapidly inspect widespread impact areas and to expedite the delivery of assistance. In most circumstances, FEMA will require applicants to provide documentation to substantiate disaster losses. Bills, contracts, estimates, and receipts for medical or dental services, durable medical equipment (DME), childcare, moving and storage, vehicle repairs, and damages to wells or septic systems and furnaces are some of the examples of the types of documentation that may be required by FEMA.

FEMA normally communicates with applicants directly in order to protect personally identifiable information (PII). In those instances where it is necessary to share an applicant's PII with a third party, the Privacy Act requires FEMA to first obtain written consent from the applicant. "FEMA may accept a Power of Attorney, Guardianship, or Conservatorship documentation from an applicant's assigned third party if it meets the state law requirements where the applicant resides."[271] The FEMA Office of Chief Counsel may be called upon to validate the documentation provided to assure compliance with the Privacy Act prior to the release of PII to a third party. Communications in the form of emails, electronic messages via the FEMA disaster assistance website, or letters sent through the U.S. Postal Service (USPS) may be sent to make eligibility notifications, advise applicants on the authorized use of IA funds, respond to appeals, and to request further information.

Unique circumstances may arise when attempting to deliver Federal assistance for insular U.S. Territories and remote locations in areas like the interior of Alaska. In those cases, FEMA may develop alternate methods to identify remote

---

[271] (FEMA, Individual Assistance Program and Policy Guide (IAPPG), Version 1.1, May 2021)

property locations utilizing Global Positioning System (GPS) coordinates, deploy teams with unique logistical support, consider financial loss for survival supplies, manually review cases where automated systems are not available, and approve the increased cost of shipping materials to remote areas. Additionally, FEMA must recognize the unique sovereignty and rights of Tribal governments respective of their capability to request a Presidential disaster declaration without regards to any State request, selection of forms of requested assistance (IA, PA, HMGP, etc...), the identification of potential obstacles to standard procedures and needed modifications, and similar issues as those for other insular and remote areas.

Public Assistance (PA) Grant Process

FEMA's public assistance (PA) grant process is concisely represented in the PA Grant Life Cycle (see Figure 7), and it all begins with pre-disaster preparedness. Everything a jurisdiction does before a disaster strikes makes up preparedness. The Department of Homeland Security defines preparedness as *"a continuous cycle of planning, organizing, training, equipping, exercising, evaluating, and taking corrective action in an effort to ensure effective coordination during incident response."*[272] All of the efforts engaged in developing emergency operation plans, building organizational structures, training personnel on the plans, identifying and procuring equipment, conducting exercises, correcting any areas for improvement, and then starting it over again and again is how we prepare for the inevitability of a disaster.

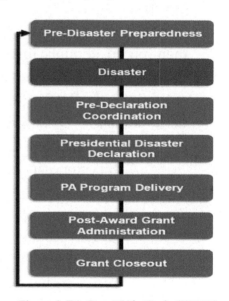

Figure 8: PA Grant Life Cycle (FEMA)

---

[272] (DHS, 2012)

Once a disaster occurs the collaboration at the Local, Regional, and State levels scales up rapidly. As has been previously provided in this text, all disasters begin and end locally. Initially, the Local jurisdiction responds utilizing their resources along with mutual aid. When a disaster exceeds the local capability, the senior elected official may issue a Local disaster declaration and request State assistance. In turn, the Governor of the State may issue a State disaster declaration to be reviewed by FEMA prior to being forwarded to the President of the United States requesting assistance. After the Presidential declaration is issued, numerous actions will take place in throughout the public assistance process and will be presented in the remainder of this chapter.

Emergency response will quickly be followed by damage assessments to determine the extent of damages to residential homes, businesses, and public (governmental) facilities. This is the beginning of the PA grant process and none of these steps can be overlooked. During the public facility damage assessments, the Local government will utilize their personnel to evaluate and document damages to government buildings, bridges, roads, and parks. The financial cost to repair damaged public facilities is calculated and submitted to the State and the State will then roll up all public financial damages across the State to FEMA. When the Presidential declaration is issued and public assistance (PA) grant funds are authorized, the PA Program Delivery process may begin as prescribed in the declaration. The PA Program Delivery is divided into four phases:

- **Phase I – Operational Planning and Applicant Coordination:** "Key milestones include conducting all Applicant Briefings, receiving and processing all Requests for Public Assistance (RPAs), and completing all Recovery Scoping Meetings."[273] The *recipient, pass-through entity*, is usually a State, Tribal, or Territorial government; however, Tribal governments may elect to apply as either a direct recipient or sub-recipient, but not both. During this phase, the recipient will provide the Applicant Briefing to explain deadlines, eligibility criteria, funding, hazard mitigation, alternate procedures, compliance issues, and

---

[273] (FEMA, Public Assistance Program and Policy Guide, Version 4, June 1, 2020)

requirements for documentation and recordkeeping. Another integral part of this phase is the Recovery Scoping Meeting to ensure applicants gather the necessary damage information and prioritize needs for assistance, understand the importance of listing all impacts, provide all required documentation, and include the appropriate attendees.

- **Phase II – Impacts and Eligibility:** Phase II revolves around the work categories of Emergency Work and Permanent Work, as presented in Chapter 7, and the PA policy covering facility eligibility. Emergency Work includes debris removal and protective measures taken to address immediate threats. The other side of the coin is Permanent Work to restore and protect buildings, bridges, roads, parks, utilities, and water control systems. In this phase, "the applicant is required to identify and report all of its incident-related impacts to FEMA within 60 days of the Recovery Scoping Meeting."[274] Work is then accurately grouped, PA grant projects are formulated, site inspections are conducted, and documentation is compiled.

- **Phase III – Scoping and Costing:** The third phase begins after FEMA, the recipient, and grant applicant have agreed upon the descriptions and dimensions of damage. At this point, the applicant will submit a Scope of Work (SOW) and calculated cost estimate for review and approval by FEMA. Cost estimates and historical pricing are taken into account by FEMA and, in some cases, FEMA may develop the cost estimates and contract third-party experts to review the submitted cost estimates.

- **Phase IV – Final Review and Obligation:** FEMA and the recipient will conduct the final review of projects and the Recovery Transition Meeting to transition field operations to the Regional or Recovery Office during the fourth phase. All PA project applications are first routed to the recipient to review before forwarding to FEMA for a final review to verify eligibility prior to the obligation of funding. The Recovery Transition Meeting, conducted during this phase, is the mechanism to ensure all damage

---

[274] (FEMA, Public Assistance Program and Policy Guide, Version 4, June 1, 2020)

claims are documented accurately, records retention is covered, deadlines and appeals are explained, applicants are fully knowledgeable of the terms and conditions, operations are transferred to the recipient, and concerns or questions are addressed.

In the Post-Award Grant Administration, the recipient submits the Large Project Quarterly Progress Report (QPR) to FEMA not later than 30 days from the end of each quarter. The sub-recipients submit quarterly information to the recipient on expenditures to date, project status, work progress, projected completion dates, and any delay issues for large projects that have not been completed. That information is compiled by the recipient to prepare the QPR along with reporting total disbursements, final payments, extensions, and approved completion deadlines. Additionally, recipients are required to submit a quarterly Federal Financial Status Report (FFR) to the FEMA Regional Office. One important requirement for applicants to understand in the Post-Award period is that PA funding may only be used for the approved eligible work for the project. Any changes to the scope of work (SOW) must be reported to the recipient and FEMA to be reviewed for eligibility and compliance prior to commencing work.

The last step in the PA Grant Life Cycle is the Grant Closeout or Final Reconciliation and Closeout. Recipients are required to report project-level completion in order to facilitate timely closeout of the recipient's prime award. "To initiate project-level closeout, the sub-recipient must inform the recipient that its project is complete and the date the work was completed."[275] Additionally, recipients report completion of Small Projects by submitting a Small Project Completion Certificate to FEMA certifying that sub-recipients have completed projects in accordance with the project agreement. While Large Projects are individually closed by FEMA based upon reporting submitted by the recipient. After receiving the report of actual costs from sub-recipients, within 90 days of completing work, the recipient will submit the Large Project Expenditure Report and Completion Certificate to FEMA certifying total incurred costs, completion in

---

[275] (FEMA, Public Assistance Program and Policy Guide, Version 4, June 1, 2020)

compliance with the PA grant agreement, and affirmation that all expenditures have been made in compliance with 2 C.F.R. § 200.305. The PA grant award final closeout is accomplished by the recipient submitting a final FFR and a written request to FEMA to close the PA award.

Hazard Mitigation Assistance (HMA) Grants

For FY2021, Hazard Mitigation Assistance Grants include the new Building Resilient Infrastructure and Communities (BRIC) grant that replaced the Pre-Disaster Mitigation (PDM) grant, Hazard Mitigation Grant Program (HMGP), and the Flood Mitigation Assistance (FMA) grant. BRIC grants "support states, local communities, tribes and territories as they undertake hazard mitigation projects, reducing the risks they face from disasters and natural hazards."[276] The BRIC program applies the principles of capability and capacity building, encouraging innovation, partnership development, supporting large projects, flexibility, and consistency. The BRIC grant program is designed to shift focus from a reactive Federal disaster funding process to a more proactive community resilience process. BRIC funding can be utilized for Capability and Capacity Building (C&CB) endeavors, mitigation projects, and costs associated with program management.

Many States establish fixed deadlines for sub-applicants that precede the Federal deadline for applicants. FEMA will review all applications based upon technical and qualitative criteria to determine feasibility in describing project strengths. A National Review Panel is then convened by FEMA to score the qualitative criteria and assigns BRIC sub-applications to one of three project statuses:

- **Identified for Further Review (IFFR):** This status is not an award notification; rather it is a notification that the sub-application meets the

---

[276] (FEMA, Building Resilient Infrastructure and Communities, 2021)

BRIC requirements. Applicants will then work with FEMA to ensure that sub-application pre-award activities are completed.

- **Not Selected:** The sub-application meets the HMA requirements, however, was not selected due to funding limitations. Applicants that are not selected may be allowed to re-submit their project for consideration for future BRIC, Flood Mitigation, or Hazard Mitigation grant proposals.
- **Does Not Meet HMA Requirements:** Simply, the sub-application did not meet eligibility requirements.

"FEMA's Hazard Mitigation Grant Program provides funding to state, local, tribal and territorial governments so they can rebuild in a way that reduces, or mitigates, future disaster losses in their communities"[277] after the occurrence of a presidentially declared disaster. Local jurisdictions may then apply for HMGP funding to retrofit existing structures to make them less subject to future disaster damages, conduct buy-outs of hazard prone properties, retrofit infrastructures and utilities, construct drainage project improvements, stabilize slopes, develop and adopt hazard mitigation plans, and protect water systems against floods and droughts. Funding approved after a presidential disaster declaration is based upon an estimate of the aggregate disaster related costs.

States, Tribal, and Territorial governments are eligible applicants for HMGP grants and may submit applications on behalf of homeowners, businesses, and non-profit organizations. Preliminary damage assessments conducted by Local jurisdictions aid in the determination of whether a major disaster declaration by the President is warranted and the determining the amount of assistance to be provided and to identify potential hazard mitigation projects. Local governments, special government districts, State agencies, and Tribal governments may be eligible HMGP sub-applicants. HMGP funding is subject to a required cost share, 75% Federal and 25% non-Federal. The non-Federal cost share for all sub-applicants may consist of cash, in-kind third-party services, donated materials, or any combination of the aforementioned. Then "the applicant must submit all sub-applications to

---

[277] (FEMA, Hazard Mitigation Grant Program (HMGP), 2021)

FEMA within 12 months of the date of the presidential major disaster declaration."[278]

The HMGP application process is similar to that of the PA process in that it begins with project scoping to determine feasibility, cost-effectiveness, and compliance with environmental planning and historic preservation (EHP) and other applicable regulatory compliance. Sub-applicants then refine project development by detailing the scope of work (SOW), projected timelines, cost-estimates, and cost-effectiveness. Applicants will review sub-applicant projects for eligibility prior to submission to FEMA. Then funding is then awarded to the applicant/recipient to be disbursed to the sub-applicants/sub-recipients. It is important to note that any "work started prior to FEMA review and approval is ineligible for funding."[279] After projects have been approved, the recipient will have thirty-six months to complete all projects and closeout the HMGP awards, during which FEMA verifies that the scope of work (SOW) was completed as approved during the award and that all reimbursable costs are eligible in regards to the conditions of the award.

The Flood Mitigation Assistance (FMA) grant is competitive funding provided to State, Tribal, Territorial, and Local (STTL) governments to reduce or eliminate risks associated with repetitive flood damage claims for facilities insured by the National Flood Insurance Program (NFIP). Projects are ranked by FEMA based upon cost-effectiveness and eligibility. STTLs are required by FEMA to develop and adopt a hazard mitigation plan to be considered eligible to receive hazard mitigation assistance (HMA) funding. Normally a State agency, such as the Texas Water Development Board, will administer FMA grants for their respective State.

---

[278] (FEMA, When You Apply: Things to Know and Do When Applying for Hazard Mitigation Grant Program Funds, 2021)

[279] (FEMA, After You Apply: Things to Know and Do After Applying for Hazard Mitigation Grant Program Funding, 2021)

Fire Management Assistance Grant (FMAG) Process

State, Tribal, Territorial, and Local (STTL) governments are eligible to receive Fire Management Assistance Grant (FMAG) funds to aid in mitigating, managing, and controlling fires in public or private property forests or grasslands that threaten to cause devastation that would constitute a major disaster. States initiate the Fire Management Assistance declaration process by submitting a request to the FEMA Regional Director advising that the "threat of major disaster exists." FEMA is able to expedite FMAG requests and render a decision on the request for assistance in the matter of a few hours in response to the potential imminent threat.

The FMAG program operates under a cost share, 75% Federal and 25% non-Federal, of the actual costs associated with fire damages. "Before a grant can be awarded, a State must demonstrate that total eligible costs for the declared fire meet or exceed either the individual fire cost threshold - which is applies to single fires, or the cumulative fire cost threshold, which recognizes numerous smaller fires burning throughout a State."[280] Calculation for the individual fire threshold is the greater of $100,000 or five percent times the State per capita indicator ($1.55 for FY2021) times the official State population. Cumulative fire costs are based on all declared and non-declared wildland fires occurring in a single calendar year. The threshold for cumulative fires is the greater of $500,000 or three times five percent of the State per capita times the population. Eligible costs include firefighting expenses for establishing facilities; repairing or replacing equipment; procuring materials, supplies, and tools; mobilizing and demobilizing resources; and utilizing equipment.

State or Tribal governments may serve as FMAG recipients and the recipient is the responsible party for administering the grant. With the exception of fires where both a State and Tribal government are recipients for the same fire, normally there is only one recipient per declared fire disaster. The recipient State or Tribal

---

[280] (FEMA, Fire Management Assistance Grants, 2021)

government "must have a FEMA approved State or Tribal Mitigation Plan that addresses wildfire risks and mitigation measures."[281] State or Tribal agencies, other than the recipient, along with Local government agencies may be eligible to receive FMAG sub-awards. Private businesses, non-profit organizations, and volunteer agencies are not eligible to receive FMAG funds but may be reimbursed under mutual aid agreements with sub-recipients.

Looking back over the last two decades, catastrophic terrorism, devastating disasters, and a worldwide pandemic have pushed the envelope of securing grant funding that has shaped our country. This chapter has served as an overview of preparedness grants associated with the prevention and protection mission areas and disaster related grants associated with the mitigation, response, and recovery mission areas that have grown out of historic tragedies. Preparedness grants, to strengthen our resolve against terrorism, are based on strategic plans and are managed at the regional level by Councils of Government (COGs) and support a number of National Campaigns and Programs. Whereas, disaster related State and Federal grants, to enhance community resilience, include the Individual Assistance (IA), Public Assistance (PA), Hazard Mitigation Assistance (HMA), and Fire Management Assistance Grant programs. The combination of the preparedness grants and disaster related grants comprise the State and Federal Emergency Management Grant Programs that work in conjunction to protect our citizens, property, and way of life.

---

[281] (FEMA, Fire Management Assistance Grant Program and Policy Guide, June 2021)

Chapter 9 Summary

Key Terms (Alphabetical Order)

Area Maritime Security Committee (AMSC)
Authorized Organizational Representative (AOR)
Authorized Equipment List (AEL)
Building Resilient Infrastructure and Communities (BRIC)
Capability and Capacity Building (C&CB)
Customs and Border Protection (CBP)
Coronavirus Aid, Relief and Economic Security (CARES) Act
Coronavirus Response and Consolidated Appropriations Act
Council of Governments (COG)
Data Universal Numbering System (DUNS)
Disaster Recovery Center (DRC)
Disaster Survivor Assistance (DSA)
Durable Medical Equipment (DME)
Emergency Management Performance Grant (EMPG)
Employer Identification Number (EIN)
Federal Financial Status Report (FFR)
Fire Management Assistance Grant (FMAG)
Flood Mitigation Assistance (FMA)
Hazard Mitigation Assistance (HMA)
Homeland Security Grant Program (HSGP)
IA Division Director (IADD)
Identified for Further Review (IFFR)
Information Bulletin (IB)
Intercity Bus Security Grant Program (IBSGP)
Intercity Passenger Rail (IPR) Program
Non-Disaster Grants Management System (ND)
Nonprofit Security Grant Program (NSGP)
Notice of Funding Opportunity (NOFO)
Operation Stone Garden (OPSG)
Personally Identifiable Information (PII)

Port Security Grant Program (PSGP)
Pre-Disaster Mitigation (PDM)
Quarterly Progress Report (QPR)
Recipient
Regional Emergency Preparedness Advisory Committee (REPAC)
Requests for Public Assistance (RPAs)
Scope of Work (SOW)
Small Unmanned Aircraft Systems (SUAS)
Social Security Number (SSN)
Soft Targets and Crowded Places (ST-CP)
State Administrative Agency (SAA)
State Homeland Security Program (SHSP)
State Preparedness Report (SPR)
Strategic Framework for Countering Terrorism and Targeted Violence (CTTV
    Framework)
System for Award Management (SAM)
Targeted Violence
Text Telephone (TTY)
Transit Security Grant Program (TSGP)
Tribal Homeland Security Grant Program (THSGP)
United States Border Patrol (USBP)
Urban Area Security Initiative (UASI)
U.S. Postal Service (USPS)
Video Relay Service (VRS)

Emergency Management Grant Program Overview

State and Federal Emergency Management grants are divided between preparedness grants to address prevention and protection efforts and disaster related grants that are associated with mitigation, response, and recovery efforts. Many of the grant programs have been established as a direct result of catastrophic terrorist attacks and the impacts of devastating natural disasters. Emergency Management grant funding is a product of implementing the National Preparedness

System, which requires estimating a jurisdiction's capability and capacity in relation to the five mission areas and thirty-two core capabilities.

Preparedness Grant Programs

Preparedness grants are based upon strategic plans, such as EOPs, THIRAs, SPRs, and the CCTV Framework. These grants are managed regionally through COGs or Regional Councils supporting National Campaigns and Programs that are aligned with the National Preparedness Goal. Grants falling into the preparedness category include EMPG, HSGP, OPSG, SHSP, and UASI grants. Additionally, the terrorism-specific NSGP and THSGP and the transportation-specific IBSGP, IPR, PSGP, and TSGP grants round out the preparedness grant programs.

Disaster Related Grant Programs

Disaster related grants are those that arise as the result of a major disaster impacting a jurisdiction and support mitigation, response, and recovery operations. IA grants focus on providing grant funding to homeowners and residents of disaster-stricken communities. PA grants offer funding for damaged governments or public properties. HMA grants are designed to prevent or eliminate the potential of damages caused by disasters. FMA grants are utilized for projects to reduce or eliminate the impact of repetitive flood damage claims for facilities insured by the National Flood Insurance Program. And, lastly, FMAG funds are eligible to State, Tribal, Territorial, and Local (STTL) governments to mitigate, manage, and control wildland fires.

In the next chapter, you will learn about Emergency Management Professional Credentialing programs.

Chapter 10: Emergency Management Professional Certification Programs

Emergency Management certificates and certification, like the documented history of Emergency Management presented throughout this book, is nothing new. In this chapter, we will trace the history of certifications and demonstrate that there are currently ninety-nine documented programs, not counting any additional certification programs through private-for-profit businesses. As with other professions, like medicine and law, the titles the career field of Emergency Management has evolved over time. However, when titles changed that does not negate everything that was accomplished up until that time. In Chapter 1, the field of Emergency Management was shown to have grown out of Civil Defense, National Defense, Federal disaster relief, colonial emergency response, and is even traced back to organized disaster response in Ancient Rome.

Even if we go back no further in history than the Civil Defense days, the United States has engaged in professional and public education and training dating back to 1941 with the establishment of the Office of Civil Defense (OCD). As a reminder, the entire concept of *Civil Defense* was defined as *"plans or activities organized by civilians and civilian authorities for the protection of civilian population and property in times of such disasters or emergencies as war or floods."*[282] Tens of thousands of Americans have received training and certifications every year over the past eighty plus years, not counting the training and certifications that were available preceding the OCD. Annual reports were produced by the OCD to document the developments and training and these reports were issued to Congress. By 1951 the OCD changed its name to the Federal Civil Defense

---

[282] (About the National Museum of Civil Defense: Mission and History, n.d.)

Administration (FCDA) which included the Federal Civil Defense Staff College (FCDSC) in Olney, Maryland, the Central Training School in Stillwater, Oklahoma, and the Western Training School in St. Mary's, California. The Federal agency name reverted to Office of Civil Defense (OCD) and in 1968 the Annual Report stated that "During fiscal year 1968, the OCD continued training and education activities designed to support civil defense operations nationwide at all levels of government and to provide civil defense education to the public."[283] The *1968 Annual Report* recorded that both professional and technical training was offered through the Office of Civil Defense Staff College (CDSC) in Battle Creek, Michigan, the Civil Defense University Extension Program (CDUEP), and the Civil Defense Adult Education Program (CDAEP). And for those who want to say those old civil defense programs don't apply to the field of Emergency Management and they don't even exist anymore; The American Civil Defense Association (TACDA) has continually existed from 1962 to present day with the same purpose of recognizing "our country's continued need for civil defense and the importance of personal emergency and disaster preparedness.[284]

The point to be made is that certificates, certifications, credentials, and credentialing have been in existence for generations relating to Emergency Management. With that fact firmly in mind, this chapter sets out to provide insight into the wide variety of Emergency Management credentials and certifications available, pertinent definitions, guidelines for credentialing, State certification programs, and professional association certificate programs. Another goal of including an entire chapter to certification is to provide a resource for those in the Emergency Management profession and those looking to enter the field to be able to see all of the options for certification that are presently available and to encourage people to consider working towards any of the varying levels of certification and to further their professional development.

---

[283] (OCD, 1968)
[284] (TACDA, n.d.)

The Foundations for Emergency Management Certificates and Certifications

It all boils down to the question, "What is so important about certificates and certifications in the first place?" The answer is that the process of certification is a means of validating and verifying a person's knowledge, skills, and abilities (KSA). When there is a standardized process, those who are familiar with the process can have some sense of confidence in the person who has been certified through one or more of the recognized certification programs and the certificate represents what the person should be capable of performing. The value of certifications is seen in the assessment process whereby an individual must submit proof of having completed prerequisite training, possessing the skills and abilities to perform specified tasks, and having met the requirements designated by the certifying agency. That process alone speaks volumes about the person being certified.

One criticism that has been leveled towards Emergency Managers is that there are far too many paths to enter into the profession. The truth, however, is that Emergency Management in some semblances resembles that of the field of medicine where there are general practitioners, specialists, and surgeons just to name a few. In the profession of Emergency Managers you will find exercise developers, planners, preparedness staff, trainers, and specialists among other established titles. Additionally, Emergency Managers can be found in all levels of the government, corporate, health care, higher education, private, volunteer sectors, and more and more industries are beginning to incorporate Emergency Managers into their profession. For those who take exception to the proliferation of Emergency Managers, consider the viewpoint that Emergency Management is a much stronger profession by having multiple paths of entry rather than a watered-down approach to attempt to force the profession to accept a single homogenous path. Emergency responders with backgrounds in emergency medical, fire, law enforcement, and the military who chose to transition into Emergency Management bring vital experience into the profession that cannot be replicated in a classroom setting. For these and many more reasons, the diverse paths and diverse Emergency Management positions available across the profession serve to make for safer and more secured communities across the nation.

The Difference between Certifications and Credentials

In the world of Emergency Management, certificates, certifications, credentials, and credentialing are extremely important for Emergency Managers and those seeking to enter into the career field. While some people may use the terms synonymously, these terms are actually very different yet inter-related terms. Taking these terms individually and progressively, we begin with *"certificates,"* which are ***documents that certify a person has completed the requirements for a specific course of study and is capable of performing tasks related to the topic***. Certificates are issued for courses of study that are completed and to document an individual's level of performance. Emergency Managers earn individual certificates from FEMA and other Federal agencies, State and Local Emergency Management agencies, and diverse public and private entities.

The next term to address is *"certification,"* which is *"**a formal process that recognizes and validates an individual's qualifications in a certain subject.**"*[285] Professional agencies and associations responsible for managing given courses or programs serve as certifying authorities, or certifying agencies, that attest to an individual having completed prescribed courses and achieving a baseline of knowledge to be capable of competently performing the tasks associated with the subject matter. The process of certification, however, applies not only to an individual's qualifications, but also verification of the quality of the course material and instruction. Dependent upon changes to techniques, new technology, or updates to course materials, the certifying authority may require periodic renewals of personnel to maintain certification standards.

---

[285] (NEHA, n.d.)

Continuing the investigation into these inter-related terms, Merriam-Webster defines *"credentials"* as *"testimonials or certified documents showing that a person is entitled to credit or has a right to exercise official power."*[286] A credential is a document or identification issued by an agency as proof of an individual's authority and competence to perform tasks for a given job. The credential speaks to the person being trained and equipped to properly carry out the job duties and it demonstrates to all interested parties that the person has acquired the training and experience to effectively function in a designated position. Obtaining a credential may require an individual to successfully pass a credentialing exam, provide official documentation of experience and training to be reviewed by the institute issuing the credential, and to provide documented proof of professional contributions to the field to be granted the credential.

Culminating the analysis of these terms, *"credentialing"* is a process that is defined as providing *"documentation that identifies personnel and authenticates and verifies the qualifications of such personnel by ensuring that such personnel possess a minimum common level of training, experience, physical and medical fitness, and capability appropriate for a particular position."*[287] Historically, Emergency Management credentialing has been de-centralized in that each agency or authority having jurisdiction (AHJ) has been responsible for establishing standards, approving courses of instruction, verifying prerequisite certificates, documenting acceptable experience, and issuing agency credentials in the form of identification cards or badges. Even at the Federal level with FEMA, "Each of the Agency's Cadres and ten Regions had its own approach for determining the proficiency of a Disaster Workforce member and for determining which tasks the Surge Capacity Force (Disaster Workforce) member was qualified to execute."[288]

Bringing it all together, a person can attend an Emergency Management course to receive a certificate of completion, agencies then may require completion

---

[286] (Merriam-Webster, 2021)

[287] (FEMA, National Incident Management System: Guideline for the Credentialing of Personnel, August 2011)

[288] (FEMA, FEMA Agency-Wide Disaster Workforce Credentialing Plan, April 2009)

of a series of courses along with other contributions to awarded certification, and then agencies can issue a credential as proof of the person's qualifications after the person successfully completes a prescribed peer or professional review as components of the credentialing process. The best news for Emergency Managers is that there are a myriad of options available to obtain certifications and, for many, the only cost is the investment of time. Therefore, people from all backgrounds and walks of life can earn certifications towards professional development in Emergency Management regardless of geo-location or financial status.

History of FEMA's Emergency Management Institute (EMI)

Illustrating how everything presented up to this point in Chapter 10 is linked, "The Emergency Management Institute started as the Civil Defense Staff College (CDSC) in Olney, Maryland, on April 1, 1951, and taught civil defense courses in program administration and finance, radiation monitoring and control, and heavy rescue."[289] The CDSC was relocated to Battle Creek, Michigan due to the potential threat of attacks on Washington, D.C. during the era of the Cold War. State and Local responders continued to be trained by the CDSC on civil defense operations, finance, natural disaster response, program administration, and radiological monitoring during this time. The Federal Civil Defense Administration (FCDA) was the parent organization of the CDSC and the FCDA was managed under the Department of Defense (DOD) which led to renaming the institute to the Defense Civil Preparedness Agency (DCPA) in May of 1972.

In 1979, President Jimmy Carter reorganized the entire national approach to disaster response, in the wake of the Three Mile Island nuclear reactor meltdown incident, by combining several agencies, including the DCPA, to form the Federal Emergency Management Agency (FEMA). The CDSC was subsequently relocated from Battle Creek, Michigan to Emmitsburg, Maryland in 1980 and as part of the

---

[289] (FEMA, Emergency Management Institute (EMI) Overview, n.d.)

move St. Joseph's College was closed and merged with Mount St. Mary's University in Emmitsburg to become FEMA's National Emergency Training Center (NETC). As an element of the shuffling and reorganization, the CDSC was renamed to the Emergency Management Institute (EMI) and NETC became the home to both EMI and the National Fire Academy (NFA) and has continued as such through present day. While EMI and the NFA are independently managed, the two institutes collaborate on course curriculum and program administration to train Emergency Management and responders throughout the United States. EMI celebrated its 65th anniversary in 2016 commemorating a distinguished lineage in Emergency Management training stretching back to 1951 and the forming of the Civil Defense Staff College (CDSC).

The current day mission of EMI is to provide online and residential training to enhance all level of government on prevention, preparedness, response, recovery, and mitigation operations. Residential training can be accomplished at the EMI and NFA facilities or through regional training requested by Local jurisdictions and through their respective State. The Federal government estimates that EMI provides training to more than 30,000 people in residence and in excess of 1.9 million people online annually. This is the result of the fact that "EMI offers a full-spectrum emergency management curriculum with more than 600 active courses available to the integrated emergency management community, which includes: FEMA staff and disaster employees; Federal partners; state, local, and tribal emergency managers; volunteer organizations; and first responders from across the nation."[290] Additionally, EMI is fully accredited by both the American Council on Education (ACE) and the International Association for Continuing Education and Training (IACET) and maintains relationships with several nationally recognized professional emergency management organizations.

---

[290] (FEMA, Emergency Management Institute (EMI) Overview, n.d.)

Responsibility for Implementing Emergency Response Credentialing and Certification Standards

Over time, the entire concept behind credentialing has progressively become more formalized just like every other existing profession worldwide. In 2006, the responsibility for credentialing emergency responders was assigned to FEMA's Administrator under *6 U.S.C. § 320*, pertaining to Credentialing and Typing. This portion of the United States Code states, "The Administrator shall enter into a memorandum of understanding with the administrators of the Emergency Management Assistance Compact (EMAC), State, local, and tribal governments, and organizations that represent emergency response providers, to collaborate on developing standards for deployment capabilities, including for credentialing and typing of incident management personnel, emergency response providers, and other personnel (including temporary personnel) and resources likely needed to respond to natural disasters, acts of terrorism, and other man-made disasters."[291]

The FEMA administrator is charged with providing standards and detailed written guidance to all levels of government to aid with credentialing and typing of all personnel engaged in response to natural and man-made disasters or acts of terrorism. The approach to typing personnel based on training and qualifications was presented in Chapter 8 of this text. It is important to note, however, that FEMA's responsibility does not diminish the sovereignty of State and Tribal governments to managing response in accordance with their statutes. Credentialing and typing of personnel is achieved through mutual respect and collaboration at all levels. Therefore, the responsibility of implementing credentialing and certification standards is collaboratively shared through the Federal, State, Tribal, Territorial, and Local governments to insure Emergency Managers and responders receive the

---

[291] (FEMA, National Incident Management System: Guideline for the Credentialing of Personnel, August 2011)

necessary training and skills to respond to disasters and emergencies within their communities and in support of other jurisdictions.

The Emergency Management credentialing and certification processes work hand-in-hand. Credentialing, throughout the profession, generally refers to position-specific qualifications for personnel assigned to All Hazards Incident Management Teams (AHIMTs) or the National Qualification System (NQS) qualified emergency operations center (EOC) staff. Certification, on the other hand, can refer to Federal, State, and Local certification programs as well as professional association certifications. Emergency Managers have the advantage of being able to earn certifications for emergency management, continuity, critical infrastructure protection, EOC management, hazmat operations, and other related professional functions. The gamut of Emergency Management certifications are tied to the official job descriptions, essential functions, and levels of training and experience associated throughout the profession.

The Fundamentals of Emergency Management Certifications

Certifications are a measurement of a base or core of Emergency Management knowledge. Levels of certifications may be established for progression through basic, intermediate, and advanced levels of knowledge and skills in a given position or topic. Offering increasing levels of certifications promotes continuous professional development and can serve as inspiration for career and entry-level Emergency Managers to embrace self-improvement from the beginning to the end of their careers. The progressive nature makes obtaining higher levels of certification much more tenable since it builds over time and allows for stepping-stone development. That is one of the more important messages that I hope readers will gain from this chapter; there may be a daunting amount of certifications attainable by Emergency Managers, but every person interested in this profession can begin the process and see some successes in a relatively short amount of time.

Emergency Management certifications are granted at the Federal level by FEMA's EMI and the NFA along with other Federal agencies and agencies that provide Department of Homeland Security (DHS) grant funded training. At the State level, the State Administrative Agency (SAA), which may vary from State to State, and other State government agencies are responsible for managing State certifications. And, at the Local level, first responder academies and Offices of Emergency Management (OEMs)/Emergency Management Agencies (EMAs) may be authorized to manage certification programs. Aside from these governmental agencies, professional associations and some private-for-profit, businesses provide a wide variety of certifications. This text will not address the private-for-profit businesses offering certifications in order to avoid favoritism and to preclude any misunderstandings of perceived recommendations. Emergency Managers who are interested in private certifications should follow their own best interests and make informed decisions.

The Starting Point to Earning Emergency Management Certifications

FEMA offers two fundamental Emergency Management certifications through EMI. The first is the Professional Development Series (PDS) that "includes seven Emergency Management Institute independent study courses that provide a well-rounded set of fundamentals for those in the emergency management profession."[292] This is the starting point to attaining Emergency Management certifications for several reasons. There are only seven online courses to complete in order to receive this certification and the required courses are free, self-paced, and developed by the agency that is responsible for designing training to improve Emergency Managers' knowledge base. Also, when you consider the topics covered for the PDS, the program covers a broad cross-section that lays a firm learning

---

[292] (FEMA, ISP Courses - Search Results: Professional Development Series, n.d.)

foundation upon which to build a lifetime of Emergency Management professional development. Additionally, FEMA automatically emails the PDS certification to the student when the final course is completed, so there is nothing more a person needs to do to complete the PDS and the program can be completed in a relative short amount of time which is a bonus to encourage people to continue a personal education cycle. The list of individual courses to be completed to earn the PDS can be viewed on FEMA's website at the following link https://training.fema.gov/is/searchis.aspx?search=PDS.

The next level of certification offered by FEMA is the Advanced Professional Series (APS) that was originally established by EMI "on November 27, 2001, to motivate and challenge students to continue emergency management training."[293] Beginning January 1, 2019, EMI transferred the administration of the APS certification program to the State Emergency Management agencies in each State. Students who complete the APS program courses are now required to provide documentation as proof of completing the required courses and to request to be issued an APS Certificate of Completion from their respective State Training Officer (STO) or State Emergency Management agency. Anyone interested in completing the APS should contact their STO and obtain information on providing documentation, applying to receive the APS, and any State specific guidance.

Where the PDS is composed solely of online courses, the APS certification is primarily comprised of courses conducted in a classroom setting with a couple of exceptions. Completion of the APS combines five required courses and an additional five courses from the approved elective course listings. Achieving the APS certification is understandably more time consuming and it requires more effort because students will need to identify when and where the courses are offered and schedule the time to attend. Most States provide the courses free of charge, but some private agencies charge fees for the same courses and in some instances private agency courses with the same name may not be accepted as equivalent and it is incumbent upon the Emergency Manager to verify acceptance prior to paying for a

---

[293] (FEMA, Advanced Professional Series, n.d.)

class that may not qualify. Depending on the availability of authorized trainers, it can be difficult to find courses being offered from the APS listing. Therefore, completion may take a year or more, however, this is a certification that can be attained with dedication and time. The list of courses to be completed for the APS can be viewed on FEMA's website at the following link https://training.fema.gov/programs/aps.

Specialized Emergency Management Certification Programs

Beyond the PDS and APS programs, this section will address four specific programs available to Emergency Managers. The certification programs to be covered are FEMA's National Continuity Program (NCP), Master Exercise Practitioner Program (MEPP), Integrated Emergency Management (IEM) Program, and the EMI Trainer Program. Each of these programs represents job functions of Emergency Management in which individuals may potentially hold a position of employment dedicated to one of these specific functions. Alternately, Emergency Managers may hold a generalized job position incorporating one or more or all of these functions. In either case, these specialized programs serve to provide a concentration of courses of study for each function. The program overviews and required courses will be illustrated along with relevant information to afford interested individuals with a snapshot of the programs to aid in selecting specialized programs that will be beneficial to professional development.

1. **National Continuity Program (NCP):** The certification programs implemented by the National Continuity Programs (NCP) guide "the planning, implementation and assessment of continuity programs that enable federal, state, local, tribal and territorial and (SLTT) governments to continue performance of essential functions and deliver critical services across a broad spectrum of emergencies when normal operations are

disrupted."[294] Continuity of operations (COOP), as introduced in Chapter 4 along with the corresponding continuity of government (COG), is a topic that is so specialized that it is a recognized professional career field unto itself in business, government, and private sectors. Nevertheless, COOP and COG are inherently functions that overlap into the duties of Emergency Managers as we seek to build and sustain resilient communities and government.

The work of COOP/COG is far too expansive for the Federal government to accomplish throughout the entire nation without the assistance of all sectors. Federal agencies and departments require the support of the STTL governments, private partners, non-governmental agencies, and the public to maintain continuity and promote resilience before, during, and after catastrophic disasters. The requisite collaborative efforts involved in COOP/COG are identified in the eight National Essential Functions (NEFs) as follows:

- "NEF 1: Preserve Our Constitutional Government
- NEF 2: Provide Viable Leadership
- NEF 3: Defend the Country
- NEF 4: Maintain Foreign Relations
- NEF 5: Protect the Homeland
- NEF 6: Provide Emergency Response/Recovery
- NEF 7: Maintain a Stable Economy
- NEF 8: Provide Critical Government Services"[295]

The Continuity Excellence Series (CES) was created by the NCP and encompasses two levels of COOP certification. The CES program merges continuity, Emergency Management, instructional development, and leadership courses to benefit professionals engaged in COOP management to encourage performance of NEFs during disasters or emergencies. The Level I program is the Professional Continuity

---

[294] (FEMA, National Continuity Programs (NCP), 2021)
[295] (FEMA, FEMA National Continuity Programs: Continuity Brochure Series)

Practitioner (PCP) that is designed to enable entry-level personnel to develop a basic understanding of COOP/COG. The PCP "courses offer a broad introduction to the range of areas involved in effective continuity planning."[296] The Level I PCP combines seven required EMI Independent Study (IS) courses along with three elective courses to choose from additional online selections and classroom courses. When the required courses have been completed, individuals may forward certificates of completion or a FEMA transcript to FEMA-Continuity-Practitioner@fema.dhs.gov for review and to request issuance of the Level I PCP certificate. The list of courses to be completed for the PCP can be viewed on FEMA's website at the following link https://www.fema.gov/emergency-managers/national-preparedness/continuity/excellence-series/level-1.

The CES Level II Master Continuity Practitioner (MCP) "program provides a training structure ideal to enable experienced continuity professionals to deepen their knowledge to become leaders in driving continuity concepts in their organizations."[297] The MCP is designed to enhance continuity expertise and knowledge for practitioners working in governmental and non-governmental capacities and to benefit private-sector critical infrastructure/key resource (CI/KR) owners in protecting our nation's most vital facilities. The National Continuity Programs (NCP), inclusive of the PCP and the MCP, operate on the behalf of the FEMA Administrator, Homeland Security Secretary, and the White House to assess, implement, and plan essential functions of continuity. Among the efforts previously mentioned, the NCP ensures timely delivery of public safety alerts and warnings in support of COOP/COG.

---

[296] (FEMA, Continuity Excellence Series - Level I Professional Continuity Practitioner Requirements, 2021)

[297] (FEMA, Continuity Excellence Series - Level II Master Continuity Practitioner Requirements, 2021)

The MCP certification process incorporates a blend of online EMI IS courses and courses delivered in a classroom, however, the process additionally requires the person seeking certification to teach the Continuity Planning and Continuity Program Management courses prior to receiving certification. Practitioners, at this higher level, are expected to be extremely knowledgeable and capable of instructing others on the components of COOP/COG. This process perpetuates not only a solid base of personnel trained in continuity, but in addition it develops a pool of qualified instructors to continue the process. In essence, the MCP process becomes self-sustaining which is a perfect example of program resilience. The list of courses to be completed for the MCP can be viewed on FEMA's website at the following link https://www.fema.gov/emergency-managers/national-preparedness/continuity/excellence-series/level-2.

2. **Master Exercise Practitioner Program (MEPP):** "The Master Exercise Practitioner Program is a series of two classroom courses (E0132, E0133) focusing on advanced program management, exercise design and evaluation practices in each phase of the Homeland Security Exercise and Evaluation Program (HSEEP)."[298] After completing the two courses, candidates must complete an MEPP Capstone project within one calendar year. The capstone entails designing, developing, facilitating, and evaluating either a functional exercise (FE) or full-scale exercise (FSE) and then presenting the exercise documentation to a panel of subject matter experts (SMEs) for review. Not until after the successful completion of the capstone project will the candidate receive the MEPP certification.

3. **Integrated Emergency Management Course (IEMC):** "The Integrated Emergency Management Course is a four day, exercise-based training activity for Emergency Operations Center personnel to practice simulated, but realistic, crisis situations, within a structured learning

---

[298] (FEMA, Master Exercise Practitioner Program (MEPP), 2019)

environment."[299] The IMEC is intended to be conducted for a team of personnel from the same, or neighboring, jurisdiction working collaboratively in an EOC. The jurisdiction for which the course is being conducted will be allowed to select the hazards and core capabilities they want to be simulated and exercised. Instructors will pull information reported in the jurisdiction's Threat Hazard and Identification Risk Assessment (THIRA) and Stakeholder Preparedness Report (SPR) to facilitate the exercise. The community-specific approach of the IEMC aids in building awareness and communication skills and promotes the refinement and implementation of plans, policies, procedures, and mutual aid agreements focusing on the whole community.

The IEMC is structured to be delivered to personnel who perform specific duties within or in support of an emergency operations center (EOC). Chief elected or appointed officials, senior level staff from response disciplines (emergency medical services, fire, law enforcement, public health, public works, etc.), and representatives from private or volunteer agencies are examples of appropriate attendees. The IEMC incorporates discussions, lectures, group planning, and exercise methodologies. Participants are assigned to roles that are equivalent to their actual EOC duties in their jurisdiction and new concepts are introduced to the participants during the IEMC to spur greater awareness and coordination between the agencies collaborating in the EOC.

4. **EMI Trainer Program:** The EMI Trainer Program is designed "to provide training professionals a means to acquire basic knowledge and skills in various areas of the training profession,"[300] including instructional design, teaching techniques, and evaluation methods. It is important to note that EMI strictly identifies the Trainer Program as a certificate program only and does not authorize those certified to utilize a certification acronym or post-nominal letters after their name in a signature line. The Trainer

---

[299] (FEMA, Integrated Emergency Management Course (IEMC), 2020)
[300] (FEMA, The Emergency Management Institute (EMI) Trainer Program, 2015)

Program encompasses the Basic Instructor Certificate and the Basic Instructional Design Certificate. Both certificates are geared towards improving the skills of entry-level personnel. The list of courses to be completed for the EMI Trainer Program can be viewed on FEMA's website at the following link https://training.fema.gov/tp.

The Emergency Management Professional Program (EMPP)

EMI developed the Emergency Management Professional Program (EMPP) to provide "a framework for acquiring the knowledge, skills, and abilities to enter and progress through the field and to meet the challenges of a dynamic and complex environment."[301] The EMPP is composed of three competency-based Emergency Management academies devised to offer progressive lifetime learning in conjunction with the Public Information Officer Programs. The three affiliated academies are the National Emergency Management Basic Academy (NEMBA), National Emergency Management Advanced Academy (NEMAA), and the National Emergency Management Executive Academy (NEMEA). This section will review the four EMPP programs individually.

1. **National Emergency Management Basic Academy (NEMBA):** The NEMBA is likened, by FEMA, to fire and law enforcement academies for those who are entering into the profession of Emergency Management. The Basic Academy specifically targets newly appointed or hired Emergency Managers possessing less than three years of experience. Candidates are trained on Emergency Management foundations, disaster science, planning, exercises, and the basics of public information. The course of study for the NEMBA is comprised of five in-residence classes that total 120 hours of Emergency Management training and prior to being approved to register for the NEMBA, individuals are required to complete

---

[301] (FEMA, Emergency Management Professional Program (EMPP), 2020)

twelve prerequisite EMI online classes. The list of courses to be completed for the NEMBA can be viewed on FEMA's website at the following link https://training.fema.gov/empp/basic.aspx.

2. **National Emergency Management Advanced Academy (NEMAA):** "The National Emergency Management Advanced Academy (NEMAA) reinforces the qualities needed to lead emergency management programs, provides relevant management theories and concepts, and utilizes appropriate case studies."[302] The Advanced Academy is designed for mid-level Emergency Managers with at least five years of experience who have a significant role in an agency directly related to Emergency Management or disaster and emergency response. The NEMAA focuses on honing the critical leadership skills of collaborative integration, effective communication, program oversight and management, and strategic thinking. The NEMAA is composed of four in-resident classes each of which is five days in length, must be completed in sequential order, is designed to be completed within a single Federal fiscal year (October to September), and culminates in the candidate submitting a comprehensive research paper. Interested candidates must apply to attend the NEMAA and be approved to attend by an annual evaluation board. The list of courses to be completed for the NEMAA can be viewed on FEMA's website at the following link https://training.fema.gov/empp/advanced.aspx.

3. **National Emergency Management Executive Academy (NEMEA):** The National Emergency Management Executive Academy (NEMEA) is a collaboration between academia, EMI, and renowned Emergency Management practitioners with the goal of producing curriculum which is both comprehensive and contemporary to support the advancement of executive leadership at the strategic and policy levels. The Executive Academy "provides an ideal setting for a diverse representation of senior emergency management leaders to come together in a collaborative

---

[302] (FEMA, National Emergency Management Advanced Academy, 2020)

learning environment to explore contemporary and emerging 21st century challenges."[303] Appropriate candidates will possess ten years of relevant Emergency Management experience, hold senior executive positions, and ideally will have served on commissions and task forces responsible for significant policy development. Participants will complete four in-residence courses in the fiscal year and prepare a collaborative capstone project by leveraging the cohort's wealth of institutional knowledge with the purpose of developing enhanced doctrine, policy, and practices to shape the Emergency Management profession for the foreseeable future. The selection process to attend the NEMEA is limited to only forty Emergency Management executives per year. The list of courses to be completed for the NEMEA can be viewed on FEMA's website at the following link https://training.fema.gov/empp/executive.aspx.

4. **Public Information Officer (PIO) Programs:** EMIs Public Information Officer (PIO) programs are designed to equip PIOs with essential knowledge, skills, and abilities (KSAs) to support leadership in effective decision-making and delivery of accurate and timely information to the whole community. Without a doubt, public information is a crucial component of every disaster operation and directly corresponds to the success of saving lives and protecting a community's property and environment. The PIO programs afford attendees with opportunities to learn and apply skills to coordinate, gather, verify, and disseminate public information at all levels of government, non-governmental organizations, and across private and volunteer sectors. Emphasis is given to planning strategic communication with a whole community approach and the 95/5 concept is interwoven throughout the programs. "The 95/5 concept relates to non-emergency and emergency PIO activities – 95% of most PIOs' work is in non-emergency times, with only 5% directly related to incident response or recovery."[304] Per EMI, the KSAs a PIO applies during non-emergency events directly relates to their success in delivering public

[303] (FEMA, National Emergency Management Executive Academy (NEMEA), 2020)
[304] (FEMA, Public Information Officer (PIO), 2021)

information during disasters. The PIO Program is comprised of the Awareness level training providing familiarization with PIO concepts, the Basic level including necessary skills for full or part-time PIOs for entry-level PIOs, the Advanced level of expanding knowledge pertaining to escalating incidents for PIOs with a minimum of 2 years of experience, and the Master level certification providing relevant concepts and theories for internal and external communications for PIOs with 5 years of experience. The Master PIO Program (MPIOP) highlights the establishment of a network of peers, the activation of the Joint Information System (JIS), and management of the Joint Information Center (JIC). At the awareness, basic, and advanced PIO levels EMI offers a single course for each, however, at the master PIO level there are three required courses to receive the certificate. Collectively, the EMI PIO Programs offer a progression of training to improve the KSAs of PIOs throughout the life of their career. The list of courses to be completed for the PIO Program can be viewed on FEMA's website at the following link https://training.fema.gov/programs/pio.

Professional Association Emergency Management Certifications

Up to this point, Chapter 10 has reviewed the certification programs that are available through the Federal Emergency Management Agency (FEMA). Next, we will turn the corner to consider the Emergency Management certification programs that are managed by professional associations. The first task to complete in this undertaking is to offer a definition of what constitutes a professional association or organization. The Indeed job search site provides the following definition, *"A professional organization, sometimes referred to as a professional association or professional body, exists to advance a particular profession, support the interests of people working in that profession and serve the public good. It facilitates innovation, communication and connection."*[305]

In this case, the professional associations to be studied exist to advance and promote the profession of Emergency Management. The selected associations are the certifying agencies for their respective Emergency Management certification programs. Other Emergency Management professional associations and organizations do support and further the profession, however, this overview will focus on selected associations maintaining certification programs. What is offered in this text does not constitute a recommendation for a specific association, but what it is offered is intended to illustrate and illuminate the variety of certifications available to Emergency Managers through such associations. Individuals interested in seeking certification are encouraged to consider all related details involved in professional association certification programs and to make an informed decision as to which program best suits their circumstances.

Where the certifications associated with FEMA are free of charge, professional associations normally require annual membership dues along with testing and certification fees. Another major difference between FEMA and professional associations is that FEMA does not mandate recertifying where professional associations may call for regulated cycles of recertification. The process to recertify may require submission of proof of continuing education, documentation of experience during the specific cycle, and other contributions to the field of Emergency Management. Additionally, most professional associations that award certifications will authorize the recipient to utilize professional acronyms or post-nominal letters in their signature block and may require the recipient to maintain membership in good standing to continue to utilize the professional acronym. Let's jump in and review some of the professional certifications that can be earned by Emergency Managers.

---

[305] (Indeed, 2020)

State Guard Association of the United States (SGAUS) Emergency Management Certificate Programs

"The mission of the State Guard Association of the Unites States (SGAUS) is to advocate for the advancement and support of regulated state military forces established by state governments under the authority of Title 32, Section 109, of the United States Code."[306] These military units are referred to as State Guards, State Defense Forces, or State Military Reserves and they are governed by State laws and the military regulations of the U.S. Army National Guard Bureau (NGB) and their respective State. Hereafter the title "State Guard" will be utilized when referring to these State military agencies in this section. Many of these State Guard units traced their heritage back to the founding era of the nation.

In 1985, the State Defense Force Association of the United States (SDFAUS) was created as a professional association supporting the States that maintain State Guard units. The organizational name was changed in 1993 to the State Guard Association of the United States (SGAUS). Throughout the U.S., State Guard units are comprised of non-Federal military members serving in the capacity of protecting their respective states in the role of defense support of civil authorities (DSCA). The majority of the missions assigned to State Guard units involves disaster response operations, which led to SGAUS creating the Military Emergency Management Specialist (MEMS) Academy program in 1998. The MEMS Academy program is organized around the standards of the National Incident Management System (NIMS) and the Incident Command System (ICS) to strengthen professional development of the military members engaged in disaster response operations.

The MEMS Academy certificate programs are open to State Guard members, Department of Defense (DOD) personnel, members of the Civil Air Patrol, U.S. Coast Guard Auxiliary, Medical Reserve Corps, Cadet Corps, Naval Militias, U.S. Uniformed Services personnel, and has recently been authorized for civilians

---

[306] (SGAUS, SGAUS Mission, n.d.)

interested in training and certification related to Emergency management. The MEMS Academy has grown in stature to be viewed as a highly respected national and international leader in Emergency Management training. Plans are currently being formulated to offer the MEMS Academy certificates internationally and to expand the MEMS realm of influence. "The Academy qualification Program fully complies with current U.S. Department of Homeland Security (DHS), Federal Emergency Management Administration (FEMA), Incident Command System (ICS), National Incident Management system (NIMS), National Response Framework (NRF), Homeland Security Presidential Directive 5 (HSPD-5), and Presidential Policy Directive / PPD-8: National Preparedness."[307]

The Commanding General of the State Guard units in a State is authorized to appoint a MEMS Academy Military State Director to manage the MEMS certificate programs for the State military members. With the addition of civilians being authorized to earn MEMS certificates, the SGAUS MEMS Academy Commandant is authorized to appoint a MEMS Academy Civilian State Director to manage the programs for civilians in the State. Academy State Directors (ASDs), both Military and Civilian, may appoint Academy Advisory Staff to serve as mentors and advisors to the ASD. The ASDs may also appoint Deputy Directors, instructors, and other staff to aid in verifying students have completed the requisite requirements to be awarded a MEMS certificate.

The MEMS Academy offers certificates at the Basic, Senior, and Master MEMS levels, as well as the Master MEMS Instructor Certificate and the Liaison Officer (LNO) All Hazard Specialist Certificate. Individuals who earn the Basic MEMS certificate will have attained a working knowledge of Emergency Management principles and the knowledge, skills, and abilities (KSAs) pertaining to preparedness, response, recovery, and mitigation operations. The Basic MEMS certificate program requires individuals to complete ten FEMA online IS courses and to write a MEMS Practicum. The practicum is the individual's demonstration of their accumulated Emergency Management knowledge and practical application of

---

[307] (SGAUS, MEMS Academy Student Guidelines, 2021)

NIMS and ICS principles during a real-world disaster response operation or an exercise lasting eight to sixteen hours at a minimum. The practicum is written after the individual works a qualifying disaster or participates in a qualifying exercise and is submitted to the ASD staff.

Personnel earning the Senior level MEMS certificate will have gained the skills to enable them to lead and plan response operations for expanding incidents. The Senior MEMS program encompasses eight FEMA online IS courses, the three-day Intermediate ICS course, the Weapons of Mass Destruction (WMD) Awareness course that is available online or in residence, and completion of a Senior level practicum. As with the Basic level practicum, the Senior level practicum is the tool for the individual to demonstrate the knowledge and practical application of NIMS and ICS principles for a qualifying real-world response or planned exercise. At the Senior level, the practicum should demonstrate increased levels of responsibility as Incident Command supervisors or managers as well as increased knowledge of NIMS/ICS.

Individuals completing the Master level MEMS certificate, will have attained the skills to serve in advanced levels of responsibility for disaster operations. The Master level MEMS program is composed of five FEMA online IS courses, the two-day in-residence Advanced ICS course, and completion of a Master MEMS practicum. The Master MEMS practicum must demonstrate advanced skills and abilities to be serve leadership roles for complex incidents. Individuals having completed the Master MEMS certificate who are interested in earning the Master MEMS Instructor must have earned the Master MEMS certificate and then complete the ICS-449 ICS Curricula Trainer class or "have advanced documented practical experience in Emergency Operations Centers."[308] A separate Master MEMS Instructor certificate will be issued upon completion of all requirements.

The MEMS Liaison Officer (LNO) All Hazard Specialist certificate is the capstone training program for the MEMS Academy. The LNO certificate requirements meld all the knowledge gained in the Basic, Senior, and Master level

---

[308] (SGAUS, MEMS Academy Student Guidelines, 2021)

programs along with the documentation of response experience serving as an LNO. To effectively serve on a command staff as the point of contact for all supporting agencies during a response operation demands the highest levels of Emergency Management knowledge. Completion of the LNO Specialist certificate requires the completion of two in-residence courses, documentation of having served as an LNO during a response operation, and completion of the FEMA All Hazards Liaison Officer Position Specific Task book. Alternately, individuals can apply for the certification requirements to be waived if they submit documentation showing that their agency has designated them as an LNO and that they actively serve in that capacity.

Award of the Basic, Senior, Master, Master Instructor, and LNO certificates authorizes the individual to wear the distinctive MEMS skill badge for the appropriate level. SGAUS designed the silver MEMS badge around the historic U.S. Civil Defense eagle with the ancient shield symbol for victory and a surrounding laurel wreath. The Senior level MEMS badge includes a five-pointed star over the eagle and the Master level MEMS badge adds a circular laurel wreath around the five-pointed star. The LNO MEMS badge is gold in color rather than silver to indicate the highest level of achievement. Military members are authorized to wear the appropriate MEMS badge on uniforms in accordance with their military regulations and civilians are authorized to wear miniature versions of the MEMS badges on the lapels of their clothing. The list of courses to be completed for the levels of MEMS programs can be viewed on the SGAUS website at the following link https://sgaus.org/sgaus-academy/mems-academy.

State Level Emergency Management Certification Programs

Forty-two States have established Emergency Management certification programs and over half of those States offer multiple levels of certification. Depending on the State, some of the certification programs are managed by the State Emergency Management Agency, a State Professional Emergency Management

Association, or both in a few States. Some of the certification programs mirror the International Association of Emergency Managers (IAEM) programs which will be covered in the next section.

The proliferation of State Emergency Management certification programs provides a wide array of options for Emergency Managers and those entering into the profession. With the sheer number of State certification programs, it is impractical to fully review every program in each of the forty-two States. Therefore, the following table listing all of the programs currently available at a State level is offered for Emergency Managers to review.

State Emergency Management Certification Programs		
State	**Certification**	**Designation**
Alabama	Basic Level Emergency Manager	BLEM
	Intermediate Level Emergency Manager	ILEM
	Advanced Level Emergency Manager	ALEM
	Certified Local Emergency Manager	CLEM
Alaska	Associate Emergency Manager	N/A
	Executive Emergency Manager	
Arkansas	Arkansas Certified Emergency Manager	ACEM
California	California Specialist Certificate Program	N/A
	Emergency Management Specialist Certificate	
Colorado	Colorado Associate Emergency Manager	CO-AEM
	Colorado Certified Emergency Manager	CO-CEM
Florida	Florida Associate Emergency Manager	FAEM
	Florida Professional Emergency Manager	FPEM
Georgia	Georgia Certified Emergency Manager	GA-CEM
	Georgia Master Certified Emergency Manager	GA-MCEM
Illinois	Illinois Professional Emergency Manager	IPEM
Indiana	Professional Emergency Manager	PEMP
Iowa	Iowa Certified Emergency Manager	IACEM
Kansas	Kansas Certified Emergency Manager	KCEM
Kentucky	Kentucky Certified Emergency Manager	KCEM
Louisiana	Louisiana Emergency Manager Basic	LEB-B
	Louisiana Emergency Manager Technical	LEMT
	Louisiana Emergency Manager Certified Professional	LEM-Pro
Maine	Certified Emergency Manager ME	CEM-ME

Maryland	Maryland Professional Emergency Manager Program	MDPEMP
Massachusetts	Massachusetts Certified Emergency Manager	MA-CEM
Michigan	Michigan Professional Emergency Manager	PEM
Minnesota	Emergency Management Certification Program	EMCP
Mississippi	Mississippi Certified Emergency Manager	MCEM
Missouri	Level 1 Missouri Associate Emergency Manager	Level 1 MAEM
	Level 2 Missouri Emergency Manager Certified (Documented)	Level 2 MEMC-D
	Level 2 Missouri Emergency Manager Certified (Grandfathered)	Level 2 MEMC-G
Nebraska	Nebraska Certified Emergency Manager Basic	NE-CEM (B)
	Nebraska Certified Emergency Manager Advanced	NE-CEM (A)
Nevada	Nevada Emergency Manager Associate	NVEM-A
	Nevada Emergency Manager	NVEM
New Jersey	New Jersey Certified Emergency Manager	NJCEM
New Mexico	New Mexico Certified Emergency Manager	NMCEM
New York	Emergency Management Certification & Training Program (Tier 2)	EMCTP (Tier 2)
North Carolina	North Carolina Associate Emergency Manager	NCAEM
	North Carolina Executive Emergency Manager	NCEEMC
North Dakota	Level I	NDEMA Level 1
	Level II	NDEMA Level 2
	Full Certification	NDEMA Full
Ohio	Ohio Emergency Manager Certification	OEMC
Oklahoma	Oklahoma Certified Emergency Manager	OCEM
Oregon	Oregon Certified Emergency Management Specialist	ORCEMS
Pennsylvania	Pennsylvania Basic Certification	PBC
	Pennsylvania Advanced Certification	PAC
	Pennsylvania Professional Certification	PPC
Rhode Island	Basic Certification in Emergency Management	BCEM
	Intermediate Certification in Emergency Management	ICEM
	Advanced Certification in Emergency Management	ACEM
South Carolina	South Carolina Certified Emergency Manager	SCCEM
South Dakota	South Dakota Certified Emergency Manager	SD-CEM
Tennessee	Emergency Manager Level 1	EM 1
	Emergency Manager Level 2	EM II
	Certified Emergency Manager	CEMP
Texas	Certified Texas Emergency Manager – Basic	TEM-B

	Certified Texas Emergency Manager	TEM
Utah	Utah Associate Emergency Manager	UAEM
	Utah Certified Emergency Manager	UCEM
Vermont	Vermont Emergency Manager Certification Level 1	VEMC 1
	Vermont Emergency Manager Certification Level 2	VEMC 2
Virginia	Emergency Management Assistant	EMA
	Emergency Management Volunteer	EMV
	Associate Emergency Manager	AEM
	Professional Emergency Manager	PEM
West Virginia	West Virginia Emergency Manager 1	WVEM 1
	West Virginia Emergency Manager 2	WVEM 2
	West Virginia Emergency Manager 3	WVEM 3
Wisconsin	Wisconsin Emergency Management Professional Certification Program Level 1	WIEMC 1
	Wisconsin Emergency Management Professional Certification Program Level 2	WIEMC 2
	Wisconsin Emergency Management Professional Certification Program Level 3	WIEMC 3
	Wisconsin Emergency Management Professional Certification Program Level 4	WIEMC 4
Wyoming	Associate Wyoming Emergency Manager	AWEM
	Wyoming Emergency Manager	WEM
Table 9: State Emergency Management Certification Programs (Chadwick)		

International Level Emergency Management Certification Programs

The International Association of Emergency Managers (IAEM) was originally founded in 1952 as the United States Civil Defense Council (USCDC). In 1985, the organization was renamed as the National Coordinating Council of Emergency Managers (NCCEM) to embrace the transition in terminology that began in 1979 with the creation of FEMA which saw the title "civil defense" shifting to "emergency management." Then the NCCEM name was changed to the International Association of Emergency Managers (IAEM) in 1997, but it wasn't until 1999 that IAEM truly began the work to become an international association by forming an

International Development Committee (IDC). The progression towards international formation continued with the establishment of an International Region in 2001; IAEM-Canada in 2003; IAEM-Europa, IAEM-Oceania, and IAEM-Asia in 2004; an IAEM-Global Board in 2006; and IAEM-Italy and IAEM-Spain in 2010. Bringing it full circle, today IAEM "has more than 6,000 members worldwide, is a non-profit educational organization dedicated to promoting the Principles of Emergency Management and representing those professionals whose goals are saving lives and protecting property and the environment during emergencies and disasters."[309]

The Associate Emergency Manager (AEM) and Certified Emergency Manager (CEM) certification programs were developed by IAEM in 1993 to address the improvement and maintenance of professional standards. The AEM and CEM certifications do not represent a guarantee or promise as to an individual's performance ability, but rather serve to demonstrate education, experience, and training criteria and an acknowledgement of an individual having met the established criteria. The IAEM certification programs serve to recognize individual achievements in the profession of Emergency Management. Both, the AEM and CEM, are certification programs that apply a professional peer review process by the CEM Commission "made up of Emergency Management professionals including representatives from allied fields, educators, military, and private industry personnel."[310] IAEM members and non-members seeking certification must complete an application, provide documentation to verify completion of all related requirements, and pay all applicable fees to be considered for either the AEM or CEM certification. After the initial award of the AEM or CEM, individuals must complete the recertification process every five years to maintain certification.

The Associate Emergency Manager (AEM) certification is the entry level professional certification. The AEM provides a level of certification for those individuals who do not yet meet the requirements to be recognized as a Certified

---

[309] (IAEM, History of IAEM, n.d.)
[310] (IAEM, IAEM Certification Brochure, 2020)

Emergency Manager (CEM). There is no requirement at the AEM level to demonstrate a minimum level of years in work experience or contributions to the profession of Emergency Management to be certified. The requirements to qualify for the AEM certification are:

- Completion of 100 hours of Emergency Management training in the past 10 years with no more than 25 hours in a single topic.
- Completion of 100 hours of General Management training in the past 10 years with no more than 25 hours in a single topic.
- Submission of an essay for review that demonstrates the knowledge, skills, and abilities (KSAs) applicable to the profession as specified in the application.
- Providing a letter of reference from the individual's immediate supervisor on official letterhead along with three additional letters of reference.
- Successfully completing the certification exam with a minimum score of 75% on the 100 question exam.
- Submission of the application along with documentation for all relevant training and required documentation.

The Certified Emergency Manager (CEM) is the premier Emergency Management certificate offered through IAEM. The CEM recognizes that an individual demonstrates the KSAs to manage comprehensive Emergency Management operations, possesses a working knowledge of the mission areas and core capabilities, has experience in whole community and collaborative planning, and can effectively accomplish the tasks pertinent to Emergency Management with their current level of training. An individual certified as a CEM possesses the capabilities to succeed in and contribute to the betterment of the profession. Achieving the certification of a CEM is not a simple task, nor should it be easy to attain. Becoming certified as a CEM is a milestone accomplish in an individual's career and marks a lifetime achievement. The requirements to be awarded the CEM certification are to provide documentation of:

- A minimum of three years of full-time equivalent work experience in managing disaster and emergency operations.

- Documentation of having held a major role and responsibilities for a real-world disaster, full-scale exercise, two separate functional exercises, or in a major planned event.
- Possessing a four-year Bachelor's degree in any subject from an accredited university; if the Bachelor degree is in the field of Emergency Management the number of years of work experience is reduced to 2 years and waives the required hours of Emergency Management training.
- Completing 100 hours of Emergency Management training in the past 10 years with no more than 25 hours in a single topic.
- Completing 100 hours of General Management training in the past 10 years with no more than 25 hours in a single topic.
- Documentation of contributions to the profession of Emergency Management; the initial certification must provide documentation of 6 separate professional contributions from the following areas:
  1. Proof of 3 years of membership in a disaster or Emergency Management organization (i.e., IAEM, State Association, Regional Association, Local Organization).
  2. Participation in at least 40 cumulative contact hours in professional conferences, seminars, workshops, etc.
  3. Serving on a board of directors, committee, special project, or task force for a professional or jurisdictional Emergency Management organization.
  4. Voluntary leadership role, not a part of their normal job duties, on a board of directors, committee, special project, or task force for Emergency Management or a jurisdictional agency supporting disasters and Emergency Management.
  5. Having been involved in a special assignment as part of a committee, task force, or work group assigned to address a substantive topic relating to disasters and Emergency Management that produces a product making a significant impact on the profession.

6. Developing and presenting for 3 professional speaking engagements, in the past 10 years, to a community or professional audience on topics related to disaster response or Emergency Management.
7. Conducting a formal 3-hour block of instruction or teaching relating to disaster response or Emergency Management.
8. Having a significant role in the development or extensive revision of an Emergency Management course consisting of a minimum of 3 hours of instruction; may not be merely in the form of a Power Point presentation.
9. Publishing a substantial disaster or Emergency Management article in a professional publication requiring independent editorial review beyond that of the individual.
10. Personal development of content for an audio-visual tool, computer software, or Emergency Management video.
11. Receiving a personal award for activities relating to disaster response or Emergency Management.
12. Earning an Emergency Management certification such as through IAEM, State agencies, or professional associations.
13. Contacting a Federal or State legislative elected official pertaining to a disaster or Emergency Management topic; include copies of the original letter sent to the elected official and the corresponding letter received from the elected official.
14. Serving a significant role in the development and execution of a research project on an Emergency Management topic.
15. Other contributions to the profession such as having volunteered to respond to assist on a disaster operation outside of your jurisdiction.

- Submission of a comprehensive essay on Emergency Management as prescribed by IAEM.
- Successfully complete the certification examination with a minimum score of 75% from a 100 question exam; IAEM produces a study guide that is available for download from their website.

- Providing a letter of reference from the individual's immediate supervisor on official letterhead along with three additional letters of reference.

Every five years, all current AEMs and CEMs must apply for recertification and submit documentation to meet the requirements for continuing education in Emergency Management and general management as well as meeting the required professional contributions. At each five-year interval the required number of hours of continuing education is reduced, however, even after 25 years of having earned the AEM or CEM individuals must complete a minimum of 25 hours of training during the preceding 5 years on Emergency Management and general management along with increasing levels of professional contributions.

IAEM does offer a Lifetime CEM designation to be bestowed as an honor by the Certification Commission to retired full-time Emergency Managers. The definition of *retired* in this regard means that *the individual is employed, self-employed, or consulting in Emergency Management less than 400 hours per year.* To receive the Lifetime designation, the individual must be a current CEM who has recertified at least one time prior to being eligible to receive the Lifetime designation. The candidate must be nominated by a fellow CEM who is familiar with the candidate's career of service and accomplishments. The nomination "shall include a narrative stating the achievements in the field of emergency management, two letters of recommendation from current CEMs stating achievements deserving of this honor, and a letter of interest (including the retirement date) from the candidate."[311] The process to receive the Lifetime designation may take several months due to the Certification Commission needing time to review the nomination for eligibility, forwarding the nomination to the USA Board of Directors meeting along with an acceptance of the nomination by the Commission, and then the approval of the nomination for the Lifetime designation may be granted by the Board of Directors. Complete information on IAEM certifications can be found at https://www.iaem.org/certification/intro.

---

[311] (IAEM, Lifertime CEM Designation, n.d.)

A mountain of information has been scaled in this chapter pertaining to certificate programs and certifications. Fundamental certifications were presented that are available through FEMA's EMI from the basic Professional Development Series (PDS), through the specialized certifications, to the Emergency Management Professional Program (EMPP) certifications. Beyond the certifications through FEMA, professional associations and States were shown to have an impressive spectrum of Emergency Management certificates and certification programs to aid in the professional development of Emergency Managers and those seeking to enter the profession. And, ultimately, IAEM maintains the AEM and CEM certification programs which are internationally recognized for Emergency Managers.

Chapter 10 Summary

Key Terms (Alphabetical Order)

Academy State Director (ASD)
Advanced Professional Series (APS)
American Council on Education (ACE)
Associate Emergency Manager (AEM)
Certificates
Certification
Civil Defense Adult Education Program (CDAEP)
Civil Defense Staff College (CDSC)
Civil Defense University Extension Program (CDUEP)
Continuity Excellence Series (CES)
Credentials
Credentialing
Defense Civil Preparedness Agency (DCPA)
Defense Support of Civil Authorities (DSCA)
Department of Defense (DOD)
Emergency Management Professional Program (EMPP)
Federal Civil Defense Administration (FCDA)
Federal Civil Defense Staff College (FCDSC)
Integrated Emergency Management (IEM) Program
Integrated Emergency Management Course (IEMC)
International Association for Continuing Education and Training (IACET)
International Association of Emergency Managers (IAEM)
International Development Committee (IDC)
Knowledge, Skills, and Abilities (KSA)
Liaison Officer (LNO)
Master Continuity Practitioner (MCP)
Master Exercise Practitioner Program (MEPP)
Master Public Information Officer Program (MPIOP)
National Continuity Programs (NCP)
National Coordinating Council of Emergency Managers (NCCEM)

National Emergency Management Advanced Academy (NEMAA)
National Emergency Management Basic Academy (NEMBA)
National Emergency Management Executive Academy (NEMEA)
National Essential Function (NEF)
Professional Continuity Practitioner (PCP)
Professional Development Series (PDS)
Professional Organization
Retired
State Defense Force Association of the United States (SDFAUS)
State Training Officer (STO)
The American Civil Defense Association (TACDA)
U.S. Army National Guard Bureau (NGB)
United States Civil Defense Council (USCDC)

The Basis of Emergency Management Certificates and Certifications

There is a long-standing and rich heritage of Emergency Management certificates and certification programs in the United States stretching back to 1941 with the founding of the Office of Civil Defense (OCD); not counting the programs pre-dating the OCD. Since that time, programs have been developed and modified over decades to strengthen and enhance the Emergency Management profession. A plethora of agencies and programs exist to provide certificates and certifications for Emergency Managers to aid in meeting the wide variety of Emergency Management professionals along with the specialists and generalists in the field. FEMA's Emergency Management Institute (EMI) has served as the backbone to a vast cross-section of the Emergency Management certificate programs available and EMI traces its distinguished history back to the formation of the Civil Defense Staff College (CDSC) in 1951 through present day.

The Cornerstones of Emergency Management Certification

FEMA's Professional Development Series (PDS) certification program requires the completion of seven online, free, and self-paced courses and provides a solid starting point for Emergency Managers seeking professional development. The Advanced Professional Series (APS) builds upon the foundational knowledge of the PDS with a combination of online and classroom courses. Then, aside from those initial programs, specialized FEMA certifications including the National Continuity Program (NCP), Master Exercise Practitioner Program (MEPP), Integrated Emergency Management (IEM) Program, and the Emergency Management Trainer Program provide options for individuals employed in various Emergency Management specializations. Lastly, FEMA developed the Emergency Management Professional Program (EMPP) for individuals with increasing levels of experience in the field and for Public Information Officers (PIOs) coordinating internal and external communications during disasters and emergencies.

Emergency Management Certification Professional Associations

The certificates and certifications managed by FEMA represent one of the many avenues leading to Emergency Management certifications. With the goal of advancing the field of Emergency Management, professional associations offer another source of professional development training and certifications. One such professional association, the State Guard Association of the United States (SGAUS) Military Emergency Management Specialist (MEMS) has developed programs that have grown to include offering certificates to military members and civilians alike in the U.S. and the association aims to broaden its horizon to envelop an international audience. Additionally, State Emergency Management agencies and associations in forty-two States currently manage a total of seventy-seven certification options within their jurisdictions. And, the International Association of Emergency

Managers (IAEM) developed the Associate Emergency Manager (AEM) and Certified Emergency Manager (CEM) certifications that has pushed the boundaries of Emergency Management professional development for twenty-eight years and has embraced a global reach.

When it is all tallied spanning the certificate and certification programs managed by FEMA, professional associations, State level programs, and IAEM, there are currently nearly one hundred potential Emergency Management certifications in existence in the United States alone. That figure does not take into account the private-for-profit programs and other programs that were not selected for review in this text. Neither were Local jurisdictional certification programs or those managed by volunteer organizations active in disasters (VOADs) considered in this chapter. These final statements are included to further illustrate that what has been presented in Chapter 10 is not the entirety of the possible certification programs Emergency Managers could potentially earn because to attempt to consolidate every possible Emergency Management or related certification into this text is quite literally impossible to accomplish.

The next chapter is the Conclusion chapter for this book.

Conclusion

The journey of writing *"Organizing Chaos"* has encompassed thousands of hours of research that has matured for many years. For more than 15 years, I have been involved in writing local courses, developing exercises for a multitude of jurisdictions, and producing workshops for professional conferences and symposiums on wide ranging Emergency Management topics. During that time, I have refined my materials and improved upon the concepts that have been incorporated in this work along with innumerable new and expanded elements. This book not only represents a literary pilgrimage, but it is also a personal expedition into the depths of Emergency Management. The final evolution of this work, over the past year, has transitioned from a burgeoning idea to the culmination of a finished product has been challenging and rewarding in the same breath.

When I started the process of writing this book, I began with a couple of simple goals in mind. First, I wanted to dispel the myths or misunderstandings that have taken hold describing Emergency Management as a new or emerging. To shed the light of truth of the Emergency Management profession, I began by documenting the factual history of this vital and wondrous career spanning centuries. Secondly, I was determined to provide a beneficial resource that current and future Emergency Managers could utilize as a comprehensive guide to the profession. Towards those ends, I have chronicled evidence from hundreds of government regulations, reports, and statutes tracing Emergency Management through a lineage inaugurated long before the founding of our nation.

Traversing through history has illuminated foundations of Emergency Management that can be seen as far into the past as ancient Rome in 21 BC when Emperor Augustus instituted his *vigiles* or "watchmen of the city." Arguably, however, common sense demands that since the history of the world catalogs disasters from the dawn of recorded time, then to people must have responded to and managed those very same disasters. Unquestionably, extensive research through the annals of time would result in continuing evidence of the genealogy of Emergency Management. I felt comfortable, though, with looking no further than two millennia in my quest. However even for those who would choose to discount the ancient lineage, it is impossible to honestly overlook the heritage of Emergency Management in America that I have presented. Since the founding colonial days there has been a progressive development of the profession which has been well-documented within this book.

The practices of disaster management that have matured in the United States have come about through a long series of catastrophes beginning with the tragedy of the Roanoake Colony and moving through the Revolutionary War, Industrial era, Native American wars, New Madrid earthquakes, Great Chicago Fire, World Wars, terrorist attack of 9/11, Hurricane Katrina, Super Storm Sandy and on and on. At each stage of the journey, disaster management has advanced based on the lessons learned and the adopted best practices that have formed what has been inherited by those entering the profession today. Soldiers returning from World War I and then again in World War II applied a military model of disaster management which led to the development of the Large Fire Organization (LFO) and the founding of the Incident Command System (ICS) that is the shining jewel of present-day Emergency Management.

The institutionalization of ICS in the Unites States has risen from the ashes of devastation and destruction. Following the 9/11 terrorist attack, the nation desperately needed a disaster management system capable of uniting all response disciplines. ICS and its ancestral foundations had been proven effective for generations and it was selected to be included as one of the critical elements of the National Incident Management System (NIMS). The adoption of ICS into NIMS has enabled agencies since to effectively mesh and collaborate through all phases of emergency response. By combining the roles and responsibilities and a tactical planning process, ICS has provided our nation with a management system which is capable of meeting the demands of any incident regardless of size or complexity.

Continuing to push the boundaries, the National Preparedness Goal of developing a secure and resilient nation has evolved to include the National Preparedness System (NPS), five mission areas, and thirty-two core capabilities that unifies the tasks of Emergency Management across all levels of the government, business and private sectors, and volunteer organizations. The Goal, in turn, led to the implementation of a comprehensive planning process for strategic and operational plans to address the greatest threats and hazards. This established planning process for emergency operation plans (EOPs) alone has proven to be far more diverse that might appear on the surface through the implementation of diverse planning options. The very nature of those options or alternate methods of performing the tasks associated with Emergency Management has fostered a success story of building and sustaining resilience in communities across the nation.

Beyond the planning and preparedness responsibilities, this book stands as a testimony of the work Emergency Managers coordinate during field operations in support of the incident at the scene and remotely from the emergency operations center (EOC). From coordinating the establishment of incident facilities and evacuation operations to conducing damage assessments and resource management, the intrinsic duties of Emergency Managers reinforce all aspects of field operations. As overwhelming as the obstacles confronted in field operations may appear, it is not the functions that are normally performed that impose the greatest levels of difficulty, but rather the most complicated challenges emerge from operations that are vastly unique and not previously experienced. It is because of the potential for unprecedented occurrences that Emergency Managers must be exceptionally trained and capable of rapidly applying creative "outside the box" solutions in the face of the unknown.

In order for effective EOC management and operations to transpire, Emergency Managers must be fully versed in the applicable statutes, policies, and procedures mandated at all levels of government. The expansive volumes of EOC regulatory guidance encompass the performance of normal daily operations, emergency activations, organizational design and management, and the infamous "other duties as assigned". To meet the distinct needs of the community served, Emergency Managers may opt to embrace the management model that is most advantageous to protect the public and government interests. Each of the EOC management and operation models incorporates a diverse assortment of roles and responsibilities that revolve around performing the common functions of managing information and resources, developing plans and policies, and coordinating all associated aspects contained in Emergency Management. Therefore, the selected model should promote a process for the proper identification and qualification of Emergency Managers and support staff and it should be founded upon established professional standards.

Navigating the Local, State, and Federal disaster declarations and the related hurdles presents a myriad of potential concerns requiring Emergency Managers to be prepared for the consequences of disasters negatively impacting our communities. That preparation starts with being grounded in the truth that all disasters are local disasters in the beginning, in the middle, and at the end. Therefore, it must be understood that the disaster declaration process begins at the local level when jurisdictional capabilities are exceeded and the senior elected official issues a local disaster declaration and requests assistance from the State. After which, the State governor may issue a State disaster declaration and request Federal assistance when the State capability has been surpassed. From that point, FEMA will review a governor's request for assistance to determine eligibility and then forward a recommendation to the President. Once a presidential declaration is issued the Stafford Acts authorizations for Public Assistance (PA) and Individual Assistance (IA) may be enacted if requisite thresholds have been met as prescribed and result in authorization of hazard mitigation grant funding related to the presidential declaration. However, the financial assistance received through Federal assistance may turn out to be far less than expected and take considerable time for reimbursement to come to fruition.

Because of the complexities inherent in this profession, Emergency Managers must adopt a life of continued training and exercises to meet the challenges that lay ahead in the unknown future. For this very purpose, NIMS and the National Qualification System (NQS) have established training standards which enlist FEMA in collaboration with various Federal, State, and Local agencies and private training providers to offer an extensive array of Emergency Management courses. The incumbent professional development training spans relevant Emergency

Management along with nearly every Incident Management Team (IMT) position. The necessary training is only half of the answer to address the challenges and must be followed with an evaluation of the effectiveness of training. The appropriate mechanism for evaluating training comes from applied exercises, both discussion- and operations-based to examine current capabilities and capacities. Which is why the Homeland Security Exercise and Evaluation Program (HSEEP) was designed to provide a fundamental set of principles for developing, facilitating, and evaluating exercises and formulating corrective action plans.

This book has demonstrated how catastrophic disasters in the United States have, in many instances, led to the establishment of a number of Emergency Management grant programs which are primarily managed at the Federal and State government levels. Generally speaking, these Emergency Management grants fall into two main categories; the preparedness grants that are relative to the prevention and protection mission areas in concert with the disaster related grants pertinent to the mitigation, response, and recovery mission areas. This text has delineated that some Emergency Management grants support national campaigns and programs to enhance preparedness, while others directly align with the National Preparedness Goal to support protection efforts to combat extreme violence and terrorism. Whereas, disaster related grants are specifically enacted to address IA, PA, hazard mitigation assistance (HMA), and fire management assistance grants (FMAGs) to aid disaster-stricken communities.

Rounding it all out, I wanted to document the abounding heritage of Emergency Management certificate and certification programs that parallel and are intertwined with the history of the profession and can be traced back more than eighty years in the United States. This text has illustrated how FEMA manages foundational certification programs along with numerous certifications for specializations in continuity, exercise design, integrated EOC operations, trainers, individuals of diverse levels of experience, and personnel responsible for managing internal and external communications. In addition to the programs managed by FEMA, professional associations and State Emergency Management agencies have been shown to administer an impressive magnitude of professional development certification programs. Of those, the State Guard Association of the United States (SGAUS) manages the Military Emergency Management Specialist (MEMS) certificate programs initially developed for military members and recently having been opened up to civilians and SGAUS is incrementally moving towards making these programs available internationally. And when it comes to global recognition, the vaunted International Association of Emergency Managers (IAEM) has created the Associate Emergency Manager (AEM) certification for entry-level professionals and the preeminent Certified Emergency Manager (CEM) certification for the professionals who have achieved the highest professional standards. All told, a staggering ninety-nine Emergency Management professional development certificate and certification programs have been documented in this book.

Were the goals of writing *"Organizing Chaos"* achieved? The answer to that question may be years in the making and come through examination of professional who have chosen to take up the yoke of Emergency Management to make our communities as safe as humanly possible and resilient to weather the storms that may come our way. I can take comfort, however, in knowing that I have been true to my intentions and that I can diligently striven to be a positive influence in this profession for which I passionately undertake my duties and responsibilities. Let me now close with this final thought, Emergency Managers are often an unseen force that holds our societies together in the worst of times and they are deserving of our admiration and caring support!

Respectfully,

Dr. Mark D. Chadwick, CEM, TEM

Acronyms

AAR	After-Action Report
ABA	American Bar Association
AC	Area Command
ACE	American Council on Education
ADA	Americans with Disabilities Act
AEL	Authorized Equipment List
AEM	Associate Emergency Manager
AHIMT	All Hazards Incident Management Team
AHJ	Authority Having Jurisdiction
AMSC	Area Maritime Security Committee
AOR	Authorized Organizational Representative
APCO	Association of Public Safety Communications Officials
APS	Advanced Professional Series
ASD	Academy State Director
ASPR	Assistant Secretary for Preparedness and Response
ATF	Bureau of Alcohol, Tobacco, Firearms and Explosives
AWR	Awareness
BCOEM	Bexar County Office of Emergency Management
BCSO	Bexar County Sheriff's Office
BRIC	Building Resilient Infrastructure and Communities

C&CB	Capability and Capacity Building
C/E	Controller/Evaluator
CAD	Computer Aided Dispatch
CARES	Coronavirus Aid, Relief and Economic Security Act
CBP	Customs and Border Protection
CBRNE	Chemical-Biological-Radiological-Nuclear-Explosive
CCP	Crisis Counseling Assistance and Training Program
CDAEP	Civil Defense Adult Education Program
CDC	Centers for Disease Control and Prevention
CDP	Center for Domestic Preparedness
CDSC	Civil Defense Staff College
CDUEP	Civil Defense University Extension Program
CEM	Certified Emergency Manager
CERT	Community Emergency Response Team
CES	Continuity Excellence Series
CHDS	Center for Homeland Defense and Security
CI/KR	Critical Infrastructure/Key Resources
CISM	Critical Incident Stress Management
CND	Council of National Defense
CPG	Comprehensive Preparedness Guide
COG	Council of Governments
CONOPS	Concept of Operations

COG	Continuity of Government
COOP	Continuity of Operations
COP	Common Operating Picture
COSIN	Control Staff Instructions
COVID-19	Corona (CO) Virus (VI) Disease (D) 19 (2019)
C-POD	Commodity Point of Distribution
CPS	City Public Service
CST	Civil Support Team
CTOS	Counter Terrorism Operations Support
CTTV Framework	Strategic Framework for Countering Terrorism and Targeted Violence
CUSEC	Central United States Earthquake Consortium
DCM	Disaster Case Management
DCPA	Defense Civil Preparedness Agency
DHS	Department of Homeland Security
DLS	Disaster Legal Services
DME	Durable Medical Equipment
DOD	Department of Defense
DOE	Department of Energy
DRC	Disaster Recovery Center
DSA	Disaster Survivor Assistance
DSCA	Defense Support of Civil Authorities
DUA	Disaster Unemployment Assistance

DUNS	Data Universal Numbering System
EAS	Emergency Alert System
ECC	Emergency Coordination Center
EEG	Exercise Evaluation Guide
EHP	Environmental and Historic Preservation
EIN	Employer Identification Number
EM	Emergency Management
EMA	Emergency Management Agency
EMAC	Emergency Management Assistance Compact
EMAT	Emergency Management Association of Texas
EMC	Emergency Management Coordinator
EMI	Emergency Management Institute
EMPG	Emergency Management Performance Grants
EMPP	Emergency Management Professional Program
EMRTC	Energetic Materials Research and Testing Center
EMS	Emergency Medical Service
EMT	Emergency Medical Technician
EOC	Emergency Operations Center
EOP	Emergency Operation Plan
ER	Emergency Room
ESD	Emergency Service District
ESF	Emergency Support Function

EvalPlan	Evaluation Plan
ExPlan	Exercise Plan
F/ASC	Finance/Administration Section Chief
FAC	Family Assistance Center
FBI	Federal Bureau of Investigations
FCDA	Federal Civil Defense Administration
FCDSC	Federal Civil Defense Staff College
FE	Functional Exercise
FEMA	Federal Emergency Management Agency
FFR	Federal Financial Status Report
FGC	Fire Ground Command System
FIRESCOPE	Firefighting Resources of Southern California Organized for Potential Emergencies
FLETC	Federal Law Enforcement Training Center
FM	Frequency Modulation
FMA	Flood Mitigation Assistance
FMAG	Fire Management Assistance Grant
FNSS	Functional Needs Support Services
FRP	Federal Response Plan
FSE	Full-Scale Exercise
GPS	Global Positioning System
HazMat	Hazardous Materials
HHS	US. Department of Health and Human Services

HHSC	Texas Health & Human Services Commission
HMA	Hazard Mitigation Assistance (HMA)
HMGP	Hazard Mitigation Grant Program
HSEEP	Homeland Security Exercise and Evaluation Program
HSGP	Homeland Security Grant Program
HSPD	Homeland Security President Directive
IA	Individual Assistance
IACET	International Association for Continuing Education and Training
IADD	IA Division Director
IAEM	International Association of Emergency Managers
IAFC	International Association of Fire Chiefs
IAFF	International Association of Fire Fighters
IAP	Incident Action Plan
IB	Information Bulletin
IBSGP	Intercity Bus Security Grant Program
ICS	Incident Command System
IDC	International Development Committee
IED	Improvised Explosive Device
IEM	Integrated Emergency Management
IEMC	Integrated Emergency Management Course
IFFR	Identified for Further Review
IFSAC	International Fire Service Accreditation Congress

IHP	Individuals and Households Program
IMS	Incident Management System
IMT	Incident Management Team
IP	Improvement Plan
IPP	Integrated Preparedness Plan
IPPW	Integrated Preparedness Planning Workshop
IPR	Intercity Passenger Rail Program
ISAC	Information Sharing and Analysis Centers
ISE	Information Sharing Environment
JIC	Joint Information Center
JIS	Joint Information System
JIT	Just-in-Time Training
KBDI	Keetch-Byram Drought Index
KSA	Knowledge, Skills, and Abilities
LER	Lodging Expense Reimbursement
LFO	Large Fire Organization
LNO	Liaison Officer
LOFR	Liaison Officer
LSC	Logistics Section Chief
LSU	Louisiana State University
MAC	Multi-Agency Coordination
MACS	Multi-Agency Coordination System

MC/EA	Mass Care and Emergency Assistance
MCM	Medical Countermeasure
MCP	Master Continuity Practitioner
ME	Medical Examiner
MEOC	Mobile Emergency Operations Center
MEMS	Master Military Emergency Management Specialist
MEPP	Master Exercise Practitioner Program
MGT	Management and Planning
MHz	Megahertz
MPIOP	Master Public Information Officer Program
MSEL	Master Scenario Events List
NASA	National Aeronautics and Space Administration
NASF	National Association of State Foresters
NBA	National Basketball Association
NCBRT	National Center for Biological Research and Training
NCCEM	National Coordinating Council of Emergency Managers
NCP	National Contingency Plan
NCP	National Continuity Programs
ND	Non-Disaster Grants Management System
NDPC	National Domestic Preparedness Consortium
NDPTC	National Disaster Preparedness Training Center
NDRF	National Disaster Recovery Framework

NEF	National Essential Function (NEF)
NEMAA	National Emergency Management Advanced Academy (NEMAA)
NEMBA	National Emergency Management Basic Academy (NEMBA)
NEMEA	National Emergency Management Executive Academy (NEMEA)
NETC	National Emergency Training Center
NFA	National Fire Academy
NFIP	National Flood Insurance Program
NFPA	National Fire Protection Association
NGB	U.S. Army National Guard Bureau
NGO	Non-Governmental Organization
NHC	National Hurricane Center
NIIMS	National Interagency Incident Management System
NIMS	National Incident Management System
NIPP	National Infrastructure Protection Plan
NNSS	Nevada National Security Site
NOFO	Notice of Funding Opportunity
NPD	National Preparedness Directorate
NQS	National Qualification System
NRF	National Response Framework
NRP	National Response Plan

NSA	National Sheriff's Association
NSGP	Nonprofit Security Grant Program
NTED	National Training and Education Division
NTES	National Training and Education System
NWCG	National Wildfire Coordinating Group
NWR	NOAA Weather Radio All Hazards
NWS	National Weather Service
OBP	Office of Bombing Prevention
OCD	Office of Civil Defense
OEM	Office of Emergency Management
ONA	Other Needs Assistance
OPSG	Operation Stone Garden
OSC	Operations Section Chief
PA	Public Assistance
PCP	Professional Continuity Practitioner
PDA	Preliminary Damage Assessment
PDM	Pre-Disaster Mitigation
PDS	Professional Development Series
PER	Performance
PGA	Professional Golfers Association of America
PII	Personally Identifiable Information
PIO	Public Information Officer

PKEMRA	Post-Katrina Emergency Management Reform Act
PNP	Private Non-Profit
POD	Point of Dispensing
POETE	Planning, Organizing, Equipping, Training, and Exercising
PPD	Presidential Policy Directive
PSC	Planning Section Chief
PSGP	Port Security Grant Program
PTT	Push-to-Talk
QPR	Quarterly Progress Report
RAP	Radiological Assistance Program
RDPC	Rural Domestic Preparedness Consortium
REPAC	Regional Emergency Preparedness Advisory Committee
RPA	Request for Public Assistance
RSF	Recovery Support Function
SA	Situational Awareness
SAA	State Administrative Agency
SAM	System for Award Management
SAMHD	San Antonio Metropolitan Health District
SAN JAC	San Jacinto
SAR	Suspicious Activity Reporting
SDFAUS	State Defense Force Association of the United States
SERTC	Security and Emergency Response Training Center

SGAUS	State Guard Association of the United States
SHSP	State Homeland Security Program
SitMan	Situation Manual
SLTT	State, Local, Tribal and Territorial
SME	Subject Matter Expert
SNS	Strategic National Stockpile
SOC	State Operations Center
SOFR	Safety Officer
SOG	Standard Operating Guidelines
SOP	Standard Operating Procedures
SOW	Scope of Work
SPR	Stakeholder Preparedness Review
SPR	State Preparedness Report
SRIA	Sandy Recover Improvement Act
SSA	Sector-Specific Agencies
SSN	Social Security Number
ST-CP	Soft Targets and Crowded Places
STAR	State of Texas Assistance Request
STO	State Training Officer
STTL	State, Tribal, Territorial, and Local Governments
SUAS	Small Unmanned Aircraft Systems
TACDA	The American Civil Defense Association

TCFP	Texas Commission on Fire Protection
TCID	Texas Center for Infectious Disease
TDEM	Texas Division of Emergency Management
TEEX	Texas Engineering Extension Service
TEM	Certified Texas Emergency Manager
THIRA	Threat and Hazard Identification and Risk Assessment
THSGP	Tribal Homeland Security Grant Program
TIA	Telecommunications Industry Association
TIFMAS	Texas Intrastate Fire Mutual System
TSGP	Transit Security Grant Program
TTCI	Transportation Technology Center, Incorporated
TTT	Triage, Treatment, and Transport
TTX	Tabletop Exercise
TTY	Text Telephone
UASI	Urban Area Security Initiative
UC	Unified Command
U.S.	United States
USBP	United States Border Patrol
USCDC	United States Civil Defense Council
USCG	United States Coast Guard
USDA	United States Department of Agriculture
USFA	United States Fire Administration

USGS	United States Geological Service
USPS	U.S. Postal Service
VAL	Volunteer Agency Liaison
VHF	Very High Frequency
VIC	Victim Information Center
VOAD	Volunteer Organizations Active in Disasters
VOC	Volunteer Operations Center
VRS	Video Relay Service
VTC	Video Teleconference
WEA	Wireless Emergency Alerts
WMD	Weapons of Mass Destruction
WTC	World Trade Center

Glossary

Actor: Role player simulating officials or disaster victims.

After-Action Report (AAR): Document to capture observations of an exercise and make recommendations for post-exercise improvements.

All-Hazards: Human-caused, natural, or technological incidents warranting actions intended to protect lives, property, environment, and safeguard basic human needs.

All Hazards Incident Management Team (AHIMT): A team of personnel who have received advanced ICS position-specific training to be able to respond to and manage incidents regardless of shape, size, or complexity.

AMBER Alerts: Emergency messages from law enforcement for child abductions.

Analysis Paralysis: Condition where a person is frozen in analyzing a situation and cannot formulate a decision.

Area Command: An organization that oversees the management of multiple incidents or oversees the management of a large or evolving situation with multiple ICS organizations.

Authority Having Jurisdiction (AHJ): The jurisdiction having the legal authority over the location where the incident occurred.

Awareness (AWR): Courses developed to provide responders with the abilities to recognize and report hazards or catastrophic incidents or to provide skills necessary to investigate hazardous materials and/or incidents involving potentially explosive devices.

Base: The main location where resources not assigned are allowed a rest cycle.

Best Practices: Proven methods, which are accepted as being reliable, based upon past experience.

Burn Rate: Calculated hourly cost of equipment, personnel, and supplies

Camp: May exist on a large operation to allow resources to have a place to rest without having to travel long distances back to a base.

Cascading Incident: A single catastrophic incident is plagued with secondary incidents occurring in rapid succession in a relatively short amount of time.

Certificates: Documents that certify a person has completed the requirements for a specific course of study and is capable of performing tasks related to the topic.

Certification: The process whereby an AHJ or third party recognize an individual for having met established standards to be qualified for holding a specific position; a formal process that recognizes and validates an individual's qualifications in a certain subject.

Chain of Command: An orderly line of authority and reporting relationships within the ranks of the organization, with lower levels subordinate to, and connected to, higher levels.

Cold Site: A cold site EOC is one, which basically has four walls and a ceiling and may require bringing in all equipment and a few hours to make fully operational.

Cold Zone: Area free of contamination.

Commodity Point of Distribution: An initial point(s) where the public can obtain life-sustaining emergency relief supplies after catastrophic disasters.

Common Operating Picture (COP): An integrated situational awareness process to collect, share, and display information.

Community Lifelines: Governmental and business functions, which are essential to economics security, health, and societal safety.

Comprehensive: Complete or nearly complete coverage of the elements of a given topic.

Congregate Shelter: Group settings utilizing community facilities holding hundreds of evacuees (schools, churches, community centers, etc…).

Context Descriptions: The details about a threat or hazard needed to identify the impacts it will have on a community and includes critical details such as location, magnitude, and time of an incident.

Control Staff Instructions (COSIN): Detailed guideline on procedures and responsibilities for control, simulation, and support; may be a component of the C/E Handbook.

Controller: Manages and monitors exercise pace and prompts actions to maintain exercise flow.

Controller/Evaluator (C/E) Handbook: Specific information for controllers and evaluators, may be contained in the ExPlan or as a standalone document.

Coronavirus Aid, Relief and Economic Security Act (CARES): Provided fast and direct economic assistance for American workers, families, small businesses, and industries.

Cost Share: The portion of the costs of a federally assisted project or program not borne by the Federal Government.

COVID-19: A disease caused by a novel or new strain of coronavirus; previously referred to as the 2019 novel coronavirus (2019-nCoV).

COVID Fatigue: A form of disaster fatigue brought on by the prolonged impact on life by the COVID virus where those affected are tired of being careful, cooped up, scared, and living in an abnormal reality.

Credentials: Testimonials or certified documents showing that a person is entitled to credit or has a right to exercise official power.

Credentialing: The process of providing documentation that identifies personnel and verifies their qualifications for certain positions; documentation that identifies personnel and authenticates and verifies the qualifications of such personnel by ensuring that such personnel possess a minimum common level of training, experience, physical and medical fitness, and capability appropriate for a particular position.

Crisis Counseling: The application of individual and group treatment procedures, which are designed to help alleviate the mental and emotional crises and their subsequent psychological and behavioral conditions resulting from a major disaster or its aftermath.

Critical Infrastructure/Key Resources (CI/KR): The 16 critical infrastructure sectors assets, networks, and systems, both physical and virtual, which are identified as vital to the United States because their destruction or disruption will have debilitating impacts upon our economy, health, or safety.

Deliberate Plans: plans to prevent, protect against, and mitigate the effects of, responding to, and recovering from threats or hazards.

Disaster Case Management (DCM): A partnership between a case manager and a disaster survivor to develop and carry out the survivor's long-term recovery plan.

Disaster Legal Services (DLS): Provides free legal help to low-income disaster survivors.

Disaster Unemployment Assistance (DUA). Provides temporary benefits to people who, as a result of a major disaster, lost or had their employment or self-employment interrupted.

Discussion-Based Exercises: Familiarize participants with plans, policies, and procedures in a guided or facilitated format.

Divert: An incident where an ER immediately shuts down receiving patients.

Drills: Coordinated evaluation of capabilities of personnel to perform a specific function or operation, such as a fire drill.

Emergency Declaration of Disaster: Supplement State and local efforts in providing emergency services, such as the protection of lives, property, public health, and safety, or to lessen or avert the threat of a catastrophe in any part of the United States where the financial cost is limited to not more than $5 million.

Emergency Management: The managerial function charged with creating the framework within which communities reduce vulnerability to hazards and cope with disasters. Emergency Management is dynamic and entails all of the actions involved in coordinating and organizing the efforts in planning for, preparing for, responding to, recovering from, and mitigating the impact of disasters upon our society.

Emergency Management Assistance Compact (EMAC): Offers assistance during governor-declared states of emergency or disaster through a responsive, straightforward system that allows states to send personnel, equipment, and commodities to assist with response and recovery efforts in other states

Emergency Work: To implement emergency protective measures and conduct debris removal.

Essential Tools: Required as a condition of employment.

Evaluation Plan (EvalPlan): Instructions for observing and evaluating an exercise.

Evaluator: Subject-Matter Experts (SMEs) selected to observe and evaluate exercise performance.

Event: A planned activity such as a concert, fair, parade, private or public gathering, sporting competition, or exercise.

Exercise Evaluation Guides (EEGs): Tools for collecting data to evaluate performance in a standardized manner.

Exercise Plan (ExPlan): General information on exercise objectives and scope for participants.

Extent of Play Agreement: Agreement outlining a participant jurisdiction or organization level of involvement in the exercise.

External Communications: Communications with the public, private sector, and volunteer agencies.

Facilitator: Leads and guides the exercise to remain focused on planned objectives.

Facilitator Guide: Instructions for facilitators to guide participants.

Facility: A building, works, system, or equipment, built or manufactured, or an improved and maintained natural feature.

Family Assistance Center (FAC): A location to provide care and support for the family members and friends whose loved ones have died during disasters.

Family Reunification: Process or location from which to manage reunifying minors with custodial parents after the occurrence of a disaster.

Field Operations: Performance of tasks in a natural setting by public safety, Emergency Managers, and assisting agencies to aid in response and recovery.

Formal Communication: Used to issue work assignments, order resources, and providing progress reports.

Full-Scale Exercises (FSE): Mobilization or movement of a large number of personnel and resources to evaluate command, control, and coordination for multi-agency/multi-discipline/multi-jurisdictional incident response.

Functional Exercises (FE): Mobilization or movement of a limited number of personnel and resources to evaluate command, control, and coordination for multi-agency/multi-discipline/multi-jurisdictional incident response.

Fusion: The overarching process of managing the flow of information and intelligence across all levels and sectors of government and the private sector.

Games: Competitive simulations involving two or more teams utilizing data, policies and procedures, and rules depicting a real-world incident.

Glide Path: A course of action that leads easily to an expected outcome.

Ground Truth: Detailed scenario elements to add to realism and guide achievement of objectives.

Hazard Mitigation Assistance: Funding for measures designed to reduce future loses to public and private property.

Heli-Base: A permanent helicopter landing area like those pre-identified and marked at a hospital.

Heli-Spot: A temporary helicopter landing area, which may be on a highway, or flat area of ground to be able to land and load patients requiring emergency air ambulance or for other urgent needs to land a helicopter outside of a heli-base.

Hot Site: A hot site EOC has all equipment, systems, and utilities required to activate the EOC on a moments' notice.

Hot Zone: Area where hazardous substances have been released.

Human-Caused Disasters: Those disasters resulting from human errors, intentional acts, and neglect.

Improvement Plan (IP): List of issues or areas to be improved, corrective action to be taken, the agency or individual responsible for implementing the corrective action, and a date for the completion of the corrective action assigned.

Incident: An occurrence, natural or human-caused, that requires a response to protect life or property.

Incident Command Post: The location from which the Incident Commander and Command Staff will manage an incident; the ICP is normally near the site of the incident.

Incident Complex: Two or more distinct incidents in the same general area that, by management action, are managed under a single incident commander or unified command in order to improve efficiency and simplify incident management processes.

Incident Complexity: Refers to the classification of the 5 incident types.

Incident Management Team (IMT): Personnel trained to hold specific Incident Command System (ICS) positions or "position-specific training.

Informal Communication: Serves the purpose of exchanging information on an incident, such as the Food Unit Leader asking the Operations Section Chief for the number of personnel working on an incident to be able to order meals.

Information: Raw unconfirmed data received through various reports.

Information hoarder: Someone who holds back information from others.

Intelligence: Analyzed and confirmed data.

Internal Communications: Those communications specific to the internal audience of elected and senior officials, jurisdictional departments, and public safety response agencies.

Interoperability: The ability of equipment or groups to operate in conjunction with one another.

Joint Information Center (JIC): A central location that facilitates operation of the Joint Information System (JIS).

Joint Information System (JIS): Provides the mechanism to organize, integrate, and coordinate information to ensure timely, accurate, accessible, and consistent messaging across multiple jurisdictions and/or disciplines, including the private sector and NGOs.

Keetch-Byram Drought Index (KBDI): an index used to determine forest fire potential.

Kind: Describes what a resource is (for example: police officer, firefighter, paramedic, etc…).

Lessons Learned: Knowledge gained from challenging experiences and failures during disasters.

Major Declaration of Disaster: Issued for any natural event, including any hurricane, tornado, storm, high water, wind-driven water, tidal wave, tsunami, earthquake, volcanic eruption, landslide, mudslide, snowstorm, or drought, or, regardless of cause, fire, flood, or explosion, that the President believes has caused damage of such severity that it is beyond the combined capabilities of State and Local governments to respond.

Management (MGT): Courses developed to provide managers with the knowledge to develop incident plans and coordinate over-arching incident coordination for catastrophic incidents.

Master Scenario Events List (MSEL): Timeline of scripted actions and events to be injected by controllers to prompt participants.

Mass Care and Emergency Assistance (MC/EA): The provision of life-sustaining services to disaster survivors as defined in the National Response Framework.

Mass Fatality Incidents: Those in which there are more bodies than can be handled using local resources.

Mega-Shelter: Extremely large facilities such as warehouses where thousands of evacuees can be housed.

Mitigation: The capabilities necessary to reduce loss of life and property by lessening the impact of disasters.

Mutual Aid Agreement: Establishes the terms under which assistance is provided between two or more jurisdictions within a state and between states, and can be with and between private sector entities, NGOs, and other whole community partners.

National Training and Education System (NTES): A network of students, training providers, and higher education partners building a more secure and resilient nation.

Natural disasters: All types of severe weather, which have the potential to pose a significant threat to human health and safety, property, critical infrastructure, and homeland security.

Necessary Expense: A cost attributed to purchasing an item, procuring a service, or payment for other activities that meet a serious need.

Non-Congregate Shelter: Shelters for single individuals or families such as hotels.

Observer: Individual who is not a direct participant who is observing, typically from a non-participant agency.

Operations-Based Exercises: Involve the mobilization or movement of personnel and resources in response to a planned hypothetical emergency.

Operational Period: The period of time scheduled for execution of a given set of tactical actions as specified in the Incident Action Plan.

Opt-In System: Citizens in the community must elect to be registered to receive communications through these systems.

Participant: Any individual involved in the exercise.

Participant Feedback Form: Tool to collect participant information to develop and After-Action-Report (AAR) and Improvement Plan (IP).

Per Capita: The per unit of population: by or for each person.

Per Capita Indicator: The multiplier (number) which is applied to the population number for the County or State to determine the specific threshold.

Performance (PER): Courses developed to train those responders who will be performing tasks related to initial response and catastrophic incidents, such as insuring safety of responders and the public, search and rescue, and HazMat decontamination.

Permanent Work: For the restoration of damaged facilities and hazard mitigation projects to protect facilities from future damages.

Player: Individual with an active role in discussion or performance of exercise tasks.

Player Handout: Supplements or replaces the SitMan; participant quick reference.

Preparedness: A continuous Emergency Management process of corrective-action, equipping, evaluating, exercising, organizing, planning, and training to enhance coordination efforts for disasters.

Prevention: Those actions intended to avoid, prevent, or stop a threatened or actual act of terrorism.

Primary Residence: The home where the applicant lives during the major portion of the calendar year, or the home that is required because of proximity to employment, including agricultural activities that provide 50% of the household's income.

Professional Organization: A professional organization, sometimes referred to as a professional association or professional body, exists to advance a particular profession, support the interests of people working in that profession and serve the public good. It facilitates innovation, communication and connection.

Protection: The ability to secure the homeland against acts of terrorism and manmade or natural disasters.

Qualification: The process through which personnel are enabled to perform position-specific duties and the documentation of performance capabilities for the assigned position.

Rainy Day Funds: Accounts set aside as emergency contingency funds.

Reasonable Cost: Cost, which does not exceed the cost a prudent person would incur under the prevailing circumstances at the time an applicant, determines to incur the cost.

Recipient: Pass-through entity; State, Tribal, or Territorial government.

Recovery: Short- and long-term efforts to stabilize and rebuild communities affected by disasters.

Redundancy: Includes backup communications, electricity, and water supply.

Response: Saving lives, stabilizing community lifelines, protecting property and the environment, and meeting basic human needs after an incident has occurred.

Retired: An individual who is employed, self-employed, or consulting in Emergency Management less than 400 hours per year; in relation to the CEM Lifetime designation.

Risk: The potential for an unwanted outcome resulting from an incident or occurrence, as determined by its likelihood and the associated consequences.

Risk Management: Actions taken to avoid, reduce, or transfer risks.

Risk Management Equation: Risk = threat x vulnerability x consequences.

Self-Dispatch: When a person or resource arrives to a disaster scene without being properly requested.

Seminars: Informal discussions or briefings to present new or revised plans, policies, or procedures.

Serious Need: The requirement for an item or service that is essential to an applicant's ability to prevent, mitigate, or overcome a disaster-caused hardship, injury, or adverse condition.

Simulator: Delivers scenario messages or injects representing actions, conversations, or changes to the scenario to prompt participants to engage in corresponding activities or decision-making.

Situation Manual (SitMan): Background and reference for participants.

Situational Awareness (SA): The perception and comprehension of the details involved in an on-going incident.

Staging Area: A staging area can be any location in which personnel, supplies, and equipment await assignment.

Statute: A statute is a law.

Strategic EOC: Determines and coordinates what is to be done during an incident(s).

Survivability: Pertains to the type of construction materials and design, such as, being built above projected flood levels and to withstand hurricane or tornado force winds.

Sustainability: Relates to mechanisms in place in the EOC, which ensure the capability to maintain extended operations.

Tabletop Exercises (TTX): Scenario-based discussion involving key leadership and decision-makers working through a hypothetical incident.

Tactical EOC: Conducts on-scene operations itself or in conjunction with first responders.

Tactics: Specific tasks to achieve strategies and objectives.

Targeted Violence: Any incident of violence that implicates homeland security and/or DHS activities in which a known or knowable attacker selects a particular target prior to the violent attack.

Technological Disasters: Include commercial explosions or fires, computer infrastructure failures, dam failures, hazards materials spills, radiation exposures, and transportation accidents.

Threshold: A minimum level of monetary costs related to disasters, which must be exceeded to qualify for Federal grant money for Public Assistance (PA).

Trigger: Triggers are events or incidents, which automatically trigger the activation of the EOC.

Type: Describes the size, capability, and staffing qualifications of a resource.

Typed: Defined by level of capability to respond to and manage incidents based upon the corresponding Incident Complexity types.

Unified Command: Through a unified command, agencies work together through the designated members of the Unified Command, often the senior person from agencies/disciplines participating in the Unified Command, to establish a common set of objectives and strategies and a single IAP.

Unity of Command: A simple way of stating that each person working on the disaster has only one supervisor.

Victim Information Center (VIC): The VIC is a location where family members can be interviewed to obtain ante-mortem (pre-death) information on a victim such as birthmarks, dental work history, surgeries or scars, and tattoos.

Warm Site: A warm site EOC is a facility that may have some equipment and systems, but would require bringing in laptops, phones, or other necessary equipment and will require a short period of time to be fully operational.

Warm Zone: Area between the Cold Zone and the area where the hazardous materials are present.

WebEOC: A web-based platform for monitoring incidents, ordering and tracking resources, and coordinating efforts between all response partners.

Whole Community: The concept whereby community residents, Emergency Managers, governmental leaders, private and nonprofit agencies, and faith-based organizations work collaboratively to improve societal resilience and security.

Workshops: Similar to seminars, however workshops include the development of a work product during the workshop in the form of a draft plan or policy.

Bibliography

(DHS) Security, D. o. (2017, February 8). *Responder News: P25 Compliance.* Retrieved from DHS.gov: https://www.dhs.gov/science-and-technology/news/2017/02/08/responder-news-p25-compliance-what-should-it-mean-you

(DHS), D. o. (n.d.). *Fusion Centers.* Retrieved from DHS.gov: https://www.dhs.gov/fusion-centers

(DHS), D. o. (n.d.). *Fusion Centers vs. Emergency Operations Centers.* Retrieved from DHS.gov: https://www.dhs.gov/fusion-centers-and-emergency-operations-centers

(DHS), D. o. (n.d.). *Natural Disasters.* Retrieved from DHS.gov: https://www.dhs.gov/natural-disasters

(EMAC), E. M. (n.d.). *What is EMAC?* Retrieved from Emergency Management Assistance Compact (EMAC): https://www.emacweb.org/index.php/learn-about-emac/what-is-emac

(FCC) Commission, F. C. (n.d.). *Wireless Emergency Alerts (WEA).* Retrieved from FCC.gov: https://www.fcc.gov/consumers/guides/wireless-emergency-alerts-wea

(HHS) Services, U. D. (n.d.). *Topic Collection: Fatality Management.* Retrieved from HHS.gov: https://asprtracie.hhs.gov/technical-resources/65/fatality-management/0

(NWCG), N. W. (June 2009). *NWCG Task Book for the Position of Incident Commander Type 3.* Washington, D.C.: National Wildfire Coordinating Group (NWCG).

(NWCG), N. W. (n.d.). *The Mission, Purpose, and Course Codes of the United States Fire Administration's National Fire Academy.* Retrieved from National Wildfire Coordinating Group (NWCG): https://training.nwcg.gov/pdfs/NFA%20Course%20Coding.pdf

(TDEM), T. D. (n.d.). *About the State Exercise Program.* Retrieved from Texas Division of Emergency Management (TDEM): https://tdem.texas.gov/about-emergency-management-workshops/

(TDEM), T. D. (November 2019). *FY2020 Local Emergency Management Performance Guide.* Austin, TX: Texas Division of Emergency Management (TDEM).

(TDEM), T. D. (n.d.). *Regions*. Retrieved from TDEM: https://tdem.texas.gov/field-response/

(TIA) Association, T. I. (n.d.). *Project 25*. Retrieved from TIAonline.org: http://standards.tiaonline.org/standards/technology/project_25/index.cfm

107th Congress. (2002, November 25). *PUBLIC LAW 107–296*. Retrieved from Department of Homeland Security: https://www.dhs.gov/sites/default/files/publications/hr_5005_enr.pdf

1918 Pandemic (H1N1 virus). (n.d.). Retrieved from CDC.gov: https://www.cdc.gov/flu/pandemic-resources/1918-pandemic-h1n1.html

(October 13, 2015). *235th Anniversary of the Great Hurricane of 1780*. Miami, FL: National Oceanagraphic and Atmospheric Administration. Retrieved from Hurricanes Science: http://hurricanescience.net/history/storms/pre1900s/1780/

9/11 Commission. (July 22, 2004). *The 9/11 Commission Report*. Washington, D.C.: National Commission on Terrorist Attacks Upon the United States.

A Brief History of the American Red Cross. (n.d.). Retrieved from American Red Cross: https://www.redcross.org/content/dam/redcross/National/history-full-history.pdf page 2

About ISACs. (n.d.). Retrieved from National Council of ISACs: https://www.nationalisacs.org/about-isacs

About SERTC. (n.d.). Retrieved from Security and Emergency Response Training Center (SERTC): https://sertc.org/about/

About the National Museum of Civil Defense: Mission and History. (n.d.). Retrieved from National Museum of Civil Defense: https://www.nationalmuseumofcivildefense.org/about

(November 21, 2008). *Actions Taken to Implement the Post-Katrina Emergency Management Reform Act of 2006*. Washington, D.C.: U.S. Government Accountability Office.

Active911. (n.d.). Retrieved from Active911.com: https://www.active911.com/

Branigin, W. (2005, August 28). Evacuation Ordered as Katrina Bears Down on New Orleans. *The Washington Post*.

Center for Domestic Preparedness (CDP). (n.d.). Retrieved from FEMA Center for Domestic Preparedness: https://cdp.dhs.gov/about

Center for Homeland Defense and Security (CHDS). (n.d.). Retrieved from Naval Postgraduate School: https://www.chds.us/c/about-chds

Center for Radiological Nuclear Training. (n.d.). Retrieved from Counter Terrorism Operations Support (CTOS) : http://www.ctosnnsa.org/pages/ctos_overview.htm

Chadwick, M. (2013). *Emergency Manager "Go Kit" List*. San Antonio, TX: Bexar County Office of Emergency Management.

Chadwick, M. (2014). *Cascading Challenges within a Single Incident*. San Antonio, TX: Bexar County Office of Emergency Management.

Chadwick, M. (2015). *Family Assistance Center and Victim Information Center*. San Antonio, TX: Bexar County Office of Emergency Management.

Chadwick, M. (2016). *The Responder Emergency Manager*. San Antonio: Bexar County Office of Emergency Management.

Chadwick, M. (April 16, 2014). *Hand Grenade - Uvalde County*. San Antonio, TX: Bexar County Office of Emergency Management.

Chadwick, M. (January 1, 2014). *United Site Services Fire*. San Antonio, TX: Bexar County Office of Emergency Management.

Chadwick, M. (January 23, 2017). *Trench Body Retrieval*. San Antonio, TX: Bexar County Office of Emergency Management.

Chadwick, M. (June 30, 2017). *Venomous Snakes Vehicle Extrication*. San Antonio: Bexar County Office of Emergency Management.

Chaos. (n.d.). Retrieved from Cambridge Dictionary: https://dictionary.cambridge.org/us/dictionary/english/chaos

Chicago Fire of 1871. (2018, August 21). Retrieved from History.com: https://www.history.com/topics/19th-century/great-chicago-fire

Civil Defense. (n.d.). Retrieved from John F. Kennedy Presidential Library & Museum: https://www.jfklibrary.org/search?f%5B0%5D=subject_organization%3AUnited%20 States.%20President.%20Office%20of%20Civil%20and%20Defense%20Mobilizatio n&f%5B1%5D=source%3A46

Civil Defense and Homeland Security: A Short History of National Preparedness. (2006, September). Retrieved from Federal Emergency Management Agency (FEMA):

https://training.fema.gov/hiedu/docs/dhs%20civil%20defense-hs%20-%20short%20history.pdf page 7

Commandant, United States Coast Guard. (September 28, 1998). *Commandant Intstruction 3120.14*. Washington, D.C. : United States Coast Guard.

Congress, U. S. (October 4 2006). *Post-Katrina Emergency Management Reform Act of 2006 (Public Law 109-295)*. Washington, D.C.: United States Congress.

Cresswell, K. (2021, May 24). *A Guide to the Four Levels of Hazardous Materials (HazMat) Response*. Retrieved from Hazmat Nation: https://www.hazmatnation.com/a-guide-to-the-four-levels-of-hazardous-materials-hazmat-response/

Defense Civil Preparedness Agency. (1972). *Civil Defense - A New Dual Mission*. Retrieved from Federal Emergency Management Agency (FEMA): https://training.fema.gov/hiedu/docs/dcpa%20-%201972%20-%20civil%20preparedness%20a%20new%20dual%20mission-annual%20r.pdf

DHS. (2012, June 19). *Plan and Prepare for Disasters*. Retrieved from Department of Homeland Security: https://www.dhs.gov/plan-and-prepare-disasters

Disaster Legal Services (DLS). (2020, August 11). Retrieved from www.disasterassistance.gov: https://www.disasterassistance.gov/get-assistance/forms-of-assistance/4464

Disaster Unemployment Assistance. (2021, January 20). Retrieved from www.disasterassistance.gov: https://www.disasterassistance.gov/get-assistance/forms-of-assistance/4466

Dr. B. Wayne Blanchard, CEM. (September 11, 2007). *Principles of Emergency Management Supplement*. FEMA.

Dunlap, D. W. (2006, December 1). *Civil Defense Logo Dies at 67, and Some Mourn Its Passing*. Retrieved from The New York Times: https://www.nytimes.com/2006/12/01/washington/01civil.html

Emergency Management Study. (n.d.). Retrieved from https://em-study.com/emsfema/

Energetic Materials Research and Testing Center (EMRTC). (n.d.). Retrieved from New Mexico Tech: http://www.emrtc.nmt.edu/training.php

Exxon Valdez Oil Spill. (2018, March 9). Retrieved from History.com: https://www.history.com/topics/1980s/exxon-valdez-oil-spill

(n.d.). *Federal Disaster Case Management Program*. Washington, D.C.: U.S. Department of Health and Human Services.

Federal Response Plan. (April 1992). Washington, D.C.: FEMA.

FEMA. (1979). *FEMA History*. Retrieved from FEMA.gov: https://training.fema.gov/history.aspx

FEMA. (2006). *National Infrastructure Protection Plan (NIPP)*. Washington, D.C.: FEMA.

FEMA. (2015, August 8). *The Emergency Management Institute (EMI) Trainer Program*. Retrieved from Training.FEMA.gov: https://training.fema.gov/tp/

FEMA. (2019, April 8). *Master Exercise Practitioner Program (MEPP)*. Retrieved from Training.FEMA.gov: https://training.fema.gov/mepp

FEMA. (2020, March 9). *Emergency Management Professional Program (EMPP)*. Retrieved from Training.FEMA.gov: https://training.fema.gov/empp/

FEMA. (2020, November 3). *Integrated Emergency Management Course (IEMC)*. Retrieved from Training.FEMA.gov: https://training.fema.gov/iemc

FEMA. (2020, November 4). *National Emergency Management Advanced Academy*. Retrieved from Training.FEMA.gov: https://training.fema.gov/empp/advanced.aspx

FEMA. (2020, November 5). *National Emergency Management Executive Academy (NEMEA)*. Retrieved from Training.FEMA.gov: https://training.fema.gov/empp/executive.aspx

FEMA. (2020). *National Incident Management System Training Program*. Washington, D.C.: FEMA.

FEMA. (2020, July 20). *National Preparedness Goal*. Retrieved from FEMA.gov: https://www.fema.gov/emergency-managers/national-preparedness/goal

FEMA. (2020, October 2). *Per Capita Impact Indicator and Project Thresholds*. Retrieved from FEMA.gov: https://www.fema.gov/assistance/public/applicants/per-capita-impact-indicator

FEMA. (2020, November 3). *Resilience*. Retrieved from FEMA.gov: https://www.fema.gov/about/offices/resilience

FEMA. (2021 , August 11). *Building Resilient Infrastructure and Communities*. Retrieved from FEMA.gov: https://www.fema.gov/grants/mitigation/building-resilient-infrastructure-communities

FEMA. (2021, February 26). *After You Apply: Things to Know and Do After Applying for Hazard Mitigation Grant Program Funding*. Retrieved from FEMA.gov: https://www.fema.gov/grants/mitigation/hazard-mitigation/after-you-apply

FEMA. (2021, February 26). *After You Apply: Things to Know and Do After Applying for Hazard Mitigation Grant Program Funding*. Retrieved from FEMA.gov: https://www.fema.gov/grants/mitigation/hazard-mitigation/after-you-apply

FEMA. (2021, March 30). *Continuity Excellence Series - Level I Professional Continuity Practitioner Requirements*. Retrieved from FEMA.gov: https://www.fema.gov/emergency-managers/national-preparedness/continuity/excellence-series/level-1

FEMA. (2021, April 2). *Continuity Excellence Series - Level II Master Continuity Practitioner Requirements*. Retrieved from FEMA.gov: https://www.fema.gov/emergency-managers/national-preparedness/continuity/excellence-series/level-2

FEMA. (2021, January 13). *EMI Course Codes*. Retrieved from FEMA.gov: https://training.fema.gov/emicourses/emicoursecodes.aspx

FEMA. (2021, March 18). *Fact Sheet: A Guide to Grant Writing for Resources or Recovery Assistance*. Retrieved from FEMA.gov: https://www.fema.gov/press-release/20210318/fact-sheet-guide-grant-writing-resources-or-recovery-assistance

FEMA. (2021, July 1). *Fire Management Assistance Grants*. Retrieved from FEMA.gov: https://www.fema.gov/assistance/public/fire-management-assistance

FEMA. (2021). *Fiscal Year 2021 Intercity Bus Security Grant Program (IBSGP)*. Washington, D.C.: FEMA.

FEMA. (2021). *Fiscal Year 2021 Intercity Passenger Rail (IPR) Program*. Washington, D.C.: FEMA.

FEMA. (2021). *Fiscal Year 2021 Nonprofit Security Grant Program (NSGP)*. Washington, D.C.: FEMA.

FEMA. (2021). *Fiscal Year 2021 Port Security Grant Program (PSGP).* Washington, D.C.: FEMA.

FEMA. (2021). *Fiscal Year 2021 Transit Security Grant Program (TSGP).* Washington, D.C.: FEMA.

FEMA. (2021). *Fiscal Year 2021 Tribal Homeland Security Grant Program (THSGP).* Washington, D.C.: FEMA.

FEMA. (2021, June 18). *Hazard Mitigation Grant Program (HMGP).* Retrieved from FEMA.gov: https://www.fema.gov/grants/mitigation/hazard-mitigation

FEMA. (2021, August 6). *Hazard Mitigation Grant Program (HMGP).* Retrieved from FEMA.gov: https://www.fema.gov/grants/mitigation/hazard-mitigation

FEMA. (2021, July 16). *Homeland Security Grant Program.* Retrieved from FEMA.gov: https://www.fema.gov/grants/preparedness/homeland-security

FEMA. (2021, January 20). *National Continuity Programs (NCP).* Retrieved from FEMA.gov: https://www.fema.gov/about/offices/continuity

FEMA. (2021, February 18). *NIMS Components - Guidance and Tools.* Retrieved from FEMA.gov: https://www.fema.gov/emergency-managers/nims/components#nqs

FEMA. (2021, June 29). *Public Information Officer (PIO).* Retrieved from Training.FEMA.gov: https://training.fema.gov/programs/pio/

FEMA. (2021, June 8). *Sandy Recovery Improvement Act of 2013.* Retrieved from FEMA.gov: https://www.fema.gov/disasters/sandy-recovery-improvement-act-2013

FEMA. (2021, March 4). *When You Apply: Things to Know and Do When Applying for Hazard Mitigation Grant Program Funds.* Retrieved from FEMA.gov: https://www.fema.gov/grants/mitigation/hazard-mitigation/when-you-apply

FEMA. (n.d.). *A Guide to the Disaster Declaration Process and Federal Disaster Assistance.* Washington, D.C.: FEMA.

FEMA. (n.d.). *Advanced Professional Series.* Retrieved from Training.FEMA.gov: https://training.fema.gov/programs/aps/

FEMA. (April 2009). *FEMA Agency-Wide Disaster Workforce Credentialing Plan.* Washington, D.C.: FEMA.

FEMA. (April 2017). *Public Assistance Program and Policy Guide FP 104-009-2 .* Washington, D.C.: FEMA.

FEMA. (April 2018). *Public Assistance Program and Policy Guide.* Washington, D.C.: FEMA.

FEMA. (April 2019). *Advanced Incident Command System for Complex Incidents, ICS 400.* Washington, D.C. : FEMA.

FEMA. (April 2019). *Intermediate Incident Command System for Expanding Incidents, ICS 300.* Washington, D.C.: FEMA.

FEMA. (August 2011). *National Incident Management System: Guideline for the Credentialing of Personnel.* Washington, D.C.: FEMA.

FEMA. (August 2019). *Distribution Management Plan Guide.* Washington, D.C.: FEMA.

FEMA. (n.d.). *Cost Sharing.* Retrieved from FEMA.gov: https://www.fema.gov/hmgp-appeal-categories/cost-sharing

FEMA. (n.d.). *Debris Removal.* Washington, D.C.: FEMA and U.S. Army Corps of Engineers.

FEMA. (December 14, 2020). *Cost of Assistance Estimates in the Disaster Declaration Process for the Public Assistance Program.* Washington, D.C.: FEMA.

FEMA. (December 16, 2013). *Fundamentals of Emergency Management, IS-230d.* Washington, D.C.: FEMA.

FEMA. (December 2012). *EOC Management and Operations (G-775).* Washington, D.C.: FEMA.

FEMA. (n.d.). *Distance Learning.* Retrieved from FEMA Emergency Management Institute: https://training.fema.gov/is/

FEMA. (n.d.). *Emergency Management Institute (EMI) Overview.* Retrieved from training.FEMA.gov: https://training.fema.gov/history.aspx

FEMA. (February 12, 2019). *Fact Sheet: Disaster Case Management.* Washington, D.C.: FEMA.

FEMA. (February 2020). *FEMA Preparedness Grants Manual.* Washington, D.C.: FEMA.

FEMA. (February 2021). *FEMA Preparedness Grants Manual, Version 2*. Washington, D.C.: FEMA.

FEMA. (n.d.). *FEMA Glossary*. Retrieved from FEMA: https://training.fema.gov/programs/emischool/el361toolkit/glossary.htm#R

FEMA. (n.d.). *FEMA National Continuity Programs: Continuity Brochure Series*. Washington, D.C.: FEMA.

FEMA. (n.d.). *Hazard Mitigation Assistance Grants*. Retrieved from FEMA.gov: https://www.fema.gov/grants/mitigation

FEMA. (n.d.). *History of FEMA*. Retrieved from FEMA.gov: https://www.fema.gov/about/history

FEMA Individuals and Households Program (IHP) - Other Needs Assistance . (2019, December 10). Retrieved from www.disasterassistance.gov: https://www.disasterassistance.gov/get-assistance/forms-of-assistance/4473

FEMA. (n.d.). *ISP Courses - Search Results: Professional Development Series*. Retrieved from Training.FEMA.gov: https://training.fema.gov/is/searchis.aspx?search=pds

FEMA. (January 2019). *Individual Assistance Program and Policy Guide (IAPPG)*. Washington, D.C.: FEMA.

FEMA. (January 2020). *Homeland Security Exercise and Evaluation Program (HSEEP)*. Washington, D.C.: FEMA.

FEMA. (July 9, 2018). *THIRA/SPR Overview and Updated Methodology*. Washington, D.C.: FEMA.

FEMA. (June 1, 2020). *Public Assistance Program and Policy Guide, Version 4*. Washington, D.C.: FEMA.

FEMA. (June 2016). *National Disaster Recovery Framework, Second Edition*. Washington, D.C.: FEMA.

FEMA. (June 2016). *National Mitigation Framework, Second Edition*. Washington, D.C.: FEMA.

FEMA. (June 2016). *National Prevention Framework, Second Edition*. Washington, D.C.: FEMA.

FEMA. (June 2016). *National Protection Framework, Second Edition.* Washington, D.C.: FEMA.

FEMA. (June 2021). *Fire Management Assistance Grant Program and Policy Guide.* Washington, D.C.: FEMA.

FEMA. (March 2018). *ICS Organizational Structure and Elements.* Washington, D.C.: FEMA.

FEMA. (March 2018). *Incident Action Planning Process.* Washington, D.C.: FEMA.

FEMA. (March 2018). *Incident Complexity and Type.* Washington, D.C.: FEMA.

FEMA. (May 2010). *Consideration for Fusion Center and Emergency Operations Center (EOC) Coordination; Comprehensive Preparedness Guide (CPG) 502.* Washington, D.C.: FEMA.

FEMA. (May 2011). *Diaster Declaration Process Fact Sheet.* Washington, D.C.: FEMA.

FEMA. (May 2013). *National Prevention Framework.* Washington, D.C.: FEMA.

FEMA. (May 2018). *Threat and Hazard Identification and Risk Assessment (THIRA) and Stakeholder Preparedness Review (SPR) Guide, Comprehensive Preparedness Guide (CPG) 201, Third Edition.* Washington, D.C.: FEMA.

FEMA. (May 2019). *Intermediate Emergency Operations Center Functions (G-2300).* Washington, D.C.: FEMA.

FEMA. (May 2021). *Individual Assistance Program and Policy Guide (IAPPG), Version 1.1.* Washington, D.C.: FEMA.

FEMA. (n.d.). *National Preparedness System.* Retrieved from FEMA.gov: https://www.fema.gov/emergency-managers/national-preparedness/system

FEMA. (n.d.). *National Response Framework.* Retrieved from FEMA.gov: https://www.fema.gov/emergency-managers/national-preparedness/frameworks/response

FEMA. (n.d.). *NIMS and the Incident Command System.* Retrieved from FEMA.gov: https://www.fema.gov/txt/nims/nims_ics_position_paper.txt

FEMA. (n.d.). *NIMS ICS All-Hazards Position Specific Training Program Official Website.* Retrieved from FEMA.gov: https://training.fema.gov/allhazards/

FEMA. (n.d.). *NIMS Resources*. Retrieved from FEMA.gov: https://rtlt.preptoolkit.fema.gov/Public/Home/LinksTools

FEMA. (November 2007). *Basic Guidance for Public Information Officers (PIOs)*. Washington, D.C.: FEMA.

FEMA. (November 2010). *Comprehensive Preparedness Guide (CPG) 101: Developing and Maintaining Emergency Operation Plans*. Washington, D.C.: FEMA.

FEMA. (November 2010). *Guidance on Planning for Integration of Functional Needs Support Services in General Population Shelters*. Washington, D.C.: FEMA.

FEMA. (November 2011). *National Preparedness System*. Washington, D.C.: FEMA.

FEMA. (November 2017). *National Incident Management System Guideline for Mutual Aid*. Washington D.C.: FEMA.

FEMA. (November 2017). *National Incident Management System Guideline for the National Qualification System*. Washington, D.C.: FEMA.

FEMA. (October 16, 2019). *Notice of Maximum Amount of Assistance Under the Individuals and Households Program*. Washington, D.C.: FEMA.

FEMA. (October 2012). *Position Qualifications for Operational Coordination: Liaison Officer*. Washington, D.C.: FEMA.

FEMA. (October 2012). *Position Qualifications for Operational Coordination: Safety Officer*. Washington, D.C.: FEMA.

FEMA. (October 2013). *ICS for Single Resource and Initial Action Incidents, Student Manual*. Washington, D.C.: FEMA.

FEMA. (October 2017). *National Incident Management System, Third Edition*. Washington, D.C.: FEMA.

FEMA. (October 28, 2019). *National Response Framework, Fourth Edition*. Washington, D.C.: FEMA. Retrieved from FEMA: https://www.fema.gov/emergency-managers/national-preparedness/frameworks/response#

FEMA. (October 3, 2011). *NIMS Training Program FAQs*. Washington, D.C.: FEMA.

FEMA. (n.d.). *Overcoming Objections*. Retrieved from www.training.fema.gov: https://emilms.fema.gov/IS1116/groups/56.html

FEMA. (n.d.). *Public Assistance Program Overview*. Retrieved from FEMA.gov: https://www.fema.gov/assistance/public/program-overview

FEMA. (n.d.). *Recovery Support Functions*. Retrieved from FEMA.gov: https://www.fema.gov/emergency-managers/national-preparedness/frameworks/national-disaster-recovery/support-functions

FEMA. (September 2011). *National Preparedness Goal*. Washington, D.C.: FEMA.

FEMA. (September 2015). *National Preparedness Goal, Second Edition*. Washington, D.C.: FEMA.

FEMA. (September 2016). *E/L0103 Planning: Emergency Operations*. Washington, D.C.: FEMA.

FEMA. (September 2017). *Resource Typing Definition for the National Qualification Sytem: Finance/Administration Section Chief*. Washington, D.C.: FEMA.

FEMA. (September 2018). *National Incident Management System: Emergency Operations Center Skillsets User Guide*. Washington, D.C.: FEMA.

FEMA. (n.d.). *Short-Term Shelter*. Retrieved from FEMA.gov: https://www.fema.gov/media-library-data/1494264802106-ba1fb3179987a4a68241d0b66c68f748/NIMS_508_Short_Term_Shelter_MAR21201 7.pdf

FEMA. (Summer 2020). *National Incident Management System Training Program*. Washington, D.C.: FEMA.

FEMA. (n.d.). *The Emergency Alert System (EAS)*. Retrieved from FEMA.gov: https://www.fema.gov/emergency-managers/practitioners/integrated-public-alert-warning-system/public/emergency-alert-system

FEMA. (n.d.). *The Integrated Public Alert & Warning System (IPAWS)*. Retrieved from FEMA.gov: https://www.fema.gov/emergency-managers/practitioners/integrated-public-alert-warning-system

FEMA. (n.d.). Unit Three: Overview of Federal Disaster Assistance. In FEMA, *A Citizen's Guide to Disaster Assistance (FEMA IS-7)* (pp. 3-2). Emmitsburg, MD: FEMA. Retrieved from FEMA.gov.

First Airplane Flies. (2019, December 17). Retrieved from History.com: https://www.history.com/this-day-in-history/first-airplane-flies

George D. Haddow, Jane A. Bullock, and Damon P. Coppola. (2011). *Introduction to Emergency Management; Fourth Edition*. Burlington, MA: Butterworth -Heinemann.

Gerald W. Williams, P. (April 2005). *The USDA Forest Service - The First Century*. Washington, D.C.: USDA Forest Service, Office of Communication.

Glide Path. (n.d.). Retrieved from Merriam-Webster Dictionary: https://www.merriam-webster.com/dictionary/glide%20path

Graham, G. (2012, July 27). *High Risk/Low Frequency*. Retrieved from YouTube.com: https://www.youtube.com/watch?v=Og9Usv82CdU

Harris, M. U. (1975, February 7). *Defense Civil Preparedness Agency (DCPA)*. Retrieved from Civil Defense Museum: http://www.civildefensemuseum.com/history.html

Hashagan, P. (n.d.). *Firefighting in Colonial America*. Retrieved from Ladies Island/St. Helena Fire Department: http://lishfd.org/History/firefighting_in_colonial_america.htm

Historic Flood Events in the Missouri River Basin. (1986, October). Retrieved from National Weather Service (NWS); National Oceanic and Atmospheric Administration (NOAA): https://www.weather.gov/mbrfc/flood

History of ICS. (n.d.). Retrieved from Emergency Management Services International (EMSI): http://www.emsics.com/history-of-ics

Homeland Security Grant Information. (n.d.). Retrieved from Alamo Area Council of Governments: https://www.aacog.com/145/Grants

(February 28, 2003). *Homeland Security Presidential Directive (HSPD) 5*. Washington, D.C.: Office of the President of the United States.

Homeland Security Presidential Directive (HSPD) 8. (December 17, 2003). Washington, D.C.: Office of the President.

(December 17, 2003). *Homeland Security Presidential Policy (HSPD) 7*. Washington, D.C.: Office of the President of the United States.

IAEM. (2020). *IAEM Certification Brochure*. Falls Church, Virginia: IAEM.

IAEM. (n.d.). *History of IAEM*. Retrieved from IAEM.org: https://www.iaem.org/History-of-IAEM#How-IAEM-Began

IAEM. (n.d.). *Lifertime CEM Designation*. Retrieved from IAEM.org: https://www.iaem.org/certification/application/lifetime-certification

Indeed. (2020, December 27). *Q&A: What Is a Professional Organization?* Retrieved from Indeed.com: https://www.indeed.com/career-advice/career-development/what-is-a-professional-organization

Individual Assistance. (2018, January 15). Retrieved from TDEM.Texas.gov: https://tdem.texas.gov/individual-assistance/

Johnstown Flood of 1889. (2020, October 16). Retrieved from History.com: https://www.history.com/this-day-in-history/the-johnstown-flood

Kiriakova, M. (n.d.). *Wall Street Bombing of 1920*. Retrieved from Britannica.com: https://www.britannica.com/event/Wall-Street-bombing-of-1920

Little, B. (2019, April 12). *How the Galveston Hurricane of 1900 Became the Deadliest U.S. Natural Disaster*. Retrieved from History.com: HTTPS://WWW.HISTORY.COM/NEWS/HOW-THE-GALVESTON-HURRICANE-OF-1900-BECAME-THE-DEADLIEST-U-S-NATURAL-DISASTER

Madison, J. (December 15, 1791). *Bill of Rights, Tenth Amendment*. Washington, D.C. : U.S. Congress.

(February 2, 2021). *Memorandum on Maximizing Assistance from the Federal Emergency Management Agency*. Washington, D.C.: Office of the President of the United States.

Merriam-Webster. (2021, August 5). *Credential*. Retrieved from Merriam-Webster.com: https://www.merriam-webster.com/dictionary/credentials

Mount St. Helens 1980 Eruption Changed the Future of Volcanology. (2020, May 14). Retrieved from USGS.gov: https://www.usgs.gov/news/mount-st-helens-1980-eruption-changed-future-volcanology#:~:text=Forty%20years%20ago%2C%20after%20two,ash%20hundreds%20of%20miles%20away.

Mulcahy, M. (February 2018). Making Sense of Disasters in Early America. *The American Historian*, 37 - 42.

Municipal Reforms of Augustus. (n.d.). Retrieved from Britannica: https://www.britannica.com/place/Rome/Municipal-reforms-of-Augustus

National Center for Biological Research and Training (NCBRT). (n.d.). Retrieved from Louisiana State University (LSU): https://www.ncbrt.lsu.edu/about/index.php

National Disaster Preparedness Training Center. (n.d.). Retrieved from University of Hawaii: https://ndptc.hawaii.edu/about/

National Interagency Incident Management System . (2004, April). Retrieved from National Wildfire Coordinating Group (NWCG): https://www.nwcg.gov/sites/default/files/hist-NIIMS-Document-April-2004.pdf

National Oil and Hazardous Substances Pollution Contingency Plan (NCP) Overview. (n.d.). Retrieved from EPA.gove: https://www.epa.gov/emergency-response/national-oil-and-hazardous-substances-pollution-contingency-plan-ncp-overview

National Training and Education Division (NTED) Course Catalog. (n.d.). Retrieved from FEMA's First Responder Training: https://www.firstrespondertraining.gov/frtserver/catalogs/NTED_course_catalog.pdf?_=1623417664418

NEHA. (n.d.). *Differnce Between Credentials and Certifications*. Retrieved from NEHA.org: https://www.neha.org/professional-development/education-and-training/differences-between-credentials-certifications

New Madrid Seismic Zone Catastrophic Planning Project. (n.d.). Retrieved from CUSEC.org: http://cusec.org/new-madrid-seismic-zone/new-madrid-seismic-zone-catastrophic-planning-project/

NOAA. (n.d.). *NOAA Weather Radio All Hazards*. Retrieved from Weather.gov: https://www.weather.gov/nwr/

NWCG Glossary - Incident Complex. (n.d.). Retrieved from National Wildfire Coordinating Group (NWCG): https://www.nwcg.gov/term/glossary/incident-complex

NWCG. (n.d.). *NWCG Glossary of Wildland Fire, PMS 205*. Retrieved from National Wildfire Coordinating Group: https://www.nwcg.gov/term/glossary

OCD. (1968). *1968 Annual Report, Department of Defense, Office of Civil Defense*. Washington, D.C.: Office of Civil Defense.

Oklahoma City Bombing. (n.d.). Retrieved from FBI.gov: https://www.fbi.gov/history/famous-cases/oklahoma-city-bombing

Operation Stonegarden (OPSG) Program. (n.d.). Retrieved from Homeland Security Grants: https://www.homelandsecuritygrants.info/GrantDetails.aspx?gid=21875

Per Capita. (n.d.). Retrieved from Merriam-Webster Dictionary: https://www.merriam-webster.com/dictionary/per%20capita

Percy, G. (1624). *A True Relation (Trewe Relacyon).* London.

Post 9/11 Federal Grants. (n.d.). Retrieved from Federal Grants Wire: https://www.federalgrantswire.com/post-911-federal-grants.html#.YN4HvOhKiUk

(February 12, 2013). *Presidential Policy Directive (PPD) 21.* Washington, D.C.: Office of the President.

Presidential Policy Directive (PPD) 8. (March 3, 2011). Washington, D.C.: Office of the President.

Prevention, C. f. (n.d.). *Fact Sheet: Medical Countermeasures (MCM) and Points of Dispensing (POD) Basics.* Retrieved from CDC.gov: https://www.cdc.gov/cpr/readiness/healthcare/closedpodtoolkit/factsheet-mcm.htm

Qualification. (n.d.). Retrieved from Cambride Dictionary: https://dictionary.cambridge.org/us/dictionary/english/qualification

Rafferty, J. P. (2010, September 24). *New Madrid Earthquakes of 1811 - 1812.* Retrieved from Britannica.com: https://www.britannica.com/event/New-Madrid-earthquakes-of-1811-1812

(March 2014). *Sandy Recovery Improvement Act (SRIA) Fact Sheet.* Emmitsburg, MD: FEMA.

Santayana, G. (1905). *Reason in Common Sense, Volume One of The Life of Reason.* New York: Charles Scribner's Sons.

Security, D. o. (September 2019). *Strategic Framework for Countering Terrorism and Targeted Violence .* Washington, D.C.: Department of Homeland Security.

Security, D. o. (September 2020). *Strategic Framework for Countering Terrorism and Targeted Violence: Public Action Plan.* Washington, D.C.: Department of Homeland Security.

Service, T. A. (2014). *Staging Area Manager.* College Station, TX: Texas A&M Forest Service.

Service, T. A. (n.d.). *Keetch-Byram Drought Index (KBDI)*. Retrieved from Texas Weather Connection: https://twc.tamu.edu/kbdi

SGAUS. (2021). *MEMS Academy Student Guidelines*. Germantown, TN: SGAUS.

SGAUS. (n.d.). *SGAUS Mission*. Retrieved from State Guard Association of the Unites States (SGAUS): https://sgaus.org/about-sgaus/sgaus-mission/

State Homeland Security Program (SHSP). (n.d.). Retrieved from Homeland Security Grants: https://www.homelandsecuritygrants.info/GrantDetails.aspx?gid=21909

TACDA. (n.d.). *About: The History of The American Civil Defense Association*. Retrieved from https://tacda.org/about/: https://tacda.org/about/

TDEM. (2021). *Emergency Management Performance Grant, FY2021 Grant Guidance*. Austin, TX: Texas Division of Emergency Management (TDEM).

TDEM. (n.d.). *Emergency Management Performance Grant*. Retrieved from Texas Division of Emergency Management (TDEM): https://tdem.texas.gov/emergency-management-performance-grant/

Texas A&M Forest Service. (July 2014). *Inicdent Command System: Situation Unit Leader (SITL) Job Aid*. College Station, TX: Texas A&M Forest Service.

(n.d.). *Texas Local Declaration of Disaster*. Austin, TX: Texas Division of Emergency Management (TDEM).

Texas. (n.d.). *Texas Government Code, Chapter 418 Emergency Management*. Austin, Texas: State of Texas.

The Different Levels of Hazardous Materials Response. (2011, August 9). Retrieved from My Firefighter Nation: https://my.firefighternation.com/profiles/blogs/the-different-levels-of-hazardous-materials-response#gref

The National Security Act of 1947 – July 26, 1947. (1947, July 26). Retrieved from Central Intelligence Agency: https://www.cia.gov/library/readingroom/docs/1947-07-26.pdf

Thomas Hall. (n.d.). Retrieved from New York State Unified Court System: http://www.nycourts.gov/history/legal-history-new-york/luminaries-dutch/hall-thomas.html

Trail of Tears. (2020, July 7). Retrieved from History.com: https://www.history.com/topics/native-american-history/trail-of-tears

Treasury, U. D. (n.d.). *About the CARES Act and the Consolidated Appropriations Act*. Retrieved from U.S. Department of the Treasury: https://home.treasury.gov/policy-issues/coronavirus/about-the-cares-act

Union Fire Company. (n.d.). Retrieved from Ben Franklin Historical Society: http://www.benjamin-franklin-history.org/union-fire-company/

Urban Area Security Initiative (UASI) Program. (n.d.). Retrieved from Homeland Security Grants: https://www.homelandsecuritygrants.info/GrantDetails.aspx?gid=17162

Vlassis, A. (2007, March 29). *Council of Governments* . Retrieved from Britannica.com: https://www.britannica.com/topic/council-of-governments

WAVE Push-to-Talk. (n.d.). Retrieved from Motorolasolutions.com : https://www.motorolasolutions.com/en_us/products/command-center-software/broadband-ptt-and-lmr-interoperability/wave.html

Weiser-Alexander, K. (2018, December). *American Life in the Late 19th Century*. Retrieved from Legends of America: https://www.legendsofamerica.com/life-late-19th-century

This page is intentionally left blank.

Made in the USA
Columbia, SC
13 February 2022